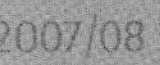
2007/08

POCKET GUIDE TO
SOUTH
AFRICA
2007/08

Pocket Guide to South Africa 2007/08
Fifth edition

Published by Government Communications (GCIS)
Private Bag X745, Pretoria, 0001, South Africa
Tel: +27 12 314-2911
Fax: +27 12 323-0557
Website: *www.gcis.gov.za*

ISBN: 978-0-621-37569-5

Editor: Delien Burger
Assistant editors: Elias Tibane and Marié Henning
Editorial support: Ongezwa Manyathi and Antonia Vermeulen
Design and layout: Neville Rabie
Photographs supplied by: GCIS, Satour, Department of Foreign Affairs and Photos.com
Printed and bound in South Africa by Formeset Printers

The editorial staff has taken all reasonable care to ensure correctness of facts and statistics. However, any person requiring confirmation of any data in the *Pocket Guide to South Africa*, or more detailed and specific information, should consult the relevant department/institution. This information is also available at *www.gcis.gov.za*.

Unless otherwise specified, information contained in this *Pocket Guide* was the latest available as at October 2007.

Contents

Foreword

As in previous editions, the *Pocket Guide to South Africa 2007/08* gives a comprehensive account of the programmes and policies of our government as well as the current state of the South African nation.

I am proud to give this brief foreword because through this *Pocket Guide* it is clear that since we attained our freedom in 1994 we have made important advances towards the goal of a better life for all.

The advances of last year, similar to those of the preceding years, indicate that while the challenges of poverty and underdevelopment are acute, we have, however, laid the necessary basis for a sustained, comprehensive and integrated development of our country.

Of particular importance, our economy is now growing at a faster rate than the country's population. This economic growth, coupled with prudent fiscal regime, have helped us to be in a better position to address poverty and underdevelopment.

FOREWORD

Clearly one of the critical challenges is the delivery of good and reliable services for our people. In this regard, in 2007, 88,6% of South Africans enjoyed access to piped water; 80% of households in South Africa are using electricity for lighting, and unemployment decreased by 2,5% since 2003. We continue to provide free healthcare to children under six years, pregnant and lactating women; and to people with disabilities.

The National Strategic Plan for HIV and AIDS and Sexually Transmitted Diseases for 2007 – 2011 gives the country a holistic view on how to respond to this challenge. It aims to reduce the number of new HIV infections by 50% by 2011; and reduce the impact of HIV and AIDS on individuals, families, communities and society by expanding access to appropriate treatment, care and support to 80% of all affected people.

Over the past year alone, an amount of R100 million was allocated for bursaries in further education and training (FET) colleges, benefiting more than 12 500 students. Government has also committed R2 billion for the systematic modernising and development of the FET college sector.

The Accelerated and Shared Growth Initiative for South Africa (AsgiSA) and the Joint Initiative on Priority Skills Acquisition are some of our country's strategic interventions for economic growth and development. The successful implementation of AsgiSA will result in greater scope for faster growth. The continued promotion of access to government programmes and economic opportunities brought by democracy is being intensified to ensure that all people, particularly women and youths, benefit. Land restitution continues apace.

The fight against crime has intensified through partnerships with various stakeholders to create safer communities for all. Our goal is to reduce crime levels by between 7% and 10%, giving special focus to crime prevention, integrated law-enforcement operations and the reduction of repeat offending. The South African Police Service's strategic plan for 2005 to 2010 sets out several operational priorities, including combating organised crime, serious and violent crime and crime against women and children.

As the first African hosts of the prestigious FIFA World Cup in 2010, we are excited about the positive spin-offs the tournament will bring for our country and Africa. Investments and programmes for the World Cup will accelerate delivery and the achievement of the development goals and the target economic growth rate in the continent. We say again: *Africa's time has come! South Africa is ready!*

Government is aware that although there have been huge strides, there are still many challenges. We remain committed to working in partnership with all South Africans to create a better life for all.

The *Pocket Guide to South Africa 2007/08* is an important resource and a critical barometer of the advances we are making towards a better life for all.

Thabo Mbeki

President Thabo Mbeki
January 2008

Size	1 219 090 km^2
Key economic sectors	Mining services and transport, energy, manufacturing, tourism, agriculture
Population	47,9 million (mid-2007)
Official languages	English, isiZulu, isiXhosa, isiNdebele, Afrikaans, siSwati, Sesotho sa Leboa, Sesotho, Setswana, Tshivenda and Xitsonga
Government	Constitutional multiparty, three-tier (local, provincial, national) democracy
Major cities	Johannesburg, Cape Town, Durban, Pretoria, Port Elizabeth, Bloemfontein, East London, Kimberley. There are nine provinces.
Currency	100 cents equals one rand
Time	GMT +2 hours
Distances	Cape Town to Johannesburg 1 400 km (880 miles) Johannesburg to Durban 600 km (380 miles) Port Elizabeth to Bloemfontein 700 km (440 miles)
Transportation	Excellent roads, rail and air facilities (both domestic and international)
Telecommunications	World-class infrastructure. Internet access is widely available. There are four mobile (cellular) networks.
Value-added tax	Levied at 14%. Tourists may apply for tax refunds on purchases over R250 on departure.
Health	Top-quality care is available throughout the country, although basic in rural areas. Inoculations are only required for those travelling from yellow-fever areas. Malaria precautions are necessary in some areas.

Total GDP (2006)	US$255,3 billion*
GDP per capita (2006)	US$5 321*
Real GDP growth (2006)	5,0%
Inflation (CPIX) (2006)	4,6%

* Based on a mid-2006 exchange rate of R6,762 to the US$

For further information on South Africa, visit *www.southafrica.info* and *www.gov.za*

LIVIERO

SOUTH AFRICA TODAY

In 1994, a new democratic South African state was born with an inheritance which was anything but auspicious. The first years of democracy saw the introduction of a new constitutional and legislative framework. The Constitution was adopted in 1996 and an average of 90 Acts of new legislation were introduced per year in the first 10 years.

Within that framework, the South African polity has seen progress in:

- voice and accountability
- political stability
- government effectiveness
- regulatory quality
- integrity and legitimacy of the State and the rule of law
- efforts to expose and deal with corruption.

Black people had previously been denied the vote and meaningful access to the economy. From the sports fields to the factory floors, schoolrooms to neighbourhoods, South Africans were divided along racial lines, a divide enforced by repression and the denial of human rights.

The economy, isolated for years by the international community, was stagnating while debt was ballooning.

Since 1994, in line with the Reconstruction and Development Programme, government has set out to dismantle apartheid social relations and to create a democratic society based on equity, non-racialism and non-sexism.

In 2003, government conducted a review covering the First Decade of Freedom. *Towards a Ten Year Review* assessed how far these objectives had been met through the work of its five clusters, and identified challenges of the Second Decade of Freedom. This was supplemented in 2006 by a report on macrosocial trends. The report, *A Nation in the Making*, concluded that South African society was making advances in terms of both hard (socio-economic) and soft (identity and social cohesion) issues, but that there were still many challenges to be overcome to fully realise the vision of a better life for all.

In 2007, government, for the first time released a set of development indicators to provide pointers to time the evolution of South Africa's society. They showed the strides the country has made towards creating a better life for all.

Governance and Administration Cluster

Since 1994, the Public Service has been transformed. On 31 March 2005, 73,9% of the Public Service was African, 3,7% Asian, 8,9% coloured and 13,5% white. With regard to gender, 53,3% was female and 46,7% male. At senior management level, 54% were African, 7,5% Asian, 7,7% coloured and 30% white. The gender breakdown for senior management was 28,5% female and 71,5% male.

Government's imbizo outreach programmes, including meetings with provincial and local government executives, enable communities to interact directly with government to help speed up the implementation of programmes to improve their lives.

Policy and implementation are more integrated thanks to the Government's cluster approach, improved provincial and local government co-ordination and a national development framework. The fight against corruption has been given muscle with legislation, national campaigns, whistle-blowing mechanisms and special courts.

Important initiatives include community development workers, the Batho Pele Gateway Portal, and Thusong Service Centres.

Social Cluster

The central programme of the social sector focuses on poverty alleviation through programmes that address income, human capital and asset poverty. It is in this intersection between access to services, income and assets that the issue of overall poverty trends since 1994 are examined.

Inequality, as measured at household level before and after factoring in social spending by the State, shows that the impact of social spending (including the tax effect) reduced the degree of inequality massively due to a redirection of spending to the poor since 1994.

Social grants are no longer allocated on a racial basis as they were under apartheid. Grants are targeted at, among others, pensioners, poor families with children, war veterans and families taking care of children and people in need.

With regard to social assistance and social insurance, 3,2% of gross domestic product goes towards social grants to 12,7 million beneficiaries. The South African Social Security Agency is in full swing, helping reduce inefficiencies in the social grant system.

Between 1994 and August 2007, government had injected more than R44,1 billion into housing and built 2,4 million houses.

By the end of the 2006/07 financial year, the Commission on the Restitution of Land Rights had settled 93% of the 79 696 claims lodged. It still had to settle an outstanding 5 279 rural claims. Access to electricity, water and sanitation has improved. South Africa has already achieved the Millennium Development Goal in respect of basic water supply, with improvement of access to 83% in 2006.

In 2006, 1,2 million people received access to basic water, contributing to government's target of eradicating the backlog of people without access to water by 2008. An additional 250 000 households received access to basic sanitation. By August 2007, 149 863 bucket toilets had been removed around the country from the initial backlog of 252 254 in February 2005.

To make the health system more equitable, efficient and effective, the Department of Health is undertaking a complete transformation of the health delivery system.

By April 2007, 1 600 clinics had either been built or upgraded since 1995 and 11 new hospitals built since 1998.

Free healthcare is being provided to children under six years of age, pregnant and lactating women; and to people with disabilities.

Social-sector programmes have helped address the apartheid legacy of poverty and inequality. However, the challenge of eradicating poverty and other social ills is compounded by societal dynamics set in motion in part by the transition itself. These are further elaborated in the macrosocial report, *A Nation in the Making,* and the *Development Indicators.*

Economic Cluster

South Africa's economy grew by 5% in 2006, representing the highest rate of economic growth in 25 years. The unemployment rate has declined for three years in a row, with over a million jobs created in this period.

The Accelerated and Shared Growth Initiative for South Africa (AsgiSA) will open the way for faster implementation of various government programmes. By addressing the binding constraints to faster growth of the economy, it will create conditions for the speeding up of economic growth to at least 6% a year between 2010 and 2014. This will help halve unemployment and poverty by 2014, as mandated by the electorate in the 2004 election. AsgiSA is a response to the following binding constraints:

- the relative volatility of the currency
- the cost, efficiency and capacity of the national logistics system
- the shortage of suitably skilled labour amplified by the cost effects on labour of apartheid spatial patterns
- barriers to entry, limits to competition and limited new investment opportunities
- the regulatory environment and the burden on small and medium businesses
- deficiencies in state organisation, capacity and leadership.

Some R500 billion has been set aside for AsgiSA infrastructure programmes between 2007 and 2010. Some of these programmes will strengthen the economy by investing in the electricity, transport and telecommunications systems.

To improve service delivery in underdeveloped urban and rural areas, AsgiSA will work through the Municipal Infrastructure Grant, Expanded Public Works Programme and other infrastructure funds. These will improve service delivery such as roads and railways, water, electricity, housing, schools and clinics, business-support centres, sports facilities and government-service centres.

Since 2004, growth has averaged over 4,5%, and thus the country seems likely to achieve the AsgiSA target of at least 4,5% for 2009, and 6% for 2010 to 2014.

According to the *Employment Equity Report 2006/07*, blacks (i.e. Africans, coloureds and Indians) represented 26,9% of all employees at the senior management level. Black females represented 8% (African female 3,6%, coloured female 2,1% and Indian female 2,3%). Black males represented 18,9% (African male 9,8%, coloured male 3,7% and Indian male 5,4%).

Whites represented 70,9% of all employees at this level. White females accounted for 19% and white males accounted for 51,9%. Foreign nationals represented 2% of all employees at this level.

Justice, Crime Prevention and Security (JCPS) Cluster

The JCPS Cluster is following a two-pronged strategy in the fight against crime in South Africa. The strategy, while confirming the central role of law-enforcement agencies in the fight against crime, also focuses on community involvement and the establishment of partnerships as key instruments in crime prevention and combating.

When the crime figures for 2006/07 were compared to those recorded during the 2005/06 financial year, the following findings were made:

Most of the contact-related, property-related and other serious crime trends experienced decreases. Eight serious crimes were grouped together as contact crime or violent crime against the person. These crimes are murder, attempted murder, rape, assault with the intent to cause grievious bodily harm (GBH), common assault, indecent assault, aggravated robbery and other robbery. These crimes account for 33,3% of South Africa's recorded crime.

Six of the eight contact crimes, namely rape, attempted murder, assault GBH, common assault, indecent assault and common robbery, decreased by between 8,7% and 3,0%. These crimes were: common assault (-8,7%), common robbery (-5,8%), indecent assault (-5,5%), rape (-5,2%), assault GBH (-4,9%) and attempted murder (-3,0%). There was an overall decrease of 3,4% in contact crimes during the period under review. Two of the eight contact crimes, namely aggravated robbery and murder, increased by 4,6% and 2,4% respectively. Aggravated robberies, that is instances of robbery accompanied by violence and/or the use of a weapon, and murder are obviously a cause of concern to the South African Police Service.

It is concentrating a great deal of its efforts on implementing operations and interventions to prevent and combat this particular crime trend.

Car hijackings and house robberies, two of the subcategories of aggravated robbery, increased by 6% and 25,4% respectively during the period under review, accounting for just more than one out of five aggravated robberies.

Government has prioritised interventions to deal with certain specific crimes. These include sexual offences, domestic violence, organised crime and corruption, cross-border crime, taxi violence and regulating the ownership and possession of firearms. The Victim-Empowerment Programme has also been a priority of government in addressing the needs of victims.

International Relations, Peace and Security Cluster

Democracy opened a remarkable new chapter in South Africa's international relations. South Africa has established itself as a respected partner and force for good within the community of nations, and has become a leading voice in the developing world for a more progressive, people-centred and multilateral rules-based global system.

Given the apartheid State's isolated and ignominious past, the country's achievements in and contributions to international, continental and regional affairs during the First Decade of Freedom have been truly spectacular.

South Africa has successfully normalised its diplomatic relations with the world and has rejoined all significant regional, continental and multilateral institutions.

The country has also developed a reputation for its positive contribution in support of United Nations-and African Union-mandated peace-support operations.

Challenges of the next decade

The next decade's challenges arise from lessons learnt in the First Decade of Freedom and new challenges created by the first stage of transformation.

Key challenges will be creating jobs for the millions seeking work, and equipping them for a changing economy in which higher skills are required.

After a decade of freedom and transformation, the Government, elected in April 2004, has embarked on a programme of action to consolidate democracy in South Africa and to put the country on a faster growth and development path. If South Africans are to make continued and faster progress towards a united, non-racial, non-sexist and democratic society in the Second Decade of Freedom, then we need to move to a higher growth and development path. This requires a major intervention: to reinforce the consolidation of democracy with measures aimed at integrating all of society into a growing economy from which they can benefit. This will require:

- an encompassing framework and vision defining a shared

approach by all sectors of society in partnership around common development objectives

- better performance by the State, with focus on efficient implementation and decisive intervention to unlock any delivery logjams
- addressing consequences of the social transition, by improving access to work opportunities and sustainable livelihoods in urban and rural areas, and by ensuring that, when people migrate, they have the skills and information to take advantage of opportunities
- improving the regional environment and implementing the New Partnership for Africa's Development, so that South Africa can weld together a number of southern African countries into a locomotive for faster growth in sub-Saharan Africa.

Modern humans have lived in what is today South Africa for over 100 000 years, and their ancestors for some 3,3 million years.

One site which is particularly rich in fossil remains, the area around the Sterkfontein caves near Johannesburg, is justifiably called the Cradle of Humankind.

More recent evidence of early humans is the many vivid rock paintings which were created by small groups of Stone Age hunter-gatherers, the ancestors of the Khoekhoen and San.

Some 2 000 years ago, the Khoekhoen (the Hottentots of early European terminology) were pastoralists who had settled mostly along the coast, while the San (the Bushmen) were hunter-gatherers spread across the region. At this time, Bantu-speaking agro-pastoralists began arriving in southern Africa, spreading from the eastern lowlands to the Highveld.

At several archaeological sites there is evidence of sophisticated political and material cultures.

European contact

The first European settlement in southern Africa was established by the Dutch East India Company in Table Bay (Cape Town) in 1652. Created to supply passing ships, the colony grew quickly as Dutch farmers settled to grow produce. Shortly after the establishment of the colony, slaves were imported from East Africa, Madagascar and the East Indies.

Conflict

From the 1770s, colonists came into contact and inevitable conflict with Bantu-speaking chiefdoms some 800 km east of Cape Town. A century of intermittent warfare ensued during which the colonists gained ascendancy over the isiXhosa-speaking chiefdoms.

At approximately this time, in the areas beyond the reach of the colonists, a spate of state-building was being launched. The old order was upset and the Zulu kingdom emerged as a highly centralised state.

In the 1820s, the celebrated Zulu leader Shaka established sway over a vast area of south-east Africa.

As splinter groups from Shaka's Zulu nation conquered and absorbed communities in their path, the region experienced a fundamental disruption. Substantial states, such as Moshoeshoe's Lesotho and other Sotho-Tswana chiefdoms were established, partly for reasons of defence.

This temporary disruption of life on the Highveld served to facilitate the expansion northwards of the original Dutch settlers' descendants, the Boer Voortrekkers, from the 1830s.

Occupation

In 1806, Britain reoccupied the Cape. As the colony prospered, the political rights of the various races were guaranteed, with slavery being abolished in 1838.

Throughout the 1800s, the boundaries of European influence spread eastwards. From the port of Durban, Natal settlers pushed northwards, further and further into the land of the Zulu.

From the mid-1800s, the Voortrekkers coalesced in two land-locked white-ruled republics, the South African Republic (Transvaal) and the Orange Free State.

The mineral revolution

The discovery of diamonds north of the Cape in the 1860s brought tens of thousands of people to the area around Kimberley. In 1871, Britain annexed the diamond fields. Independent African chiefdoms were systematically subjugated and incorporated.

The most dramatic example was the Zulu War of 1879, which saw the Zulu state brought under imperial control, but only after King Cetshwayo's soldiers inflicted a celebrated defeat on British forces at Isandlwana.

Gold

The discovery of the Witwatersrand goldfields in 1886 was a turning point in the history of South Africa. The demand for franchise rights for English-speaking immigrants working on the new goldfields was the pretext Britain used to go to war with the Transvaal and Orange Free State in 1899.

The Boers initially inflicted some heavy defeats on the British but eventually the might of imperial Britain proved too strong for the guerilla bands and the war ended in 1902. Britain's scorched-earth policy included farm burnings and the setting up of concentration camps for non-combatants in which some 26 000 Boer women and children died.

The incarceration of black (including coloured) people in racially segregated camps has only recently been acknowledged in historical accounts of the war.

Union and opposition

In 1910, the Union of South Africa was created out of the Cape, Natal, Transvaal and Free State. It was to be essentially a white union.

Black opposition was inevitable, and the African National Congress (ANC) was founded in 1912 to protest the exclusion of blacks from power. In 1921, the Communist Party came into being at a time of heightened militancy.

In the face of a groundswell of opposition to racially defined government, the seminal Natives Land Act was legislated in 1913. This defined the remnants of blacks' ancestral lands for African occupation. The homelands, as they were subsequently called, eventually comprised about 13% of South Africa's land. More discriminatory legislation – particularly relating to job reservation favouring whites, and the disenfranchisement of coloured voters in the Cape – was enacted. Meanwhile, Afrikaner nationalism, fuelled by job losses arising from worldwide recession, was on the march.

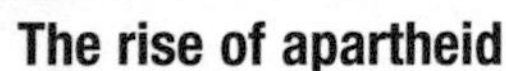

The rise of apartheid

After the Second World War, in 1948, the pro-Afrikaner National Party (NP) came to power with the ideology of apartheid, an even more rigorous and authoritarian approach than the previous segregationist policies.

While white South Africa was cementing its power, black opposition politics were evolving. In 1943, a younger, more determined political grouping came to the fore with the launch of the ANC Youth League, a development which was to foster the leadership of figures such as Nelson Mandela, Oliver Tambo and Walter Sisulu.

Repression

In 1961, the NP Government under Prime Minister HF Verwoerd declared South Africa a republic after winning a whites-only referendum.

A new concern with racial purity was apparent in laws prohibiting interracial sex and in provisions for population registration requiring that every South African be assigned to one discrete racial category or another.

Residential segregation was enforced, with whole communities being uprooted and forced into coloured and black "group areas".

Separate development

At a time when much of Africa was on the verge of independence, the South African Government was devising its policy of separate development, dividing the African population into artificial ethnic "nations", each with its own "homeland" and the prospect of "independence". The truth was that the rural reserves were by this time thoroughly degraded by overpopulation and soil erosion.

Forced removals from "white" areas affected some 3,5 million people, and vast rural slums were created in the homelands. The pass laws and influx control were extended and harshly enforced.

The introduction of apartheid policies coincided with the adoption by the ANC in 1949 of its Programme of Action, expressing the renewed militancy of the 1940s.

The programme embodied a rejection of white domination and a call for action in the form of protests, strikes and demonstrations.

Defiance

The Defiance Campaign of the early 1950s carried mass mobilisation to new heights under the banner of non-violent resistance to the pass laws. In 1955, the Freedom Charter was drawn up at the Congress of the People in Soweto. The charter enunciated the principles of the struggle, binding the movement to a culture of human rights and non-racialism.

Soon the mass-based organisations, including the ANC and the Pan-Africanist Congress (PAC), were banned. Matters came to a head at Sharpeville in March 1960 when 69 PAC anti-pass demonstrators were killed. A state of emergency was imposed, and detention without trial was introduced.

Struggle days

Leaders of the black political organisations at this time either went into exile or were arrested. In this climate, the ANC and PAC abandoned their long-standing commitment to non-violent resistance and turned to armed struggle, waged from the independent countries to the north.

Top leaders still inside the country, including members of the ANC's newly formed military wing, Umkhonto we Sizwe (Spear of the Nation), were arrested in 1963. At the Rivonia Trial, eight ANC leaders, including Nelson Mandela, convicted of sabotage (instead of treason, the original charge), were sentenced to life imprisonment.

While draconian measures kept the lid on activism for much of the 1960s, the resurgence of resistance politics in the early 1970s was dramatic.

The year 1976 marked the beginning of a sustained anti-apartheid revolt. In June, school pupils in Soweto rose up against apartheid education, followed by youth uprisings all around the country. Strong, legal vehicles for the democratic forces tested the state, whose response until then had been invariably heavy-handed repression.

Reform

Shaken by the scale of protest and opposition, the government embarked on a series of limited reforms in the early 1980s, an early example being the recognition of black trade unions.

In 1983, the Constitution was reformed to allow the coloured and Indian minorities limited participation in separate and subordinate houses of parliament, which enjoyed limited support.

In 1986, the hated pass laws were scrapped. At this time, the international community strengthened its support for the anti-apartheid cause. However, these steps fell far short of the democratic aspirations of the majority of South Africans.

Mass resistance increasingly challenged the apartheid state, which resorted to intensified repression accompanied by eventual recognition that apartheid could not be sustained.

Apartheid's last days

In February 1990, newly elected President FW de Klerk announced the unbanning of the liberation movements and the release of political prisoners, notably Nelson Mandela.

Democracy at last

After a difficult negotiation process, South Africa held its first democratic election in April 1994 under an interim Constitution.

The ANC emerged with a 62% majority. South Africa, now welcomed back into the international community, was divided into nine new provinces in place of the four provinces and 10 homelands that existed previously. In terms of the interim

Constitution, the NP and Inkatha Freedom Party participated in a government of national unity under President Mandela, South Africa's first democratically elected president.

The ANC-led Government embarked on a programme to promote the reconstruction and development of the country and its institutions.

The second democratic election, in 1999, saw the ANC increasing its majority to a point just short of two thirds of the total vote. South Africa was launched into the post-Mandela era under the presidency of Thabo Mbeki.

In the election on 14 April 2004, the ANC won the national vote with 69,68%. 27 April 2004 saw the swearing in of President Mbeki and the celebration of 10 Years of Freedom attended by heads of state and government delegations from across the world. In his speech, President Mbeki vowed to fight poverty as a central part of the national effort to build the new South Africa.

The sense of national unity among South Africans and confidence in the direction of the country have since 2004 been at levels not seen since the dawn of freedom in 1994. In this context of an unprecedented confluence of encouraging possibilities and confidence, described by President Mbeki as the beginning of South Africa's Age of Hope, the conditions for a national effort for faster and shared growth have never been better.

Working with its social partners, the Government has developed AsgiSA, the Accelerated and Shared Growth Initiative for South Africa, systematically to raise the trajectory of growth to an average of at least 6% between 2010 and 2014. Such rates of growth, combined with improved labour absorption, will ensure that South Africa is able to halve unemployment and poverty by the end of the Second Decade of Freedom. The year 2007 saw the anniversary of the deaths of Oliver Reginald Tambo (14 years ago), Inkosi Albert Luthuli (40 years ago) and Steve Biko (30 years ago). It also marked the 60th anniversary of the Doctors Pact of leaders of African and Indian communities (AB Xuma, GM Naicker and Yusuf Dadoo) and the 20th anniversary of the visit to Dakar by Afrikaner intellectuals to meet the ANC.

These commemorations reiterated the role of social partnerships in achieving long-term goals, to the benefit of the country. This is in keeping with government's commitment to build, in partnership with the people, a better life for all.

The fabric of South African society is continually changing, creating not only new challenges but also greater stability and peace, and laying the foundation for a society in which the individual and collective human potential of the nation can come to full fruition.

SOUTH AFRICA'S PEOPLE

South Africa is a country where various cultures form a unique nation, proud of their heritage and unity in diversity.

People

According to the 2001 Census, there were 44 819 778 people in South Africa on the night of 10 October 2001. They classified themselves as follows:

- Nguni people (the Zulu, Xhosa, Ndebele and Swazi)
- Sotho-Tswana people (including the Southern, Northern and Western Sotho [Tswana])
- Tsonga
- Venda
- Afrikaners
- English speakers
- coloureds
- Indians
- those who have immigrated to South Africa from the rest of Africa, Europe and Asia and maintain their own strong cultural identities
- a few members of the Khoi and the San.

The mid-2007 population was estimated at 47,9 million people.

Languages

The Constitution of the Republic of South Africa, 1996 states that everyone has the right to use the language and to participate in the cultural life of his/her choice, but no one may do so in a manner inconsistent with any provision of the Bill of Rights. Each person also has the right to instruction in the language of his/her choice where this is reasonably practicable.

Official languages

To cater for South Africa's diverse peoples, the Constitution provides for 11 official languages, namely Afrikaans, English, isiNdebele, isiXhosa, isiZulu, Sesotho sa Leboa, Sesotho, Setswana, siSwati, Tshivenda and Xitsonga.

Total population by province

Provinces	Census 1996	Census 2001	% Change 1996/2001	CS 2007	% Change 2001/2007
Eastern Cape	6 147 244	6 278 651	2,1	6 527 747	4,0
Free State	2 633 504	2 706 775	2,8	2 773 059	2,4
Gauteng	7 624 893	9 178 873	20,4	10 451 713	13,9
KwaZulu-Natal	8 572 302	9 584 129	11,8	10 259 230	7,0
Limpopo	4 576 133	4 995 534	9,2	5 238 286	4,9
Mpumalanga	3 124 203	3 365 885	7,7	3 643 435	8,2
Northern Cape	1 011 864	991 919	-2,0	1 058 060	6,7
North West	2 936 554	3 193 676	8,8	3 271 948	2,5
Western Cape	3 956 875	4 524 335	14,3	5 278 585	16,7
South Africa	**40 583 573**	**44 819 778**	**10,4**	**48 502 063**	**8,2**

Source: Census 1996, 2001 and *Community Survey 2007*

Recognising the historically diminished use and status of the indigenous languages, the Constitution expects government to implement positive measures to elevate the status and advance the use of these languages.

National and provincial governments may use any two or more official languages. While communication with the public tends to be produced in more than one language, internal communication takes place mostly in English.

In 2003, Cabinet approved the National Language Policy Framework to promote the equitable use of the 11 official languages and to ensure redress for previously marginalised indigenous languages.

The National Language Service (NLS) provides a range of language services for official documentation, develops and promotes national language policy, and advises on standardising and disseminating information on a range of terminology. The NLS, which was allocated R50 million in 2007/08, is responsible for implementing the National Language Policy Framework.

By mid-2007, successful prototypes of spell checkers for Afrikaans, isiXhosa, isiZulu, Sesotho sa Leboa and Setswana had been developed. Progress on corpus acquisition and annotation had been made for a machine-aided translation system.

The development of a multilingual telephone-based information system was signed. The National Strategy for Human Language Technologies (HLT) has been completed.

Projects planned to be implemented between 2007 and 2010 include:

- full implementation of the HLT National Strategy
- open-source HLT software for tasks such as speech recognition and speech synthesis in the South African official languages
- trained HLT developers, including fluent speakers of all of the South African official languages
- a machine-aided translation system optimised for the 11 official languages
- promulgation of the South African Language Practitioners Council Act
- establishment of the South African Language Practitioners Council
- establishment of language units within government departments.

The Telephone Interpreting Service for South Africa provides telephone-interpreting services to people who need to access government and aims especially to improve verbal communication between citizens and government agencies, thus allowing citizens to exercise their right to use the language of their choice when dealing with government.

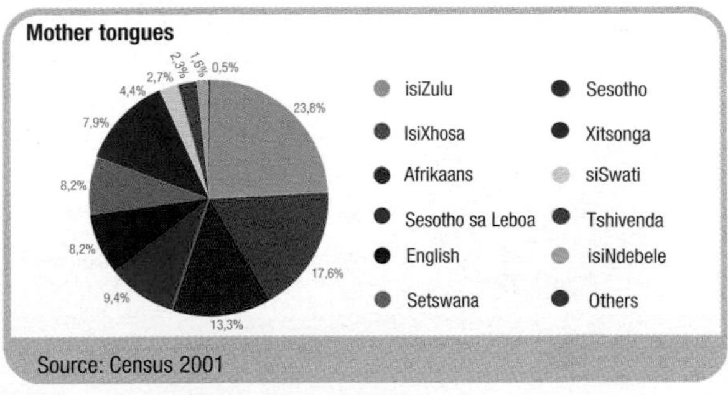

Source: Census 2001

The service was installed at over 300 sites in government departments as a pilot project, and has begun to set up sign-language sites to enable the deaf community to access the project's services.

Religion

Almost 80% of South Africa's population is Christian. Other religious groups include Hindus, Muslims and Jews. A minority of South Africa's population do not belong to any of the major religions, but regard themselves as traditionalists or of no specific religious affiliation. The Constitution guarantees freedom of worship.

Christian churches

Churches continue to play a critical role as agents of social change and transformation in pursuit of equality and the creation of a human-rights culture.

African independent churches (AICs)

The largest grouping of Christian churches is the AICs, and one of the most dramatic aspects of religious affiliation has been the rise of this movement.

There are 4 000 or more independent churches with a combined membership of more than 10 million. Most are regarded as Zionist or Apostolic churches. The Zion Christian Church is the largest of these

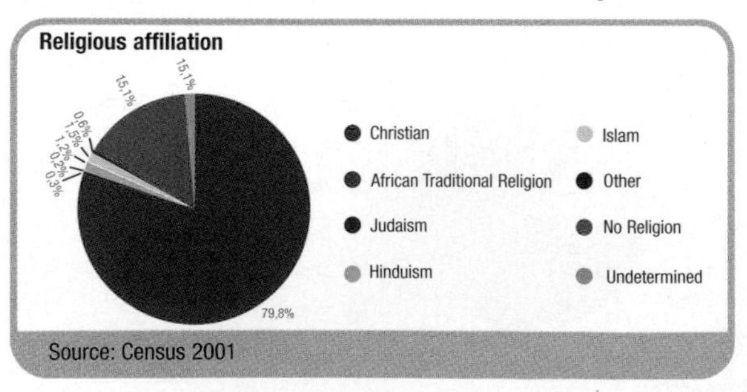

Source: Census 2001

churches in South Africa and the largest church overall, with over four million members.

Afrikaans churches

The Dutch Reformed family of churches represents some 3,5 million people. The Nederduits Gereformeerde Kerk has about 1 200 congregations countrywide. The other churches are the Uniting Reformed Church of South Africa and the smaller Reformed Church in Africa, with predominantly Indian members. The Nederduitsch Hervormde Kerk and the Gereformeerde Kerk are regarded as sister churches.

Roman Catholic Church

In recent years, the Roman Catholic Church has grown strongly in numbers and influence, even though South Africa is predominantly Protestant. It works closely with other churches on the socio-political front.

Other Christian churches

Established churches in South Africa include the Methodist Church, the Church of the Province of Southern Africa (Anglican Church), and various Lutheran, Presbyterian, Congregational and Baptist churches. Together, these churches form the nucleus of the South African Council of Churches.

The largest traditional Pentecostal churches are the Apostolic Faith Mission, the Assemblies of God and the Full Gospel Church, but there are numerous others.

A number of charismatic churches have been established in recent years. Also active in South Africa, among the smaller groups, are the Greek Orthodox and Seventh Day Adventist churches.

African Traditionalists

Because the traditional religion of the African people has a strong cultural base, the various groups have different rituals, but there are certain common features.

A supreme being is generally recognised, but ancestors are of great significance. As a result of close contact with Christianity, many people find themselves in a transitional phase somewhere between Traditional African Religion and Christianity.

Other religions

Two thirds of South Africa's Indians are Hindus.

The Muslim community in South Africa is small but growing strongly. The Cape Malays, who mostly descended from Indonesian slaves, make up most of this group, with the remaining 20% being of Indian descent.

The Jewish population is less than 100 000. Of these, the majority are Orthodox Jews.

Commission for the Promotion and Protection of the Rights of Cultural, Religious and Linguistic Communities

The Commission for the Promotion and Protection of the Rights of Cultural, Religious and Linguistic Communities is a constitutional body, which became active in January 2004.

The commission is funded through transfers from the Department of Provincial and Local Government. Its mission is to develop and promote peace, friendship, humanity, tolerance and national unity among cultural, religious and linguistic communities.

This will be achieved by facilitating the development of programmes to foster sensitivity, respect and understanding for cultural, religious and linguistic diversity and also by mediating in intercommunity conflict situations and facilitating harmonious co-existence.

South Africa's Constitution was the result of remarkably detailed and inclusive negotiations – difficult but determined – that were carried out with an acute awareness of the injustices of the country's non-democratic past.

The Constitution is the supreme law of the country. No other law or government action may supersede its provisions.

The Preamble to the Constitution states that its aims are to:

- heal the divisions of the past and establish a society based on democratic values, social justice and fundamental human rights
- improve the quality of life of all citizens and free the potential of each person
- lay the foundations for a democratic and open society in which government is based on the will of the people and every citizen is equally protected by law
- build a united and democratic South Africa able to take its rightful place as a sovereign state in the family of nations.

Government

Government consists of national, provincial and local spheres. The powers of the legislature, executive and courts are separate.

Parliament

Parliament consists of the National Assembly and the National Council of Provinces (NCOP). Parliamentary sittings are open to the public. Several measures have been implemented to make Parliament more accessible and accountable. The National Assembly consists of no fewer than 350 and no more than 400 members elected through a system of proportional representation for a five-year term. It elects the President and scrutinises the executive.

National Council of Provinces

The NCOP consists of 54 permanent members and 36 special delegates, and aims to represent provincial interests in the

Parliament launched its new logo in Cape Town on 27 March 2007. The new emblem is an important step in the identity of Parliament, representing its values, vision and mission.

national sphere of government. On 11 April 2007, the NCOP celebrated its 10th anniversary.

The Presidency

The President is the head of state and leads the Cabinet. He or she is elected by the National Assembly from among its members, and leads the country in the interest of national unity, in accordance with the Constitution and the law. The President of South Africa is Mr Thabo Mbeki.

The Deputy President

The President appoints the Deputy President from among the members of the National Assembly. The Deputy President is Ms Phumzile Mlambo-Ngcuka.

Cabinet

Cabinet consists of the President, as head of the Cabinet, the Deputy President and ministers. The President appoints the Deputy President and ministers, assigns their powers and functions and may dismiss them. No more than two ministers may be appointed from outside the National Assembly.

Provincial government

Each of the nine provinces has its own legislature of 30 to 80 members. They elect the Premier who heads the Executive Council.

Provinces may have legislative and executive powers concurrently with the national sphere, over:

- agriculture
- casinos, horse racing and gambling
- cultural affairs
- education at all levels, except university and university of technology education
- environment and nature conservation

Cabinet ministers, 1 January 2008		
Portfolio	**Minister**	**Deputy Minister**
Agriculture and Land Affairs	Lulama Xingwana	Dirk du Toit
Arts and Culture	Pallo Jordan	Ntombazana Botha
Communications	Ivy Matsepe-Casaburri	Radhakrishna Padayachie
Correctional Services	Ngconde Balfour	Loretta Jacobus
Defence	Mosiuoa Lekota	Mluleki George
Education	Naledi Pandor	Enver Surty
Environmental Affairs and Tourism	Marthinus van Schalkwyk	Joyce Mabudafhasi
Finance	Trevor Manuel	Jabu Moleketi
Foreign Affairs	Nkosazana Dlamini Zuma	Aziz Pahad and Sue van der Merwe
Health	Manto Tshabalala-Msimang	
Home Affairs	Nosiviwe Mapisa-Nqakula	Malusi Gigaba
Housing	Lindiwe Sisulu	
Intelligence Services	Ronnie Kasrils	
Justice and Constitutional Development	Brigitte Mabandla	Johnny de Lange
Labour	Membathisi Mdladlana	
Minerals and Energy	Buyelwa Sonjica	
Provincial and Local Government	Sydney Mufamadi	Nomatyala Hangana
The Presidency	Essop Pahad	
Public Enterprises	Alec Erwin	
Public Service and Administration	Geraldine Fraser-Moleketi	
Public Works	Thoko Didiza	Ntopile Kganyago
Safety and Security	Charles Nqakula	Susan Shabangu
Science and Technology	Mosibudi Mangena	Derek Hanekom
Social Development	Zola Skweyiya	Jean Swanson-Jacobs
Sport and Recreation	Makhenkesi Stofile	Gert Oosthuizen
Trade and Industry	Mandisi Mpahlwa	Rob Davies and Elizabeth Thabethe
Transport	Jeff Radebe	
Water Affairs and Forestry	Lindiwe Hendricks	

- health, housing and welfare
- language policy
- police services, public transport, traffic regulation and vehicle licensing
- regional planning and development and urban and rural development.

Provinces are also responsible for promoting trade, investment and tourism.

They have exclusive competency over:

- abattoirs
- ambulance services
- liquor licences
- museums other than national museums
- provincial planning
- provincial cultural matters
- provincial recreation
- provincial roads and traffic.

Local government

Local governments are not merely instruments of service delivery, but are expected to act as key agents for economic development.

Premiers, 1 January 2008	
Province	**Premier**
Eastern Cape	Nosimo Balindlela
Free State	Beatrice Marshoff
Gauteng	Mbhazima Shilowa
KwaZulu-Natal	S'bu Ndebele
Limpopo	Sello Moloto
Mpumalanga	Thabang Makwetla
North West	Edna Molewa
Northern Cape	Dipuo Peters
Western Cape	Ebrahim Rasool

Municipalities

There are 282 municipalities focused on growing local economies and providing infrastructure and services.

The Constitution provides for three categories of municipalities:

- metropolitan municipalities
- local municipalities
- district areas or municipalities.

South Africa has nine metropolitan municipalities, namely:

- Buffalo City (East London),
- City of Cape Town
- Ekurhuleni Metropolitan Municipality (East Rand)
- City of eThekwini (Durban)
- City of Johannesburg
- Mangaung Municipality (Bloemfontein)
- Msunduzi Municipality (Pietermaritzburg)
- Nelson Mandela Metropolitan Municipality (Port Elizabeth)
- City of Tshwane (Pretoria).

Municipalities enjoy significant powers to corporatise their services. Legislation provides for them to report on their performance, and for residents to compare this performance with that of other municipalities.

Local Government Strategic Agenda (2006 – 2011)

The five-year Local Government Strategic Agenda aims to ensure that the three spheres of government focus on a systematic and co-ordinated local development programme that can be monitored periodically.

Municipal Infrastructure Grant (MIG)

The MIG is a key instrument for addressing municipal infrastructure and basic service backlogs. A process of re-allocating MIG funds between municipalities (as provided for in the Division of Revenue Act, 2006) has been adopted with the

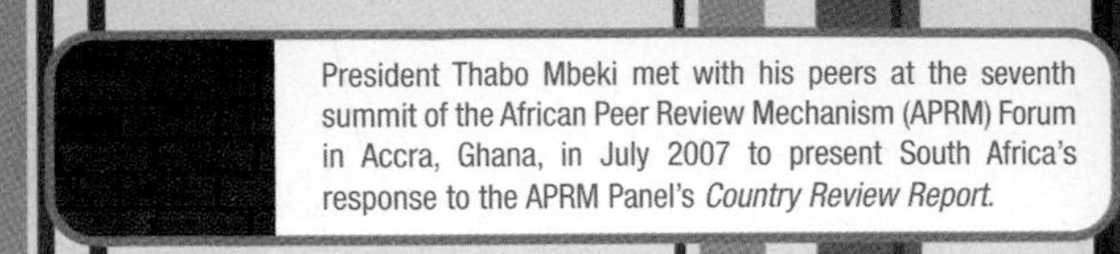
President Thabo Mbeki met with his peers at the seventh summit of the African Peer Review Mechanism (APRM) Forum in Accra, Ghana, in July 2007 to present South Africa's response to the APRM Panel's *Country Review Report*.

primary intention of using available funds in the most efficient manner, to eradicate backlogs in municipalities which have demonstrated capacity to spend. At the same time, various measures to strengthen the ability of poor-spending municipalities to better spend their MIG funds are being instituted.

Project Consolidate

In 2004, Project Consolidate, a hands-on support and engagement programme focusing on targeted municipalities, was launched. This project was informed by a growing concern that, although some municipalities were able to discharge their responsibilities, some required additional technical and institutional support. Project Consolidate is addressing these capacity challenges.

It also resulted in the mobilisation and deployment of technical support, service-delivery facilitators, engineers and project managers to the identified municipalities. All in all, this initiative introduced a new culture and method of working by national-sector departments, provinces, the private sector and the non-governmental sector to provide direct and sustained support to municipalities.

By mid-2001, 51 retired engineers, 45 graduates and 99 students had been deployed at 75 municipalities. Development and infrastructure implementation support was being given to R2,2 billion worth of projects.

Communicating with the people

The Government Communication and Information System (Government Communications) is primarily responsible for facilitating communication between government and citizens. A high premium is placed on communication that emphasises direct dialogue, especially with people in disadvantaged areas.

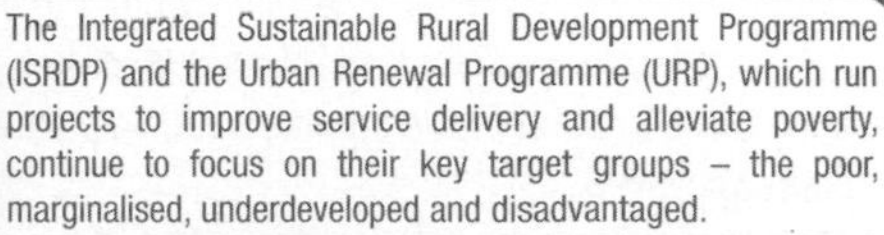

The Integrated Sustainable Rural Development Programme (ISRDP) and the Urban Renewal Programme (URP), which run projects to improve service delivery and alleviate poverty, continue to focus on their key target groups – the poor, marginalised, underdeveloped and disadvantaged.

The programmes aim to maximise the impact of all government resources and know-how in the 21 identified rural and urban nodes. Following a review of progress on the nodes, Cabinet approved the proposed financial interventions to support the nodes, within the framework of government's priority programmes.

A guide for national departments' participation in implementing the ISRDP and URP has been finalised. Provincial and local government intend on upping the pace of implementing government programmes, which seek to cultivate conditions for sustainable economic development in geographic spaces that were previously neglected.

The Urban Renewal Nodes Investment Atlas identifies 25 investment opportunities, while its rural counterpart identifies 88 investment opportunities, mainly in agriculture, tourism and mining.

A market development approach to creating jobs, building capacity for economic development and reducing poverty in the nodes was being piloted by mid-2007 at the Maruleng and Bushbuckridge nodes.

This pilot is a R30-million partnership between the Department of Provincial and Local Government and the Business Trust.

Government Communications is responsible for maintaining the Government's website (*www.gov.za*), which includes both an information portal for general information about government, and a services portal that is a source of information about all the services offered by national government.

Government Communications leads or is involved in various communication partnerships and joint processes, including:

- An intersectoral programme to set up Thusong Service Centres (formerly multipurpose community centres), providing information about accessing government services, as well as some government services at the centres themselves. In

The toll-free, 24-hour National Public Service Anti-Corruption Hotline facility (0800 701 701) was established for the reporting of fraud and corruption. By the end of March 2007, a total of 4 726 cases had been generated by the hotline.

October 2007, 96 Thusong Service Centres were in place and more centres were being established. A strategy for setting up one centre in each of the country's municipalities by 2014 has been approved.

- The process towards the transformation of the advertising and marketing industry.
- The Academy of Government Communication and Marketing, in collaboration with the School of Public and Development Management, Unilever and the Mandela-Rhodes Foundation.
- The Imbizo Campaign of direct interaction between government and the public.

Government Communications publishes, among other things, the *South African Yearbook,* the *Pocket Guide to South Africa* and *Vuk'uzenzele.*

The following entities report to Government Communications:

- the International Marketing Council (IMC)
- the Media Development and Diversity Agency.

International Marketing Council

The IMC of South Africa was established in 2000 as a public-private partnership aimed at creating a positive, united image for South Africa to give the country a strategic advantage in an increasingly competitive marketplace.

The IMC's threefold mission is to:

- articulate a brand for South Africa, which positions the country to attract tourism, trade and investment, as well as realise international relations objectives
- establish an integrated approach within government and the private sector towards the international marketing of South Africa
- build national support for Brand South Africa.

The Public Service

Government believes that the Public Service exists to create a better life for all.

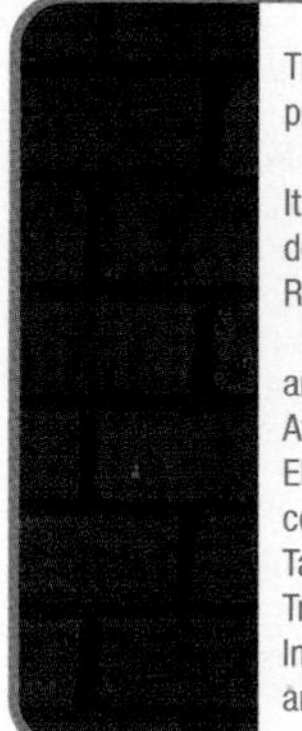

The Independent Electoral Commission (IEC) will intensify its preparations for the next general election in 2009.

The IEC is not only responsible for South Africa's elections. It has guided and supported the successful transition to democracy in a number of countries, such as the Democratic Republic of Congo.

Election-management bodies in east and southern Africa are investing in their training by sending their experts to South Africa to participate in a specialised training programme. Election administrators from eight east and southern African countries (Kenya, Lesotho, Malawi, Mozambique, South Africa, Tanzania, Zanzibar, Uganda and Zambia) all took part in the Train the Trainer course in May 2007, conducted by the International Institute for Democracy and Electoral Assistance and the IEC, with funding from the Australian Government.

Community development workers (CDWs) are part of government's drive to ensure that service delivery reaches poor and marginalised communities. CDWs act as a bridge between government and citizens, providing information on services, benefits and economic opportunities. They are in a position to inform the Government of the needs of the people.

Since the inception of the CDW Programme in 2003, 4 160 CDW learners had been recruited and deployed to municipalities. By February 2007, some 2 600 of these had subsequently been employed by provincial departments of local government. In 2007, it was envisaged that CDWs would be trained on co-operatives to enable them to mobilise and train communities on this type of business entity.

The Batho Pele (People First) policy promotes integrated and seamless service delivery.

Various projects are being delivered through Batho Pele. These include:

- the Batho Pele Gateway Portal, maintained by government, to facilitate access to all government services and information
- modernising government, for example, through the Centre for Public Service Innovation

Government's Programme of Action is available on Government Online (*www.gov.za*). The information is updated regularly to keep the public informed of the implementation process.

- creating new service-delivery mechanisms such as Thusong Service Centres and one-stop centres
- the Government Information Technology Officers' Council to alert government when and how to intervene to improve service delivery
- active auditing of national and provincial departments' anti-corruption capabilities by the Public Service Commission.

Home affairs

The Department of Home Affairs has a network of offices in all provinces. Where the establishment of fixed offices is not warranted, mobile offices or units service such areas regularly.

The Population Register is being reproduced, and an associated document-management system will be developed and rolled out gradually. This will consist of a large database, an online document-storage system, and a query interface for the retrieval and viewing of electronically stored documentation. The system will reduce processing time for each business transaction, while enhancing information integrity.

Permanent residence

The department is responsible for admitting people suitable for immigration, such as skilled workers who are in short supply locally.

The South African Government hosted the Global Forum Five on Fighting Corruption and Safeguarding Integrity, from 2 April to 5 April 2007 at the Sandton Convention Centre in Johannesburg. The conference was attended by ministers, senior officials and representatives of state bodies from over 100 countries. Heads of anti-corruption and law-enforcement agencies as well as officials from government agencies dealing with governance, the Public Service, anti-corruption, money laundering and customs attended the forum.

The Minister in The Presidency, Dr Essop Pahad, announced in May 2007 that Brand South Africa's weight in the global marketplace was valued at over half a trillion rand (over R500 billion).

This valuable imprint on popular consciousness coincides with a move by the International Marketing Council (IMC) to extend the South African country brand formula from the borders of the United Kingdom and the United States of America to emerging economic giant India.

The IMC, now a registered public entity, has brought about a sharper international profiling of South Africa as a dynamic emerging market with an image now less tied to its dramatic liberation from apartheid.

Applications are particularly encouraged from industrialists and other entrepreneurs who wish to relocate their existing concerns or establish new concerns in South Africa.

Those wishing to enter the country as work seekers or for study purposes must have the relevant permit, which is issued outside the country.

Independent Electoral Commission (IEC)

The IEC is a permanent body created by the Constitution to promote and safeguard democracy in South Africa. Although publicly funded and accountable to Parliament, the commission is independent of government. Its immediate task is the impartial management of free and fair elections at all levels of government.

A total of 250 municipal councillors crossed the floor successfully in this period, affecting the composition of 128 municipalities.

By September 2007, 12 new political parties had registered since June 2007 – the Christian Democratic Alliance, Federal Congress, National Alliance, Social Democratic Party, National People's Party, People's Democratic Movement, African People's Convention, New Vision Party, Civic Alliance of South Africa, South African Political Party, Federal African Convention and the Eden

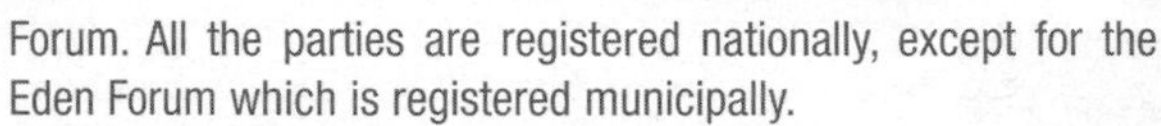

Forum. All the parties are registered nationally, except for the Eden Forum which is registered municipally.

The three parties with the largest net gain were:

- African National Congress with 53
- African People's Convention with 36
- National People's Party with 31.

In terms of loss, the three parties with the biggest net loss were:

- Pan Africanist Congress of South Africa with 41
- Independent Democrats with 27
- National Democratic Convention with 22.

THE CONSTITUTION OF THE REPUBLIC OF SOUTH AFRICA
BILL OF RIGHTS
One *law* for one *nation*

South Africa comprises nine provinces, namely Western Cape, Eastern Cape, KwaZulu-Natal, Northern Cape, Free State, North West, Gauteng, Mpumalanga and Limpopo.

Each province has its own legislature, premier and executive council.

The country has common boundaries with Namibia, Botswana and Zimbabwe, while Mozambique and Swaziland lie to the north-east. Completely enclosed by South African territory in the south-east is the mountain kingdom of Lesotho.

Western Cape

This is a region of majestic mountains; well-watered valleys; wide, sandy beaches; and breathtaking scenery.

Cape Town, the legislative capital, is one of the world's most beautiful cities and is a must-see for tourists. Other important towns in the province include Worcester and Stellenbosch, known for their winelands; George, renowned for indigenous timber and vegetable produce (and, nowadays, for world-class golf courses); and Oudtshoorn, known for its ostrich products and the celebrated Cango caves.

Provincial economy

The Western Cape's economy has grown at 5% a year in gross domestic product (GDP). By mid-2007, it was growing at 5,7%, resulting in 99 900 jobs being created since 2004.

The construction sector showed an average growth rate of 8% a year since 2004, resulting in full employment in the industry, which is poised to grow at an average of 12% a year up to 2010 and beyond.

Some tourist attractions include:

- Robben Island, where former President Nelson Mandela was imprisoned for a number of years, in Table Bay off Cape Town
- Table Mountain, with its modern cableway which takes visitors to the top, providing breathtaking views
- the National Botanical Gardens at Kirstenbosch

- whale-watching at Hermanus
- a wine-tasting tour of the spectacular winelands
- the Cape Floral Region, a world heritage site.

Western Cape

Capital:	Cape Town
Principal languages:	Afrikaans 55,3%
	isiXhosa 23,7%
	English 19,3%
Population:	4 839 800
	(*Mid-Year Population Estimates, 2007*)
Area (km^2):	129 370
% of total area:	10,6%
GDPR* at current prices (2004):	R199 412 million
% of total GDP**:	14,4%

* GDPR (Gross Domestic Product by Region)
** GDP (Gross Domestic Product)

Source: Statistics South Africa

2010 FIFA World Cup™

The 70 000-seater Greenpoint Stadium in Cape Town will host eight 2010 World Cup matches, including a semi-final.

The Western Cape Government has allocated R212 million for preparations for the tournament, in addition to the R1,9 billion contributed by national government.

The R2,7-billion investment into the Greenpoint Stadium was expected to attract at least another R7 to R8 billion in linked public investments for transport and infrastructure.

A similar amount in private-sector investments into the leisure, tourism and retail sectors of the surrounding economy in the Victoria and Alfred Waterfront, the Somerset Hospital Precinct and the larger inner-city bowl is expected.

This investment is expected to benefit ordinary citizens through employment in the construction, leisure, transport, tourism and service sectors.

Other benefits include:

- dedicated bus and taxi lanes from the R300 route right into Cape Town along the N2 Highway
- expanding the Cape Town International Airport through a R2-billion investment
- a dedicated rail link from the airport into town
- doubling the capacity of the Cape Town Convention Centre
- building at least six new hotels in the Western Cape by 2010.

Eastern Cape

The Eastern Cape, a land of undulating hills, endless sandy beaches, majestic mountain ranges and deep green forests, is the second-largest of the nine provinces. The region ranges from the dry, desolate Great Karoo to the lush forests of the Wild Coast and the Keiskamma Valley, and the mountainous southern Drakensberg region.

Provincial economy

The provincial economy has peformed well over the past three years. Provincial GDP increased by an estimated 4,7% in 2006 (4,8% in 2005), compared with the national GDP growth of 5% in 2006 (5,1% in 2005).

The metropolitan economies of Port Elizabeth and East London are based primarily on manufacturing, the most important being motor manufacturing. The Coega Industrial Development Zone near Port Elizabeth is one of the biggest initiatives ever undertaken in South Africa.

Some tourist attractions include:

- Grahamstown, the City of the Saints, a historical, educational and religious centre
- the endless golden beaches of Port Alfred and Kenton-on-Sea
- a walking tour of the Wild Coast
- the pachyderms of the Addo Elephant National Park.

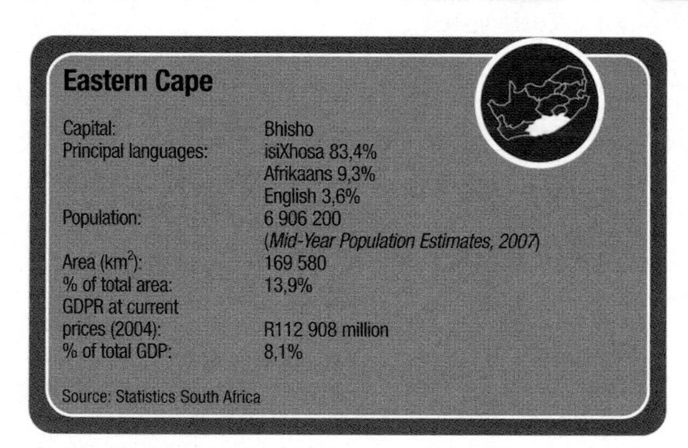

Eastern Cape

Capital:	Bhisho
Principal languages:	isiXhosa 83,4%
	Afrikaans 9,3%
	English 3,6%
Population:	6 906 200
	(*Mid-Year Population Estimates, 2007*)
Area (km^2):	169 580
% of total area:	13,9%
GDPR at current prices (2004):	R112 908 million
% of total GDP:	8,1%

Source: Statistics South Africa

2010 World Cup

The new 50 000-seater Nelson Mandela Bay Stadium in Port Elizabeth will host seven matches. By March 2007, construction of the stadium had started.

In King Sabata Dalindyebo Municipality, the final design for a new 15 000-seater stadium had been approved.

In Buffalo City, two stadiums – Absa Stadium, which seats 10 000 and Bhisho Stadium with 20 000 seats – were being refurbished.

Fan parks – public viewing areas with big-screen TVs, entertainment and food and beverage stands – will be established. Port Elizabeth will spend more than R500 million upgrading the city's transport system ahead of the World Cup.

KwaZulu-Natal

South Africa's garden province boasts a lush subtropical coastline, sweeping savanna in the east, and the magnificent Drakensberg mountains in the west. The warm Indian Ocean washing its beaches makes KwaZulu-Natal one of the country's most popular holiday destinations. Some of South Africa's best-protected indigenous coastal forests are found along the subtropical coastline.

The bustling metropolis of Durban has the busiest port in Africa.

Provincial economy

The GDP per region (GDPR) of KwaZulu-Natal is now the second-largest in the country after Gauteng. The GDPR growth rate rose over fivefold from 1% in 1999 to 5,3% in 2005, suggesting the potential to reach a 10% growth rate by the year 2014, which is far above the Accelerated and Shared Growth Initiative for South Africa's target of 6%.

Tourist attractions include:

- the 19th-century battlefields where imperial Britain clashed with the Zulu nation
- Durban's fascinating mix of eastern and western cultures
- dolphin-spotting on the coast between the Umdloti and Tugela rivers
- experiencing Zulu traditions and culture at authentic villages
- deep-sea fishing off Sodwana Bay
- the Simangaliso and Ukhahlamba-Drakensberg world heritage sites.

KwaZulu-Natal

Capital:	Pietermaritzburg
Principal languages:	isiZulu 80,9% English 13,6% Afrikaans 1,5%
Population:	10 014 500 (*Mid-Year Population Estimates, 2007*)
Area (km^2):	92 100
% of total area:	7,6%
GDPR at current prices (2004):	R231 616 million
% of total GDP:	16,71%

Source: Statistics South Africa

2010 World Cup

The stadium in Durban, with a capacity of 70 000, will host five first-round and one second-round match, as well as one of the semi-finals.

Starting from March 2007, R2,2 billion will be spent on the construction of the new soccer stadium.

Some R4 billion was expected to be spent on the construction of the new international airport and the Dube Tradeport at La Mercy. By mid-2007, the R350-million P700 Corridor from Richards Bay to Ulundi and the R300-million P577 Corridor from Mtubatuba to Hlabisa and Nongoma were under construction.

eThekwini Municipality will spend more than R1 billion over the next three years leading to the 2010 World Cup to overhaul the public transport system by making it rail-based.

Northern Cape

The Northern Cape lies to the south of the mighty Orange River, which provides the basis for a healthy agricultural industry. Away from the Orange, the landscape is characterised by vast arid plains with outcroppings of haphazard rock piles.

The province is renowned for its spectacular display of spring flowers, which, for a short period every year, attracts thousands of tourists.

Provincial economy

The Northern Cape has the smallest economy of the nine provinces. The gross geographic product represents approximately 1,8% of South Africa's GDP.

The unemployment rate is 26%, slightly below the national percentage. Nevertheless, the households under the poverty line of R800 per month are 38%, much higher than the national rate.

Mining, particularly the production of diamonds and iron ore, dominates the economy. The province is also rich in asbestos, manganese, fluorspar and marble. Strong growth areas include game farming and food production.

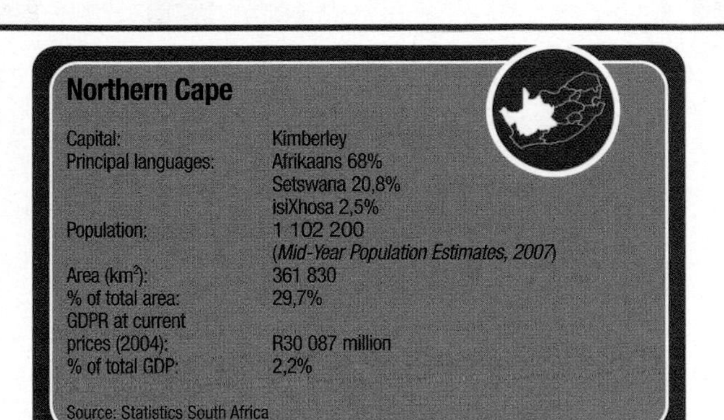

Northern Cape

Capital:	Kimberley
Principal languages:	Afrikaans 68%
	Setswana 20,8%
	isiXhosa 2,5%
Population:	1 102 200
	(*Mid-Year Population Estimates, 2007*)
Area (km²):	361 830
% of total area:	29,7%
GDPR at current prices (2004):	R30 087 million
% of total GDP:	2,2%

Source: Statistics South Africa

Tourist attractions include:

- the Kalahari Gemsbok National Park, which, together with the Gemsbok National Park in Botswana, forms Africa's first transfrontier conservation area, the Kgalagadi Transfrontier Park
- the Augrabies Falls, among the world's greatest cataracts
- the Sol Plaatje Museum in Kimberley
- the Southern African Large Telescope.

Free State

The Free State lies in the heart of South Africa. Between the Vaal River in the north and the Orange River in the south, this immense rolling prairie stretches as far as the eye can see.

The capital, Bloemfontein, houses the Supreme Court of Appeal, a leading university and some top schools.

Provincial economy

Mining, particularly gold, is the biggest employer, followed by manufacturing. A gold reef of over 400 km stretches across Gauteng and the Free State. The province accounts for 30% of South Africa's total gold production, and contributes significant amounts of silver, bituminous coal and diamonds. The Free State has cultivated land covering 3,2 million hectares. Field crops yield almost two thirds of the province's agricultural income, with most of the balance being contributed by animal products.

Some tourist attractions include:

- the sandstone formations at Golden Gate
- the spectacular scenery of the town of Clarens
- the King's Park Rose Garden in Bloemfontein
- the Basotho Cultural Village in the QwaQwa National Park
- the desolate beauty – and watersports – of Sterkfontein Dam.

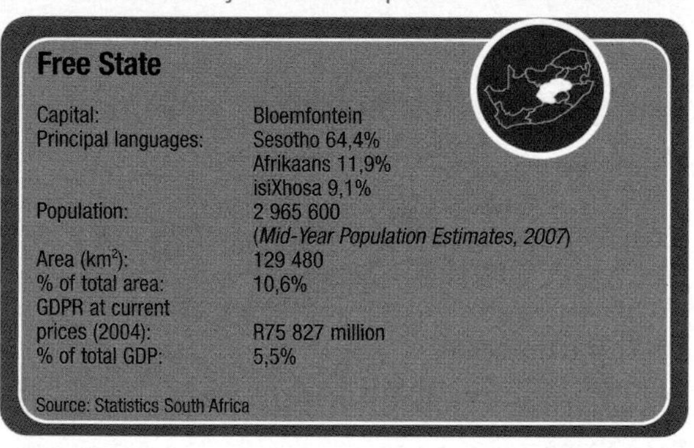

Free State

Capital:	Bloemfontein
Principal languages:	Sesotho 64,4% Afrikaans 11,9% isiXhosa 9,1%
Population:	2 965 600 (*Mid-Year Population Estimates, 2007*)
Area (km²):	129 480
% of total area:	10,6%
GDPR at current prices (2004):	R75 827 million
% of total GDP:	5,5%

Source: Statistics South Africa

2010 World Cup

The 48 000-seater Mangaung Stadium in Bloemfontein will host five first-round and one second-round match.

The province was expected to embark on the following projects from 2007:

- developing the N8 Corridor road network
- rehabilitating and reviving the rail network from Thaba Nchu to Bloemfontein
- constructing an international convention centre, which will be linked to other 2010 initiatives such as the revamping of the Bloemfontein airport, Mangaung African Cultural Festival and the intermodal transport facility.

North West

North West borders Botswana, fringed by the Kalahari Desert in the west, and the Witwatersrand in the east. A province of varied attractions, North West is home to some of South Africa's most visited national parks, the celebrated Sun City and Lost City resorts, picturesque dams and dense bush.

Provincial economy

North West is, thanks to platinum in particular, the dominant province in terms of mineral sales, which contribute 25,6% to the provincial economy. Diamonds are also mined here. Manufacturing activities include fabricated metals, food and non-metals. North West is South Africa's leading producer of white maize. Some of the world's largest cattle herds are found in the area around Vryburg.

Mining and quarrying, the flagship economic sector of the North West, continued to contribute approximately 25% to the provincial economy in 2005. This sector contributed 7,3% and 7,9% respectively in 2005 and 2006. The North West hopes to

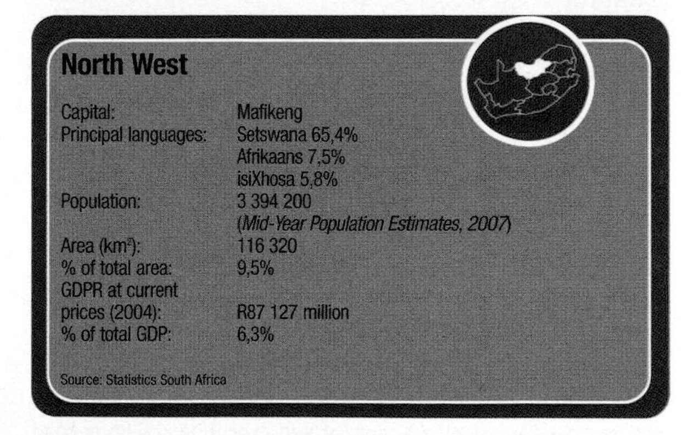

North West

Capital:	Mafikeng
Principal languages:	Setswana 65,4% Afrikaans 7,5% isiXhosa 5,8%
Population:	3 394 200 (*Mid-Year Population Estimates, 2007*)
Area (km^2):	116 320
% of total area:	9,5%
GDPR at current prices (2004):	R87 127 million
% of total GDP:	6,3%

Source: Statistics South Africa

reduce its dependence on the mining sector with an increased diversification to tourism and non-mining-related manufacturing industries.

Some tourist attractions include:

- Mafikeng, site of the Anglo-Boer/South African War siege
- the mampoer (moonshine) country of Groot Marico
- entertainment, gaming and sports at Sun City and the Palace of the Lost City
- a game drive or walk in Madikwe Game Reserve
- spotting the Big Five in the Pilanesberg National Park
- Vredefort Dome World Heritage Site.

2010 World Cup

Rustenburg is the official hosting city in the North West, with the 42 000-seater Royal Bafokeng Stadium as official match venue.

More than R400 million will be spent on road and traffic infrastructure in Rustenburg and Phokeng ahead of the 2010 World Cup.

Gauteng

Although geographically the smallest of the nine provinces, Gauteng (Sotho word for "place of gold") contributes more than a third of South Africa's GDP.

The main cities are Johannesburg, the biggest city in southern Africa, and Pretoria, the administrative capital of the country.

Provincial economy

Manufacturing, financial and business services and logistics make Gauteng the economic powerhouse of southern Africa. Success in attracting value-added new-economy investment is borne out by the burgeoning high-tech corridor in Midrand.

Gauteng has a greater proportion of its labour force in professional, technical, managerial and executive positions than any other province. Johannesburg houses the JSE Limited, the largest securities exchange in Africa.

Hundreds of leading local companies have their head offices here, as do the regional operations of many multinationals.

Some tourist attractions include:

- Soweto, home to two million people and the site of much of the anti-apartheid struggle
- Pretoria in spring, when some 50 000 flowering jacaranda trees turn the city purple
- the Cradle of Humankind, the richest source of pre-hominid fossils on the planet, and a world heritage site
- Maropeng, near the Cradle of Humankind
- bustling, funky downtown Johannesburg, City of Gold.

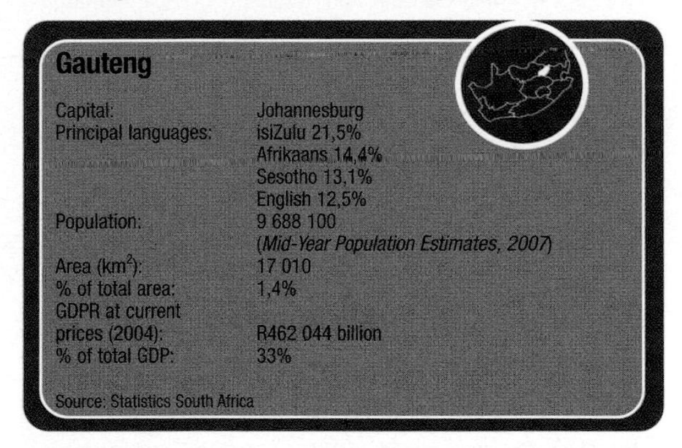

Gauteng

Capital:	Johannesburg
Principal languages:	isiZulu 21,5% Afrikaans 14,4% Sesotho 13,1% English 12,5%
Population:	9 688 100 (*Mid-Year Population Estimates, 2007*)
Area (km^2):	17 010
% of total area:	1,4%
GDPR at current prices (2004):	R462 044 billion
% of total GDP:	33%

Source: Statistics South Africa

2010 World Cup

Soccer City in Johannesburg will host the final match of the 2010 World Cup. It will accommmodate 94 700 soccer fans. Ellis Park, the venue of the 1995 Rugby World Cup final, will undergo a major renovation before the World Cup. It will have 61 000 seats.

Loftus Versfeld Stadium (50 000 seats) in Pretoria will also host 2010 World Cup games. Some R40 million was set aside in 2007/08 for the rehabilitation of the R21 road to improve connectivity between Pretoria and the OR Tambo International Airport.

In 2006/07, phase one of the refurbishment of George Thabe Stadium in Sharpeville, Sinaba Stadium in Daveyton and HM Pitje Stadium in Mamelodi was completed. Phase two of the Sinaba and HM Pitje stadiums was expected to be completed at the end of the 2007/08 financial year. These stadiums will be used as practice venues for the tournament.

The Mary Fitzgerald Square in Newtown was turned into a fan park for the Telkom Challenge matches in July 2007.

The province has won the right to host SoccerEx, the largest football business exhibition in the world, over the next three years. It provides an international platform to showcase the province's readiness to host the 2010 World Cup.

Mpumalanga

Mpumalanga ("place where the sun rises") is bordered by Mozambique and Swaziland in the east, and Gauteng in the west. It is situated mainly on high plateau grasslands which roll eastwards for hundreds of kilometres. In the north-east, the

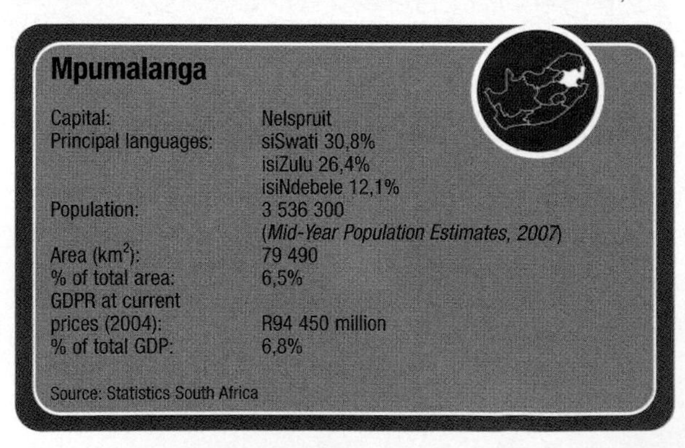

Mpumalanga

Capital:	Nelspruit
Principal languages:	siSwati 30,8% isiZulu 26,4% isiNdebele 12,1%
Population:	3 536 300 (*Mid-Year Population Estimates, 2007*)
Area (km²):	79 490
% of total area:	6,5%
GDPR at current prices (2004):	R94 450 million
% of total GDP:	6,8%

Source: Statistics South Africa

province rises towards mountain peaks and then terminates in an immense escarpment. In some places, this escarpment plunges hundreds of metres down to the low-lying Lowveld, home to the Kruger National Park.

Provincial economy

Mpumalanga combines mining and heavy industry with the cultivation of citrus, tropical and subtropical fruits and extensive forests. The southern hemisphere's three biggest power stations are located in the province, supplied by the Witbank coalfields which are among the most extensive in the world. Middelburg is a major steel producer, and Secunda has a key oil-from-coal installation.

Some tourist attractions include:

- Kruger National Park and its ultra-luxurious, privately owned adjoining lodges
- the spectacular Mac Mac Falls outside Sabie
- the well-preserved historical gold-rush towns of Pilgrim's Rest and Barberton
- the stunning scenery of the Blyde River Canyon
- spectacular scenery at God's Window
- the historic train ride between Waterval-Boven and Waterval-Onder.

2010 World Cup

The Mbombelo Stadium in Nelspruit, with a capacity of 46 000, will host four first-round matches.

Construction of the stadium started in June 2007 and is expected to be completed in May 2009. Some R15 million was put aside in 2007/08 for the first phase.

By mid-2007, the Mpumalanga Government was establishing the Intergrated 2010 Office to streamline all the preparatory work for the 2010 World Cup and ensure co-ordination among the implementing institutions, such as the Mbombela Municipality, the Office of the Premier and the Department of Culture, Sports and Recreation.

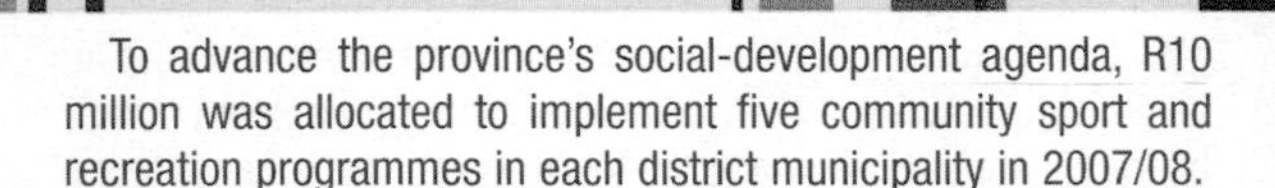

To advance the province's social-development agenda, R10 million was allocated to implement five community sport and recreation programmes in each district municipality in 2007/08.

Limpopo

In the extreme north of South Africa, Limpopo is a province of dramatic contrasts: bush, mountains, indigenous forests and plantations. Well situated for economic growth and trade with other parts of southern Africa, between 1995 and 2001 the province recorded the highest real economic growth rate in South Africa. The greater part of the Kruger National Park is located within Limpopo.

Provincial economy

Limpopo is rich in minerals, including copper, asbestos, coal, iron ore, platinum, chrome, diamonds and gold. While exports are mostly primary products, the province is rich in resources, particularly in tourism, agriculture and minerals. Cattle ranching is frequently combined with hunting. Tropical and citrus fruits are extensively cultivated while tea, coffee and forestry are important economic contributors.

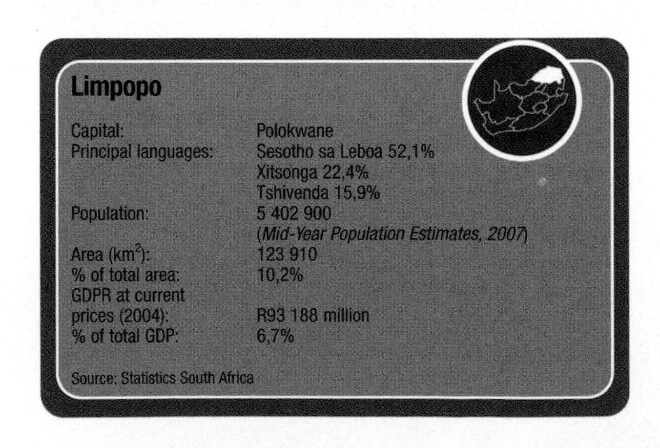

Limpopo

Capital:	Polokwane
Principal languages:	Sesotho sa Leboa 52,1% Xitsonga 22,4% Tshivenda 15,9%
Population:	5 402 900 (*Mid-Year Population Estimates, 2007*)
Area (km²):	123 910
% of total area:	10,2%
GDPR at current prices (2004):	R93 188 million
% of total GDP:	6,7%

Source: Statistics South Africa

About 60% of South Africa's tomatoes, 33% of its oranges and 70% of its mangoes come from Limpopo. More than 45% of the R2-billion annual turnover of the Johannesburg Fresh Produce Market is from the province.

Some tourist attractions include:

- the unforgettable bushveld scenery of the Waterberg
- fun and relaxation in the mineral baths of Bela-Bela
- the Big Tree near Tzaneen
- the springs of Tshipise, which attract a million visitors a year
- the Modjadji Nature Reserve
- the Mapungubwe iron age site.

2010 World Cup

By mid-2007, construction of the new 46 000-seater Peter Mokaba sports complex in Polokwane was under way. The Limpopo Department of Roads and Transport will spend R76 million upgrading airport facilities ahead of the World Cup.

The money will be used to improve the Giyani and Thohoyandou airports, as well as upgrading the Polokwane Gateway International Airport.

POCKET GUIDE TO SA 2007/08 | ECONOMY

South Africa's economy grew by 5% in 2006, the highest rate of economic growth in 25 years. After years of rising unemployment, the unemployment rate has declined for three years in a row, with over a million jobs created in this period.

All the major indicators of economic growth are showing that the present economic boom represents one of the longest sustained increases in income in about 40 years.

This growth has been relatively broad-based, with the share of income going to Africans rising to above 50% in 2005, from about 40% in 1996. The number of black people entering what is called "the middle class" increased by 30% in a single year to 2,6 million in 2006. This represents a substantial shift in the purchasing power in South Africa towards the historically disadvantaged.

According to a study by the Department of Trade and Industry, the number of small businesses has grown by 150% since 1995 and 87% of these businesses are black-owned.

Accelerated and Shared Growth Initiative for South Africa (AsgiSA)

Government's AsgiSA aims to ensure that economic growth is accelerated to at least 4,5% between 2005 and 2009 and about 6% between 2010 and 2014. This will assist in halving unemployment and poverty by 2014.

AsgiSA includes developing infrastructure to upgrade and build railway lines, harbours, ports and roads from 2005 to 2009.

With South Africa's unemployment rate at 25,5% by March 2007, the infrastructure programme is geared towards creating and sustaining jobs.

Overall government expenditure for infrastructure spending would have totalled some R410 billion between 2007 and 2010. Of this, about 40% will be spent by public enterprises, mostly Eskom and Transnet

Airports Company South Africa will spend R5,2 billion, which includes airport improvement and the Dube Tradeport, while R19,7 billion will go towards water infrastructure.

Because South Africa will host the 2010 FIFA World Cup™, existing stadiums will be improved or new ones built, and an investment will be made in the environment around stadiums and access to these venues.

Joint Initiative for Priority Skills Acquisition (Jipsa)

Jipsa is the skills empowerment arm of AsgiSA.

AsgiSA has identified six factors that constrain economic growth. One of these is the shortage of skilled labour.

Jipsa is a two-tiered structure comprising a joint task team and a technical working group. The joint task team has the task of unblocking the acquisition of targeted skills, overseeing the work of Jipsa and ensuring that it delivers on its mandate of acquiring scarce and priority skills in the shortest possible time, building partnerships with different institutions and ensuring that Jipsa initiatives are sustainable.

Based on AsgiSA's priorities, Jipsa's work areas are:

- high-level world-class engineering and planning skills for the network, transport, communications and energy industries

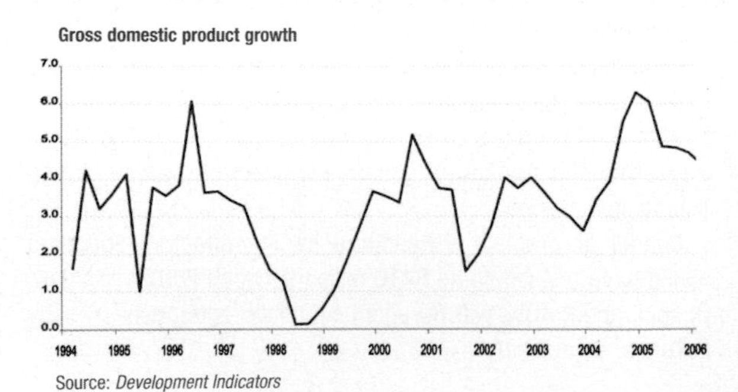

Source: *Development Indicators*

- city, urban and regional planning and engineering skills desperately needed by South African municipalities
- artisan and technical skills, with those needed for infrastructure development enjoying priority
- management and planning skills in education, health and in municipalities
- teacher training in Mathematics, Science, information communications technology (ICT) and language competence
- specific skills needed by priority AsgiSA sectors starting with tourism- and business-process outsourcing and cross-cutting skills needed by all sectors, especially financial and project managers
- skills relevant to the local economic development needs of municipalities, especially developmental economists.

Jipsa will support citizens who are trapped in the Second Economy, giving them a chance to participate in the First Economy and in the growing South African economy in general. Jipsa aims to boost empowerment through education.

Domestic output

The South African economy registered a real growth rate of 5% in 2006. This solid performance followed the attainment of brisk rates of growth in the preceding two years of 4,8% in 2004 and 5,1% in 2005.

On a quarterly basis, real economic growth expanded further in the fourth quarter of 2006, from an annualised growth rate of 4,5% in the third quarter to 5,6% in the fourth quarter. The acceleration in aggregate economic growth in the fourth quarter of 2006 resulted from improved growth in the real value added by all the main sectors of the economy.

Domestic expenditure

Growth in aggregate real gross domestic expenditure accelerated from an annualised rate of 1,4% in the third quarter of 2006 to

12,3% in the fourth quarter. All the expenditure components contributed to the acceleration, but it was especially due to a turnaround in real final consumption expenditure by general government and strong inventory accumulation, partly reflecting a surge in oil imports during the fourth quarter.

For the calendar year 2006, aggregate real gross domestic expenditure increased by 8,7% compared with an increase of 5,9% in 2005. Growth in real final consumption expenditure by households accelerated from 7,6% in the third quarter of 2006 to an annualised rate of 7,8% in the fourth quarter. The annual growth in real final consumption expenditure by households amounted to 7,3% in 2006, compared with a growth rate of 6,6% recorded in 2005.

Real disposable income of households increased in the fourth quarter of 2006, albeit at a slower rate than in the third quarter. The moderation in growth could partly be ascribed to lower farm income recorded over this period. The level of indebtedness of households also increased at a slower pace in the fourth quarter of 2006 due to a slowdown in mortgage advances during this period.

Price inflation

During recent years, remarkable progress has been made in lowering South Africa's inflation rate to levels more consistent with those of its main trading partners. This has been done through the consistent application of prudent fiscal and monetary policies which have contributed to a progressive deceleration in inflation expectations.

Overall consumer price inflation decelerated markedly from a high of 9,2% in 2002; to 5,8% in 2003; and 1,4% in 2004; before it increased to 3,4% in 2005; and 4,7% in 2006.

Also, the year-on-year rate of increase in the consumer price index (CPI) for metropolitan and other urban areas, less mortgage interest cost (CPIX), decelerated within the inflation target range of 3% to 6% in the 43 consecutive months to March 2007.

Exchange rates

On balance, the nominal effective exchange rate of the Rand declined by 4,4% during the first quarter of 2007, compared with a 7,7% increase in the fourth quarter of 2006.

The domestic market for foreign exchange experienced some volatility in the first quarter of 2007 following a reassessment of risk towards emerging-market economies, movements in commodity prices, periodic nervousness regarding the size of the current-account deficit, a sharp correction in the Chinese stock exchange and a report of a proposed windfall tax on the entire South African resources industry.

The exchange value of the Rand recovered somewhat during April 2007, partly as a result of further United States (US) dollar weakness following weaker-than-expected US gross domestic product (GDP) data for the first quarter of 2007 and expectations of a further domestic interest rate increase in response to higher-than-expected South African inflation data.

The average daily turnover in the domestic market for foreign exchange increased from US$14,6 billion in the fourth quarter of 2006 to US$15,3 billion in the first quarter of 2007, mainly as a result of non-resident investors' participation in the South African securities markets. The value of transactions in which non-residents participated accordingly increased from US$10,6 billion per day to US$11,9 billion over the period.

Foreign trade and payments

A substantial decline in crude oil imports more than compensated for a decrease in mining exports in the first quarter of 2007. South Africa's trade deficit subsequently narrowed from R65,6 billion in the fourth quarter of 2006 to R50,9 billion in the first quarter of 2007.

While the improvement in the trade deficit was partly countered by a further widening of the deficit on the country's services and income account with the rest of the world, the current-account deficit nevertheless shrank from R143 billion in the fourth quarter of 2006 to R131 billion in the first quarter of 2007. As a ratio of GDP, the deficit shrank from 7,8% to 7% over the period.

The impact of the decline in the volume of exported goods was partly offset by an increase of about 2% in the Rand prices of such goods as the Dollar price of international commodities rebounded in the first quarter of 2007. In dollar terms, international commodity prices rose by 6,5% from the fourth quarter of 2006 to the first quarter of 2007.

This decline in production was partly offset by a 4,5% increase in the average realised price of gold. The value of net gold exports accordingly fell by 5,5% over the period. On the London market, the fixing price of gold rose by 6% to a new all-time-high quarterly average of US$650 per fine ounce in the first quarter of 2007 before rising further to US$673 per fine ounce in April and May.

Higher commodity export prices alongside receding import prices gave rise to a moderate improvement in South Africa's terms of trade in the first quarter of 2007.

Trade relations

Internationally, open economies with an export base perform much better in terms of economic growth than closed economies. Increasingly, production is becoming globally integrated, and South Africa forms a vital part of international supply chains.

Therefore, dismantling barriers to trade, especially those faced by South African exporters, is a critical component of any economic strategy that promotes sustainable growth.

Africa's economic development

South Africa's global economic strategy focuses on Africa and a strong development agenda. Partnerships with countries on the continent are therefore considered vital and strategic. South Africa's economy is inextricably connected to that of the southern African region, and its success is linked to the economic recovery of the continent through the New Partnership for Africa's Development (Nepad).

In 2006, about 23% of South Africa's exports were destined for the continent. There was also a large increase in imports from the continent. In 2003, only 4% of total imports came from Africa. However, this increased to 40% in 2004.

This trade imbalance has largely been offset by South Africa's investment on the continent, aimed at infrastructural projects designed to enhance the productive capacities of African economies. Besides forging bilateral trade and economic relations, the Department of Trade and Industry is committed to increasing South Africa's involvement in large capital projects on the continent. The following areas have been prioritised:

- infrastructure and logistics (roads, ports, etc.)
- energy and ICT
- water and waste management
- transport
- construction
- oil and gas infrastructure
- agribusiness
- mining
- human-resource development.

New Partnership for Africa's Development

The Department of Trade and Industry provides supportive services to Nepad, which has a critical role in accelerating trade and economic development on the continent to realise its primary objectives, namely alleviating poverty. The department aims to contribute to the Nepad agenda by mobilising the necessary support from relevant stakeholders internally and externally, and providing leadership and strategic guidance on trade and economic issues. It also contributes to the national project co-ordinated through the African Renaissance Cluster on the formulation of a national response to Nepad through the Nepad Implementation Strategy of South Africa.

Southern African Development Community (SADC)

The SADC comprises Angola, Botswana, the Democratic Republic of Congo, Lesotho, Madagascar, Malawi, Mauritius, Mozambique, Namibia, South Africa, Swaziland, Tanzania, Zambia and Zimbabwe.

Since attaining democracy in 1994, South Africa has put regional integration by SADC member states on the top of its foreign economic agenda. This approach follows from the belief in the economic benefits that can be brought to all member states by closer economic co-operation in the region. To support this approach, South Africa has reviewed its trade relationship with other SADC members, adopted the SADC Trade Protocol, promoted investment by South African firms in the SADC and helped to facilitate greater volumes of trade by South Africa and other SADC members.

Europe

Trade relations with Europe, particularly with the European Union (EU), are pivotal to South Africa's economic development. The Trade, Development and Co-operation Agreement with the EU forms a substantial element of South Africa's reconstruction and development efforts.

Europe remains South Africa's largest trading region and source of investment. In 2006, Europe accounted for 38,8% (R139 574 billion) of South Africa's total exports, and 36,4%

(R168 198 billion) of its total imports. During the same year, the EU accounted for the bulk of this trade, with exports to the EU reaching R126 373 billion (up from R106 465 billion in 2005), and imports reaching R161 053 billion in 2005 (up from R128 360 billion in 2005).

Six European countries, namely the United Kingdom (UK), Germany, the Netherlands, Spain, Belgium and Italy are among South Africa's top-10 export destinations. Germany, the UK, Italy and France are among the top-10 countries from which South Africa's imports originate.

United States of America (USA)

The USA is one of South Africa's leading trade partners. The country ranks second after Japan as a destination of South African exports and is third – after Germany and China – as a source of South African imports.

Exports to the USA increased in nominal terms from R30 billion in 2004 to R41 billion in 2006, while imports recorded an increase from R26 billion to R35 billion for the same period. Since 2000, the trade balance has been in South Africa's favour, with the trade surplus increasing in nominal terms from R3,5 billion to R6 billion between 2000 and 2006.

South Africa is a beneficiary of the USA's Generalised System of Preferences (GSP), which grants duty-free treatment for more than 4 650 products, and benefits from the Africa Growth and Opportunity Act (AGOA), which was promulgated in May 2000.

In terms of the AGOA, 1 783 more products were added to the existing GSP product list. Although the AGOA was initially due to lapse in 2008, the US Government met African countries' requests for it to run until 2015 under what is called the AGOA III amendments.

The AGOA also allows duty-free entry of clothing and selected textiles into the USA, subject to certain criteria and policy reforms.

Canada

Another significant trading partner in the Americas is Canada. Since the lifting of sanctions in 1994, bilateral trade between South Africa and Canada increased from R904 million in 1993 to R6,6 billion in 2006. South Africa is a beneficiary of Canada's General Preferential Tariff (GPT). GPT rates range from duty-free to reductions in the Most Favoured Nation rates.

Latin America

South Africa's major trading partners in Latin America are Brazil, Argentina, Chile, Mexico, Colombia and Peru. Most trade is with Brazil and Argentina, which are members of the Mercusor trade bloc.

A framework agreement, committing South Africa and Mercusor to a free trade agreement, was signed in 2000. However, as a first step towards achieving this goal, the parties signed a preferential trade agreement (PTA) in December 2004. Upon ratification by all signatories, the PTA will offer businesses from both sides preferential access to a broad range of product lines.

Trade between South Africa and Mercusor grew substantially from R2,7 billion in 1994 to R20,7 billion in 2006. South Africa recorded a trade deficit of about R12,8 billion against the bloc for 2006. Within Mercosur, Brazil is by far the leading trading partner, accounting for 56% of South Africa's trade with the group in 2006.

South and south-east Asia and Australasia

Bilateral trade with south-east Asia, particularly the Association of Southeast Asian Nations (Asean) members, increased rapidly from a low base in 1990. Asean presents South Africa with a potential market in excess of 520 million people.

South African trade with Asean totalled R34,8 billion in 2006, and is set for continued growth. Within the region, key partners for South Africa include Singapore, Thailand, Indonesia, Malaysia, Vietnam and the Philippines.

South Africa co-operates with India in areas of common interest in the World Trade Organisation and other forums, and works closely in the India-Brazil-South Africa (IBSA) Forum. IBSA is not only an economic initiative but also an undertaking by countries with shared interests in a multilateral system that equitably addresses political, social and economic matters. South Africa and India co-operate in the G20, a grouping of developing countries that seeks to address developmental challenges in the global economic system.

Total trade between Australia and South Africa reached R18,6 billion in 2006.

North-east Asia

Economic and trade relations between South Africa and the People's Republic of China have grown rapidly since the formal establishment of diplomatic relations. Total trade grew from R5,3 billion in 1998 to R60,7 billion in 2006.

Japan is South Africa's largest trading partner in Asia and became the country's primary export partner in 2005, with total trade reaching R71,6 billion in 2006.

Economic transformation

Government aims to boost small enterprises, equalise income and wealth and create long-term jobs. Fostering entrepreneurship among women is a particular focus.

Developing small, medium and micro-enterprises has attracted increasing attention in South Africa in recent years, as an engine for general economic growth, and for employment creation and equity acceleration.

The Small Enterprise Development Agency (Seda), which provides non-financial support to small and medium enterprises (SMEs), was formed by merging the Ntsika Enterprise Promotion

Agency and the National Manufacturing Advisory Centre. It aims to:
- improve geographic outreach
- achieve the desired impact on small enterprises
- provide a single access point for small enterprises
- be inclusive of all relevant stakeholders
- leverage resources in service delivery
- optimise resource usage
- align government's service-delivery strategy coherently.

By July 2007, Seda had eight provincial offices, 39 branches and 102 enterprise information centres.

National Empowerment Fund (NEF)

The NEF was established by the NEF Act, 1998 to promote and facilitate economic equality and transformation. The fund received R150 million in 2004/05 and R400 million in 2005/06.

The NEF leverages its funding by setting up strategic alliances with other private-sector financial institutions to further increase funding for Black Economic Empowerment (BEE). It operates at several different levels, providing finance and business support to rural women and fledgling entrepreneurs, and large-scale financial support to BEE groups.

The NEF partners with business organisations that focus on serving women. It deploys its resources to optimise the empowerment dividend to government and provides pre- and post-investment management assistance.

The NEF's funding comprises a hybrid of loans and equity, and is designed to lower the cost of capital for BEE participants. This approach to BEE funding is aimed at overcoming existing funders' traditional risk aversion.

Industrial Development Corporation (IDC)

The IDC provides financing to entrepreneurs engaged in competitive industries. Its primary objectives are to contribute to balanced, sustainable economic growth in Africa and to the economic empowerment of the South African population, thereby promoting the economic prosperity of all citizens of the African continent.

The IDC received the top Development Financier for BEE Award for 2003, 2005 and 2006 from Business Map Foundation.

Through its funding projects, the IDC was expected to create more than 29 300 jobs and save over 3 800. In 2006/07, the IDC made a record profit of R4 345 billion.

The IDC contributed significantly to the equitable distribution of economic growth by supporting BEE companies. In 2006/07, BEE accounted for 160 approvals, more than half the total approvals, with more than R3,4 billion in financing for BEE start-ups or in the form of expansions of existing BEE enterprises.

Business Partners Limited

Business Partners Limited is a specialist investment group, providing customised investment, mentorship and property-management services to SMEs in South Africa.

In March 2006, Business Partners launched two new specialist investment funds, the Business Partners Empowerment Fund and the Business Partners Tourism Fund. Business Partners will be investing R6,6 billion into entrepreneurial enterprises over the next five years.

State-owned enterprises (SOEs)

The Department of Public Enterprises is the shareholder representative for government with oversight responsibility for the folowing SOEs: Alexkor, Broadband Infraco, Denel, Eskom and the Pebble-Bed Modular Reactor; South African Airways; South African Express Airways, South African Forestry Company and Transnet.

SOEs have a critical role to play in advancing economic growth, since they are responsible for the development of key infrastructure and manufacturing capacity. Infrastructure investments are a core part of the accelerated growth strategy, and SOEs are implementing comprehensive investment programmes to ensure that significant and sustained opportunities for investment are created in supplier industries. This follows 30 years of declining government capital investment.

Expanded Public Works Programme (EPWP)

The EPWP is the largest job-creating initiative to be undertaken by government.

The EPWP is operational in all nine provinces. Projects include the construction of rural or low-volume roads, water and sanitation trenches and sidewalks.

In addition, government will increase spending on the maintenance of schools, clinics and other government buildings. EPWP projects will also be launched in the area of home-based care for people affected by HIV and AIDS, childcare projects, and in environmental projects like LandCare and clearing alien vegetation from river banks.

By December 2006, the EPWP had created 573 269 job opportunities ahead of the target for the same period and exceeding its targets for women and the youth.

National Treasury aims to promote economic development, good governance, social progress and rising living standards through accountable, economic, efficient, equitable and sustainable public finances.

In support of government's Accelerated and Shared Growth Initiative for South Africa, National Treasury's work on fiscal policy and budget reform is focused on strengthening infrastructure investment and maintenance, broadening participation in the economy and improving the quality of social services. Improved budget planning, better documentation and greater transparency in public finances continue to be key priorities. National Treasury is expanding its capacity to provide technical support, particularly for infrastructure planning and project management.

Fiscal policy framework

The Minister of Finance, Mr Trevor Manuel, presented the Budget for 2007/08 in February 2007.

Spending changes for the next three years included:

- an additional R13,3 billion for the 2010 FIFA World Cup™, bringing the total contribution from national government to R17,4 billion – R8,4 billion for stadiums and R9 billion for transport infrastructure
- the provincial equitable share was increased by R24,6 billion to improve the quality and access to health, school education, welfare services and economic services
- an additional R5 billion to the local government equitable share provides further support to municipalities for the delivery of free basic services
- an additional R4,6 billion for teacher bursaries, curriculum development and an increase in higher education subsidies
- R11,6 billion for housing and community development
- R3,7 billion for the HIV and AIDS and STI Strategic Plan for South Africa, and modernising hospitals and health facilities

- R2,4 billion for industrial development, science and technology
- R6,8 billion for justice and crime prevention and improved access to justice services
- R4,7 billion for international relations and defence.

Main tax proposals included:

- net tax relief of R12,4 billion, replacing the secondary tax on companies with a dividend tax and reducing the rate from 12,5% to 10%
- personal income tax relief for individuals amounting to R8,4 billion
- abolishing the tax on retirement funds
- reducing the withholding of tax on lump-sum pension and provident-fund payments to zero for persons earning below R43 000 per year
- increases in excise duties on tobacco products and alcoholic beverages.

Debt management

Sound macroeconomic policy and fiscal management have played a central role in building South Africa's reputation as a credible and competitive borrower. The approach to debt management has assisted towards developing the financial sector as a source of capital for the public and private sectors. Improved access to capital and the development of specialised debt instruments for private borrowers have given a boost to domestic economic activity.

Twelve years of prudent macroeconomic policy have contributed to a robust economy capable of both sustaining and accelerating the growth trajectory. The uniqueness of South Africa's economic landscape is reflected in the fact that government is increasing capital and socioeconomic expenditure, even as it continues to enjoy a positive fiscal balance and is reducing the amount of money it needs to borrow. As a result, government's net loan debt as a percentage of gross

Government expenditure

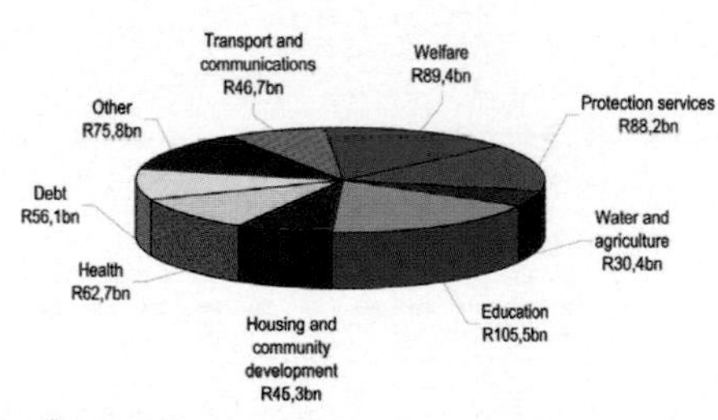

Source: *www.treasury.gov.za*

domestic product (GDP) came down, from 48,1% in 1996/97 to 27,1% in 2006/07.

South Africa's public finances do not centre on servicing debt, but on the essential pillars of human development – poverty reduction, health, education and job creation. Interest costs measured as a percentage of revenue and GDP have fallen to historically low levels, as a result of a favourable interest rate outlook and lower debt stock.

A decade ago, government spent 18 cents of every rand on servicing debt. This decreased to 11 cents in 2007 and by 2009 the figure is expected to fall to eight cents. Consequently, the debt burden on future generations continues to decline, releasing additional resources for economic development and poverty relief.

Market performance

Bond turnover

Since market turnover reached its record level in 2002 at R11,7 trillion, annual bond turnover reported on the Bond Exchange of South Africa (Besa) has ebbed, dropping to R8,1 trillion in 2005.

Government debt as a percentage of gross domestic product

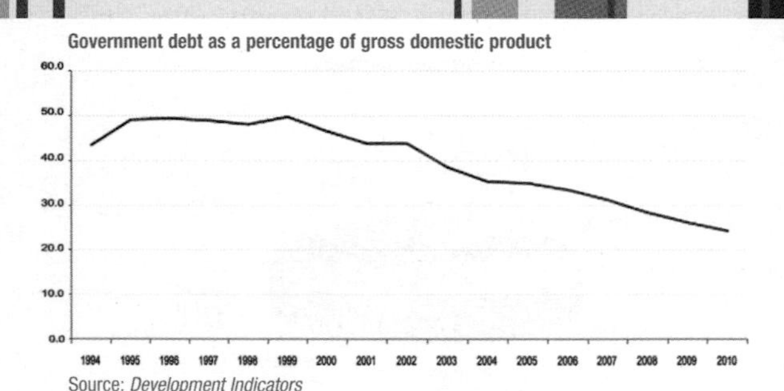

Source: *Development Indicators*

The R153 yield declined from 11,86% on 1 January 2002 to 7,31% at 31 December 2005. At the beginning of 2006, Besa estimated that market turnover for the year ahead would be in the order of R7,8 trillion. However, against all expectations nominal turnover increased during 2006 by 41% to R11,4 trillion.

The number of matched trades increased marginally, by 4%, from 298 000 trades in 2005 to 311 000 in 2006. At R11,4 trillion, the turnover velocity of the bond market stood at 13,8 times that at the end of 2006.

Government bonds remained the most traded instruments, contributing 93% to the total nominal turnover. Monthly market turnover in 2006 has been higher year on year, reaching a near-record level of R1,2 trillion in October 2006.

Where non-residents were net sellers (R5,5 billion) of South African bonds in 2005, they became net purchasers of bonds totalling R26,8 billion in 2006, while their participation in trading activity increased from 32% in 2005 to 38% of turnover in 2006.

Listed and unlisted derivative trades reported on the Bond Exchange of South Africa

Besa launched a fixed-income derivative platform (Intersec) in September 2005 to facilitate the capture and confirmation of plain vanilla forward rate agreements and swaps traded over-the-counter (OTC).

Since 2005, OTC trades reported on Intersec increased from a total of 627 trades with a value of R159 billion to 1 063 trades with a value of R589 billion in 2006.

Besa launched its Financial Services Board (FSB)-approved listed fixed-income derivatives during the course of 2006 and established the Derivatives Traders' Association, which had 12 members by mid-2007.

Listed derivative trading activity has been slower in uptake, and at the end of 2006 swaps had a value of R2,5 billion.

Listed bonds

The number of listings on Besa Increased from a nominal value in issue of R637 billion at the end of 2005 to R725 billion in 2006, with a market cap of R830 billion. The listed debt instruments totalled 725 issues issued by 91 issuers.

Most significant was the annual increase in corporate listings from 22% of the total nominal value in issue to 29% in 2006.

The nominal value of the corporate listings increased from R140 billion in 2005 to R208 billion in 2006.

In 2006, exchange-control regulations were relaxed, allowing foreign issuers to list ZAR-denominated bonds on Besa and allowing investment managers an increased investment allowance should these funds be deployed for development into Africa.

Besa listed its first such "inward listing" towards the end of 2006, when Mauritius Commercial Bank raised funding of R350 million in the South African market.

Managing public finances

Transforming public-sector financial management is one of National Treasury's key objectives. To this end, National Treasury has been implementing the Public Finance Management Act (PFMA), 1999 since 1 April 2000.

Since implementation of the PFMA, 1999, there have been measurable improvements in financial management in both the national and provincial spheres of government which include, among other things:

- an improved linkage between planning and budgeting, whereby departments are now required to compile and table strategic plans that are consistent with their budget envelope
- strategic plans and budget documentation containing improved information on measurable objectives expressed in terms of quantity, quality and timeliness
- departments submitting monthly expenditure reports on actual expenditure incurred, and on projected expenditure for the remainder of the financial year
- risk-management processes, which are now being implemented by institutions
- establishing internal-audit functions and audit committees in all departments
- setting accounting standards in accordance with best accounting practices, both locally and internationally
- finalising and submitting financial statements to the Auditor-General (AG) within two months of the end of the financial year
- tabling annual reports in the legislature within six months of the end of the financial year.

Taxation

The South African Revenue Service (Sars) collected R497,197 billion in taxes during 2006/07, exceeding its revised target of R489,7 billion.

Sources of revenue

Income tax

Income tax is government's main source of income and is levied in terms of the Income Tax Act, 1962.

In South Africa, income tax is levied on South African residents' worldwide income, with appropriate relief to avoid double taxation. Non-residents are taxed on their income from a South African source. Tax is levied on taxable income, which, in essence, consists of gross income less allowable deductions as per the Act.

The income threshold below which no tax is payable by individuals under 65 years was raised to R43 000 for the tax year beginning March 2007, and for taxpayers over the age of 65 to R69 000 a year. The maximum marginal rate of tax remains at 40%, while the threshold was raised from R400 000 to R450 000.

The domestic interest and dividend exemption for taxpayers under the age of 65 was raised from R16 500 to R18 000, and for senior citizens the threshold increased from R24 500 to R26 000. The proportion of the exemption applicable to foreign-interest income and dividends was raised from R2 500 to R3 000.

Value-added tax (VAT)

VAT is levied on the supply of all goods and services rendered by registered vendors throughout the business cycle. Effectively, VAT is levied on the value added by an enterprise. Vendors levy and pay over the tax included in their prices, resulting in VAT being paid by the final consumer. VAT is also levied on the importation of goods and services into South Africa. It is levied at the standard rate of 14% but certain supplies are zero-rated or are exempt from VAT.

Monetary Policy

Growth in broad money supply (M3) rose during the course of 2005 and early 2006, accelerating from 13% in the early months of 2005 to 21% in February 2006.

Banks' loans and advances to the domestic private sector remained relatively strong during 2005 and early 2006, registering average growth rates of 21% to 22%. Asset-backed credit (mortgage advances, leasing finance and instalment sale credit) constituted the

In 2007, the South African Revenue Service (Sars) launched a simpler income tax return and filing process for individual and business taxpayers.

Individuals now receive their returns by mid-July and have until 31 October to submit them, while companies receive returns in September and have six to 12 months after the end of their financial year to submit the returns. Previously, the deadline for the submission of completed tax returns was early July.

Sars will also in future pay moneys electronically into taxpayers' bank accounts and no longer issue cheques, unless taxpayers state otherwise.

Some of the benefits of the new system include e-filing that allows taxpayers to file their tax returns via the Internet.

bulk of the increase in banks' total loans and advances throughout 2005 and early 2006.

Growth in M3 and banks' total loans and advances was consistent with firm increases in nominal income, expenditure and wealth.

In June 2007, the repurchase rate was increased by 50 basis points to 7,5%. In August 2007, it was increased to 10%. October 2007 saw another increase to 10,5%

Auditor-General

The Constitution guarantees the independence of the AG. The office audits national, provincial and local government. The AG has the power to audit the activities of public entities without the approval of the chief executive officer or directors.

South African Reserve Bank

The bank, which is independent, formulates and implements monetary policy and regulates the supply of money by influencing its cost.

An important responsibility of the bank is to ensure that the banking system as a whole is sound and meets the requirements of the community.

The bank acts as a banker to other banking institutions. It is also the custodian of the statutory cash reserves and provides facilities for the clearing and settlement of inter-bank obligations.

The banking industry

At the end of December 2006, 34 banks, including 14 branches of foreign banks and two mutual banks, were registered with the Office of the Registrar of Banks. Furthermore, 43 foreign banks had authorised representative offices in South Africa. By the end of December 2006, the banking institutions collectively employed 129 161 workers.

Insurance companies

By December 2006, 82 long-term insurers and 106 short-term insurers were registered with the FSB. The total net premiums received and outstanding for 2004 (unaudited figures) amounted to R153 billion, while total assets amounted to R908,1 billion.

Development Bank of Southern Africa

The primary purpose of the bank is to promote economic development and growth, human-resource development and institutional capacity-building. The bank's mandate is focused on infrastructure.

Interest rates

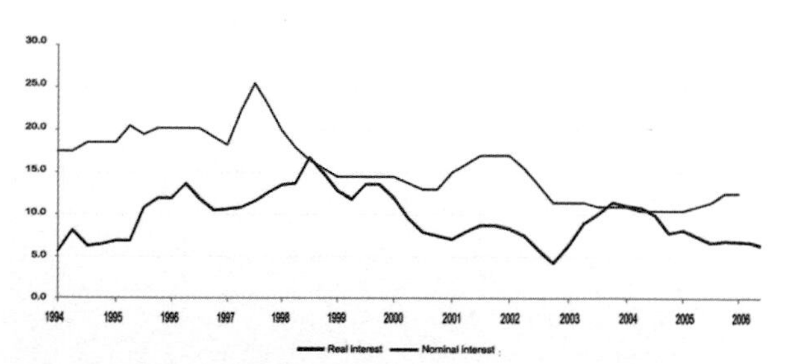

Source: *Development Indicators*

Financial Services Board

The FSB is an independent statutory body financed by levies imposed on regulated institutions and persons.

The FSB supervises institutions and services, in terms of several parliamentary Acts that entrust regulatory functions to the registrars of long-term insurance, short-term insurance, friendly societies, pension funds, collective investment schemes, financial services providers, exchanges and financial markets.

Attracting investment

In line with promoting foreign investment in South Africa and positioning the country as a financial centre for Africa, government announced in February 2004 that foreign companies, governments and institutions may list on South Africa's bond and securities exchanges.

Increasing competitiveness

A number of incentives are being offered to both large and small businesses to improve their competitiveness, including those under the:

- Small and Medium Enterprise Development Programme, which has benefited over 12 000 enterprises
- Competitiveness Fund, which supports over 1 200 enterprises
- Sector Partnership Fund, which has assisted over 85 successful partnerships consisting of over 600 individual enterprises
- Black Business Supplier Development Programme, which has assisted over 600 small, black-owned enterprises to improve systems, quality, skills and marketability.

In line with promoting inclusivity and fulfilling its mandate as a promoter of long-term savings and investment opportunities to black people, the National Empowerment Fund (NEF) launched the NEF Asonge Share Scheme in 2007.

The share scheme allows black individuals and black savings and investment groups such as stokvels, burial services, trusts, co-operatives, church groups and others, to invest in MTN shares at a 20% discount.The shares retailed at a minimum subscription of R2 000, with a maximum of R50 000 for individuals and R100 000 for stokvels and other savings groups.

The offering was available from 23 July to 16 August 2007.

Broadening economic participation

Broad-Based Black Economic Empowerment (BBBEE) is a government policy aimed at redressing past economic

During recent years, remarkable progress has been made in lowering South Africa's inflation rate to levels more consistent with those of its main trading partners. This has been done through the consistent application of prudent fiscal and monetary policies, which have contributed to a progressive deceleration in inflation expectations.

imbalances. Moreover, BEE is an important policy instrument aimed at broadening the economic base of the country, further stimulating economic growth and creating jobs while eradicating poverty.

The Codes of Good Practice for BBBEE were gazetted on 9 February 2007. These codes are the culmination of the development of the BBBEE Strategy that seeks to enhance the economic participation of black people by growing the economy and reducing income inequality.

Trade and Investment South Africa (Tisa)

Tisa, a division of the Department of Trade and Industry, aims to develop the South African economy by focusing on investment development and promotion, export development and promotion, and sector policy development.

Tisa is responsible for developing the following priority sectors:

- agroprocessing
- chemical and allied industries
- clothing, textiles, leather and footwear
- cultural industries
- exportable services (business process outsourcing)
- information and communications technology and electronics
- metals and mineral-based industries
- tourism
- transport industries.

The unit is dedicated to promoting investment opportunities, marketing investment projects, providing guidance with plant/site locations, especially in industrial development zones (IDZs) and inputting into policy formulation by providing investment information. In 2006/07, the unit undertook 12 investment seminars, six investment pavilions, 21 sector-specific presentations, 46 sector-specific briefs and 29 inward/outward customised targeted investment presentations.

National Industrial Participation Programme (NIPP)

There are two elements to the NIPP in South Africa, namely a national non-defence and a defence element.

The Department of Trade and Industry manages the NIPP, which becomes obligatory when the foreign content of the procurement, purchase or lease contracts of government departments and parastatals exceeds US$10 million, in which case an NIPP obligation of 30% on the foreign content is attracted. The NIPP focuses on national objectives, mainly in the commercial environment.

The objectives of the NIPP include fast-tracking investment, fostering partnerships in technology transfer and creating market opportunities for locally manufactured goods abroad.

By mid-2007, the total value of NIPP obligations being monitored was estimated at US$15 billion. The programme has benefited South Africans to the tune of US$3,5 billion over the last eight years as a consequence of the country's Strategic Defence Procurement and other government purchases. This includes investment credits estimated at US$1 billion, with export and local sales, technology transfer, BEE and small, medium and micro-enterprise promotion making up the balance. The benefits cover the areas of BEE, partnerships between participating entities and skills development.

Spatial development

One of South Africa's key industrial policies remains its commitment to fostering sustainable industrial development in areas where poverty and unemployment are at their highest. This objective is implemented through spatial development initiatives (SDIs), which focus high-level support on areas where socio-economic conditions require concentrated government assistance, and where inherent economic potential exists.

The SDI programme consists of 11 local SDIs and four IDZs that were at varying stages of delivery by September 2007. The SDIs are the Maputo Development Corridor; Lubombo SDI; Richards Bay SDI, including the Durban and Pietermaritzburg nodes; Wild Coast SDI; Fish River SDI; West Coast Investment Initiative; Platinum SDI; Phalaborwa SDI; and the Coast-2-Coast Corridor. The IDZs are in Coega/Ngqura, East London, Saldanha and Richards Bay.

The SDI concept focuses on:

- industry by means of the KwaZulu-Natal and Fish River SDIs
- agritourism, as in the Lubombo and Wild Coast SDIs
- a sectoral mix, for example the Maputo Development Corridor
- IDZs such as those in Coega/Ngqura, Saldanha and East London.

IDZs are located near major transport nodes such as ports or airports. The benefits of IDZs include support to investing companies, especially for greenfield development projects; access to transport for export purposes; waiver of import duties for products that are produced for export; and subsidies for providing skills training to employees. In 2006/07, some R850 million was spent on infrastructure development in the Coega IDZ, including water, sewers, electricity, facilities and services.

Some 11 796 people were employed and three investors would be involved in the textiles, chemicals and automotive sectors with a total combined investment value of R3,2 billion.

The Enterprise Organisation (Teo)

Teo's purpose is to stimulate and facilitate the development of sustainable competitive enterprises through the efficient provision of effective and accessible supply-side incentive measures.

The 2005 – 2010 National Skills Development Strategy (NSDS) has been finalised and R21,9 billion in funding allocated to it over five years.

The new NSDS is expected to play a key role in realising government's goal of halving the country's unemployment by 2014.

It contributes to the realisation of the Department of Trade and Industry's strategic objectives by:

- developing incentives in support of identified policies and sector strategies
- efficiently administering the department's incentive programmes
- facilitating access to and impact of products and services rendered by Teo through a focused business-development effort.

Department of Trade and Industry

The aim of the Department of Trade and Industry is to lead and facilitate access to sustainable economic activity and employment for all South Africans.

The department also aims to catalyse economic transformation and development, and to provide a predictable, competitive, equitable and socially responsible environment for investment, enterprise and trade for economic citizens.

The July 2007 Cabinet Lekgotla approved the Industrial Policy Action Plan for the Economic Cluster, to faciliate and support industrial development through the implementation of targeted programmes.

By August 2007, key action plans in four broad sectors – capital goods; transport equipment and metals, automotive assembly and components; chemicals, plastics and pharmaceuticals; and forestry, pulp and paper – had been finalised for immediate implementation.

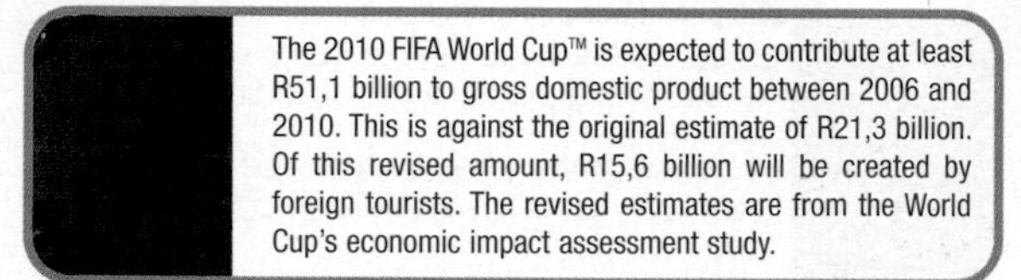

The 2010 FIFA World Cup™ is expected to contribute at least R51,1 billion to gross domestic product between 2006 and 2010. This is against the original estimate of R21,3 billion. Of this revised amount, R15,6 billion will be created by foreign tourists. The revised estimates are from the World Cup's economic impact assessment study.

An industrial upgrading programme was expected to be developed to address the issue of outdated equipment, including in sectors such as clothing and textiles. A review of selected import duties was expected to be undertaken as a means to drive down input costs and enhance the competitiveness of downstream industries that are more labour-intensive.

Taxation

International tax agreements are important for encouraging investment and trade flows between nations, by providing certainty about the tax framework. By reaching agreement on the allocation of taxing rights between residence and source countries of international investors, double taxation agreements provide a solid platform for growth in international trade and investment. South Africa has tax agreements with a wide range of countries.

Exchange control

Exchange control is administered by the South African Reserve Bank (SARB) on behalf of the Minister of Finance. The bank is assisted in this task by a number of banking institutions that have been appointed by the Minister of Finance as authorised dealers in foreign exchange. These institutions undertake foreign-exchange transactions for their own account with their clients, within limits, and subject to conditions laid down by the SARB.

The Government is committed to an open capital market and the gradual relaxation of exchange controls.

Part of the process of gradual exchange-control liberalisation and financial-sector strengthening is the shift to a system of prudential regulation governing the foreign portfolio investment of institutional investors, such as long-term insurers and pension funds.

Prudential regulations are applied internationally to protect policy-holders and pensioners from excessive risk, and typically include restrictions on foreign-asset holdings, set at a certain percentage of an institution's total assets or liabilities.

As an interim step towards prudential regulation, retirement funds, long-term insurers, collective investment-scheme management companies and investment managers are allowed to transfer funds from South Africa for investment abroad:

- Institutional investors will be allowed to invest, on approval, up to existing foreign-asset limits. These foreign-asset limits are 15% of total retail assets for retirement funds and long-term insurers. Investment managers registered as institutional investors for exchange-control purposes and collective investment-scheme management companies are restricted to 25% of total assets under management.
- Institutional investors will, on application, be allowed to invest an additional 5% of their total retail assets by acquiring foreign-currency transfers from South Africa or by acquiring approved inward-listed instruments based on foreign reference assets or issued by foreign entities listed on the Bond Exchange of South Africa, respectively.
- Foreign companies, governments and institutions may list instruments, including derivative instruments, based on foreign reference assets, on South Africa's bond and securities exchanges.
- Institutional investors will be required to submit additional information when making an application for a foreign-investment allowance.

With effect from 26 October 2004, limits on foreign direct

investment (FDI) by South African corporates were abolished. Exchange-control approval is, however, required. Requests by corporations are considered in light of national interest, such as the benefit to South Africa's foreign reserves by, for example, generating exports of goods and services. The Exchange-Control Department of the SARB reserves the right to stagger capital outflows relating to very large foreign investments, to manage any potential impact on the foreign-exchange market.

Interest payments on loans raised abroad to finance or partly finance new approved foreign investments must be repaid from offshore resources.

As a further alternative mechanism of financing offshore investments or to repay existing offshore debt, applications by corporates to engage in corporate asset or share-swap transactions and requests for share placements offshore by locally listed companies will be considered.

Corporates that have existing approved subsidiaries abroad are allowed to expand such activities without prior approval, subject to certain conditions.

Dividends declared by the offshore subsidiaries of South African corporates may be retained offshore and used for any purpose, without recourse to South Africa.

Authorised dealers may also extend foreign currency-denominated facilities to South African corporates for financing approved FDI.

JSE Limited (JSE)

Founded on 8 November 1887, the JSE is the sole licensed securities exchange in South Africa. In July 2005, after 188 years as a mutual association, the JSE celebrated its demutualisation and is now known as JSE Limited, a public unlisted company.

In 2001, the JSE incorporated the South African Futures Exchange, presenting two new divisions – the Financial Derivatives Division, which covers the equity and interest-rate futures and options markets, and the Agricultural Products Division, which covers commodities futures and options.

JSE

14.0578
6.8770
9.7977
DOW JONES RISERS
Bloom
Intel 26.30 1.70%
Citigroup 47.41 1.59%
Pfizer 24.79 1.47%
Verizon 44.90 1.40%
Caterpillar Inc 79.48 1.34%
TUI Gains After Wyser-Pratte Says He May Back
Volume
Price
2144372 30250
1428889 4561
423888 108601
7884716 25200
1312528 47150
374016 8474
826002 7970
3439182 7085
701825 7240
217572 15660

FOREIGN AFFAIRS

The Department of Foreign Affairs formulates, co-ordinates, implements and manages South Africa's foreign-policy and international-relations programmes throughout the world. These are guided by a commitment to promoting human rights, democracy, justice and international law; international peace and internationally agreed-upon mechanisms for resolving conflicts; Africa in world affairs; and economic development through regional and international co-operation.

South Africa and Africa

South Africa's development is inextricably linked to the development of Africa and the southern African region. Africa faces the challenge of positioning itself to address the marginalisation of the continent by engaging global role-players on socio-economic development, and facilitating a fair and just global order.

African Union (AU)

The AU is Africa's premier institution and principal organisation for promoting the continent's accelerated socio-economic integration, which will lead to greater unity and solidarity between African countries and peoples. South Africa was instrumental in establishing the AU and its organs, namely the:

- Assembly
- Executive Council
- specialised technical committees
- financial institutions
- Permanent Representative Council
- Peace and Security Council
- Pan-African Parliament (PAP)
- Economic, Social and Cultural Council
- Court of Justice
- African Court on Human and People's Rights
- African Commission on Human and People's Rights.

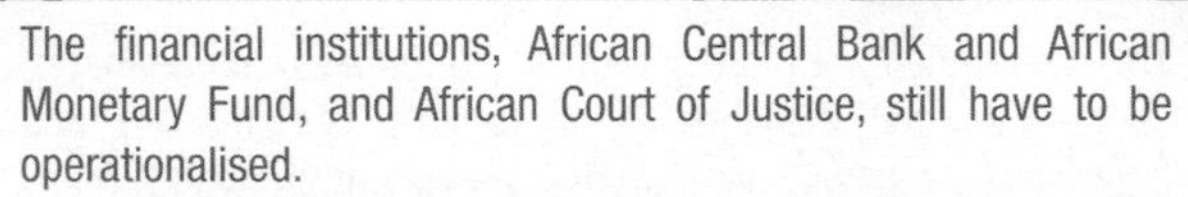

The financial institutions, African Central Bank and African Monetary Fund, and African Court of Justice, still have to be operationalised.

Through active interventions in the Democratic Republic of Congo (DRC), Burundi, Ethiopia/Eritrea, Côte d'Ivoire and Sudan, South Africa supports peace and security efforts in Africa.

The PAP will occupy its current temporary premises in Midrand, Johannesburg, until 2010. Preparations are under way to identify a suitable site and construct the permanent headquarters of the PAP in South Africa.

New Partnership for Africa's Development (Nepad)

South Africa is a key driver of Nepad, a socio-economic initiative to promote good governance, eradicate poverty and create sustainable economic growth.

The Department of Foreign Affairs will continue to facilitate implementing Nepad's priority sectors, namely infrastructure, agriculture, environment, tourism, information and communications technology, health, human resources, and science and technology (S&T). Attention will increasingly be paid to establishing structures in South Africa to enable the country to maximise the increased trade and investment benefits arising from Nepad.

Missions

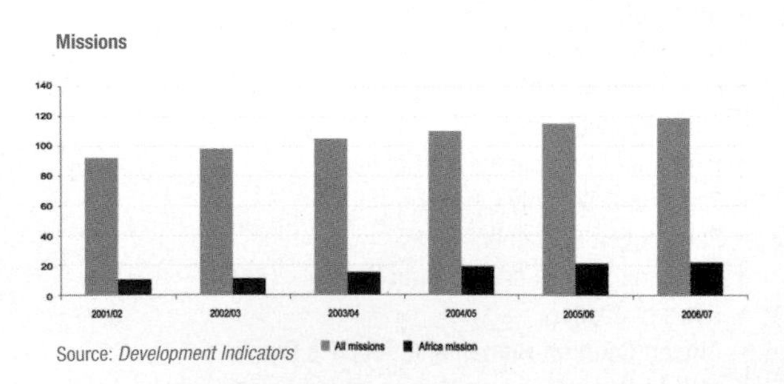

Source: *Development Indicators*

In July 2007, President Thabo Mbeki presented South Africa's response to the African Peer Review Mechanism (APRM) Panel's *Country Review Report* at the seventh summit of the APRM Forum in Accra, Ghana.

The review report identified 18 South African best practices worthy of emulation. They include co-operative governance, popular participatory governance practices, Batho Pele, Thusong Service Centres (formerly multipurpose community centres), the highly consultative budget formulation process, achievements of the South African Revenue Service, the Johannesburg Securities Exchange, Triple Bottom Line Reporting, the Mzansi Account for the unbanked, the Financial Service Charter, the King Commission reports, self-reliance in development funding, provision of basic needs and socio-economic rights and the successful promotion of gender equality in the public sphere.

The APRM's purpose is to foster the adaptation of policies, standards and practices that lead to political stability, high economic growth, sustainable development and accelerated subregional and continental economic integration by sharing experience and reinforcing successful and best practices, including identifying deficiencies and assessing the needs for capacity-building.

South Africa and the Southern African Development Community (SADC)

The SADC is a critical vehicle for southern African regional development.

It provides for regional peace and security, sectoral co-operation and an integrated regional economy. The SADC member states are Angola, Botswana, the DRC, Lesotho, Malawi, Mauritius, Mozambique, Namibia, the Seychelles, South Africa, Swaziland, Tanzania, Zambia and Zimbabwe.

The SADC is South Africa's major trading partner after the European Union (EU).

Asia and Australasia

South Africa continues to strengthen its relations with the region through increased two-way trade; personal exchanges between high-level dignitaries; and the finalisation of new instruments of co-operation in the scientific and technological fields, through technology transfer, investments and overseas development assistance (ODA) in capacity-building.

While Japan, Malaysia and Taiwan already rank among the foremost sources of foreign direct investment (FDI) in South Africa, the significance of China and India, as sources of investment, is growing. South Africa's multinational companies are finding attractive investment opportunities in Australia, China, Indonesia and Thailand in diverse fields such as mining, minerals processing, electronic media and the petrochemical industry.

South Africa also plays a leading role in the Indian Ocean Rim Association for Regional Co-operation, which creates an opportunity for countries of the South to serve their economic interests.

The India-Brazil-South Africa (IBSA) Dialogue Forum remains of strategic importance to all three countries as a powerful global forum to drive South-South co-operation and the agenda of the South, and to champion the needs of the developing world.

The fourth meeting of the Trilateral Commission of the IBSA Dialogue Forum took place in July 2007 in New Delhi, India. The Minister of Foreign Affairs, Dr Nkosazana Dlamini Zuma, used the opportunity to hold bilateral talks with her Indian and Brazilian counterparts. The second IBSA Forum was held in October 2007.

The Middle East

The Department of Foreign Affairs distinguishes between two clearly identifiable subregions in the Middle East. There is the Levant, which comprises Israel, Iraq, Jordan, Lebanon, Palestine and Syria, and on the other hand, the Arabian/Persian Gulf Region, consisting of the member states of the Gulf Co-operation

Council, namely Bahrain, Kuwait, Oman, Qatar, Saudi Arabia, the United Arab Emirates (UAE), Iran and Yemen.

The Middle East is an important economic region as it occupies a unique geopolitical position in the tricontinental hub of Europe, Asia and Africa.

South Africa's leading trade partners in the region are Saudi Arabia, Iran, Kuwait, Qatar, Israel and the UAE.

South Africa supports a just, equitable and comprehensive peace process in the Middle East and an end to the illegal occupation of land that has led to conflict and violence between the peoples of the region.

The Americas

The United States of America (USA) has been the largest single foreign investor in the South African economy since 1994, one of the largest single-country trading partners, and the largest donor of ODA.

South Africa has, in the past two years, been the top recipient of development assistance from among the 27 African countries supported by the USA Agency for International Development (USAid). Support for Nepad within the US Administration, Congress and the business sector, with particular focus on implementing infrastructure-development projects, remains a high priority.

Building local capacity for research and effective delivery is another area of co-operation with the USA in the continuing battle against communicable diseases such as malaria, tuberculosis, HIV and AIDS.

Consultation between the South African Government, through National Treasury and USAid, on the alignment of the USAid programmes with the domestic developmental priorities of South Africa, remains ongoing, and is reviewed annually.

In the multilateral sphere, South Africa and Canada share a like-minded approach to a number of issues such as human rights and the need for United Nations (UN) reform. Canada remains a strong supporter of the African Agenda and Nepad, particularly in the G8 context.

Canada is actively seeking closer co-operation with South Africa in peacekeeping on the continent.

Intensive interaction takes place between a number of South African government departments and their Canadian counterparts. Closer co-operation has been developing in the fields of minerals and energy, health, S&T, agriculture as well as arts and culture, with the emphasis on research, skills transfer and capacity-building.

The year produced significant investment outcomes with the announcement of major Canadian direct investment in the Gautrain, McCain Plant and Alcan totalling R27 billion.

South Africa maintains formal diplomatic relations with all the Latin American countries. In November 2006, President Mbeki and a South African delegation participated in the first-ever Africa-South American Summit, which took place in Abuja, Nigeria. The summit provided an opportunity for the two continents to meet for the first time to discuss issues of mutual importance.

The Caribbean

South Africa's relations with the independent member states of the Caribbean community have been further strengthened and expanded during 2006/07. South Africa opened a high commission in Port-of-Spain, Trinidad and Tobago in early 2007 and, together with the High Commission in Kingston, Jamaica, these two missions now maintain responsibility for Antigua and Barbuda, the Bahamas, Barbados, Belize, Dominica, Grenada, Guyana, Haiti, St Kitts and Nevis, St Lucia, St Vincent and the Grenadines, and Suriname. The mission in Havana, Cuba, is also responsible for relations with the Dominican Republic.

Europe

The advent of a new democratic political dispensation marked the dawn of a new era in South Africa relations. The legal framework that governs South Africa's relationship with the EU is the Trade, Development and Co-operation Agreement (TDCA), which is premised on three main areas of co-operation, namely, political dialogue, trade and economic co-operation, and development co-operation. The EU accounts for almost 40% of South Africa's imports and exports. In 2006 alone, the EU's FDI into South Africa amounted to R4,6 billion.

The TDCA provides for a free trade agreement by 2012. The Trade Chapter of the agreement provisionally entered into force in January 2000. The TDCA also provides the legal basis for continued EU support for development co-operation activities in South Africa. This support is channelled through the European Programme for Reconstruction and Development (EPRD), which is the largest single development programme in South Africa financed by foreign donors. Further assistance from the EU comes in the form of soft loans from the European Investment Bank.

Germany has made substantial new investments into the South African economy since the 1994 democratic election and remains one of the country's most important trading partners.

By 2007, German commitments towards development in South Africa amounted to about Euro 262 million of bilateral financial and technical assistance.

Germany's Chancellor, Ms Angela Merkel, paid an official visit to South Africa in October 2007.

The United Kingdom (UK) consistently occupies the third position in terms of South African exports. With the number of tourists per year approaching half a million, the UK also is one South Africa's most important overseas tourism markets.

Former UK Prime Minister Tony Blair paid an official visit to South Africa from 31 May to 1 June 2007. This was his last official visit to South Africa before stepping down in June 2007.

In April 2007, President Mbeki, supported by Deputy Minister Aziz Pahad, visited Paris, France, at the invitation of his French counterpart, President Jacques Chirac, for consultations and to bid him farewell ahead of the presidential elections in France in April 2007.

The President of the Czech Republic, Prof. Václav Klaus, paid a state visit to South Africa in December 2006.

The visit was of historical importance since it was the first visit of a head of state from the Czech Republic since the Velvet Revolution and their separation from Slovakia in 1991. The visit was also the first visit of a head of state from Central Europe to sub-Saharan Africa.

The strategic nature of South African-Russian relations was significantly consolidated over the past year through continued high-level political dialogue with the Russian Federation.

United Nations

South Africa remains an active participant in ongoing discussions on the reform of the UN and believes that the multilateral system should be fully engaged in the endeavour for human development and poverty eradication, starting with the achievement of the millennium development goals; the common struggle to address

In August 2007, the statue of former South African President Nelson Mandela was unveiled at Parliament Square in London, in honour of his contribution to the struggle against apartheid.

Dignitaries at the unveiling included British Prime Minister Gordon Brown, London Mayor Ken Livingstone, philanthropist Lord Richard Attenborough and anti-apartheid campaigner Wendy Woods.

The nine-foot statue has been placed among statues of other statesmen such as Winston Churchill and Abraham Lincoln.

environmental degradation; the pursuit of an overarching human-rights agenda; the promotion of democracy and good governance; and all efforts to combat terrorism and the proliferation of weapons of mass destruction and small arms.

As a party to the UN conventions on climate change, desertification and biodiversity, South Africa is committed to reducing poverty and the loss of biodiversity. South Africa is also firmly committed to the protection of the oceans and the sustainable management of its marine resources.

South Africa continues to reinforce its role as an active and substantive role-player on disarmament, non-proliferation and arms-control issues at national, regional and international levels.

It actively participated in the various nuclear disarmament and non-proliferation forums, including the 2005 Nuclear Non-Proliferation Treaty Review Conference.

From 2007, South Africa is serving on the UN Security Council in a non-permanent capacity for a period of two years.

United Nations Development Programme (UNDP)

The UNDP has a office in Pretoria, which is headed by the resident representative, who is also the resident UN co-ordinator for all UN operational activities for development in South Africa.

Commonwealth

The Commonwealth comprises 53 member countries on every continent and major ocean, making up a quarter of the world's population and generating 20% of global trade.

Members range from micro-states in Polynesia to members of the G8, from the smallest and poorest to the richest and most populous, with cross-cutting affiliations straddling the North-South divide.

The Commonwealth is united by its shared ideals and common traditions manifested in similar structures of governance; public administration and law; and a common working language, commercial and business practices, and understanding. It is an important multilateral institution, both uniting and serving its member countries and providing a lobby on global issues.

Its programmes of action, such as the Commonwealth Fund for Technical Co-operation, the Commonwealth Youth Programme and the Commonwealth Foundation, are focused on capacity-building, economic and social development, the removal of disparities in living standards across the world and the alleviation of poverty and illiteracy.

TASCAM

COMMUNICATIONS

South Africa boasts an outstanding telecommunications infrastructure and a diversity of print and broadcast media. South Africa is also the largest consumer of information technology (IT) products and services in the world.

With a network that is 99% digital and includes the latest in fixed-line, wireless and satellite communications, South Africa has the most developed telecommunications network in Africa.

Information society

In February 2007, Cabinet approved the National Information Society and Development Plan. According to the plan, different departments will initiate programmes according to their mandate. The Department of Communications will launch a programme that supports a strategy and plan to bring initiatives that contribute to building an information society in South Africa under one banner – *ICT for All*.

The goal is to build an enabling environment that supports the ability of the citizenry to use information and communications technologies (ICTs) to access new services.

Access

The Electronic Communications Act, 2005 seeks to remove policies that hinder the development of cross-sector applications, services and businesses. The Act enables the sector to reflect the integration of telecommunications with IT, broadcasting and broadcasting signal distribution.

It also empowers citizens with better access to knowledge and information. The Telecommunications Amendment Act, 2001 has enabled the Department of Communications to liberalise the South African telecommunications market, increase competition and, as a by-product, stimulate the sector to bring down the costs of communications and remove constraints on growth.

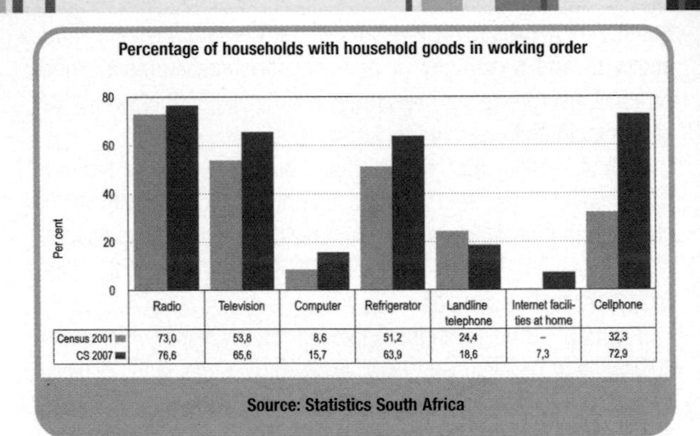

	Radio	Television	Computer	Refrigerator	Landline telephone	Internet facilities at home	Cellphone
Census 2001	73,0	53,8	8,6	51,2	24,4	–	32,3
CS 2007	76,6	65,6	15,7	63,9	18,6	7,3	72,9

The Department of Communications has identified the following areas:

- Broadcasting Digital Migration Strategy: The Cabinet declared that the first terrestrial digital signal will be switched on on 1 November 2008 and the analogue one switched off on the same date in 2011, giving the country a dual illumination period of three years.
  The Broadcasting Digital Migration Strategy was expected to be gazetted in 2007. This is an historic milestone in the country and one more area in which South Africa will join pioneer countries in the ICT sector.
- Universal Service and Access Policy and Strategy: The Universal Service and Access Agency of South Africa was established in terms of Section 58 of the Telecommunications Act, 1996. The main role of the agency is to promote universal service and access to ICTs and services for all South Africans. It also facilitates and offers guidance in evaluating, monitoring and implementing schemes which propose to improve universal access and service. In addition, it is involved in setting up telecentres, which provide ICT services, especially in rural areas, on a cost-recovery basis.

Mobile communications

In recent years, South Africa has witnessed tremendous growth in the cellular phone industry. South Africa has four operators, namely Vodacom, MTN, Cell C and Virgin Mobile.

Internet

According to Internet market research company Nielsen//Netratings, South Africa's online audience has grown tremendously over the past two years, as high broadband prices have slowly started to decrease.

The number of people using the Internet in the northern hemisphere has seen a plateauing of growth over the last year. In contrast, South Africa has seen phenomenal expansion – growing by around 50% in each of the last two years.

In May 2007, some 3,9 million active browsers were registered in South Africa, representing a 120% increase on the number in May 2005. Over the same period, page impressions grew by 129%, from 91 million in May 2005 to 207 million in May 2007.

Composition of South African Internet population by age and language

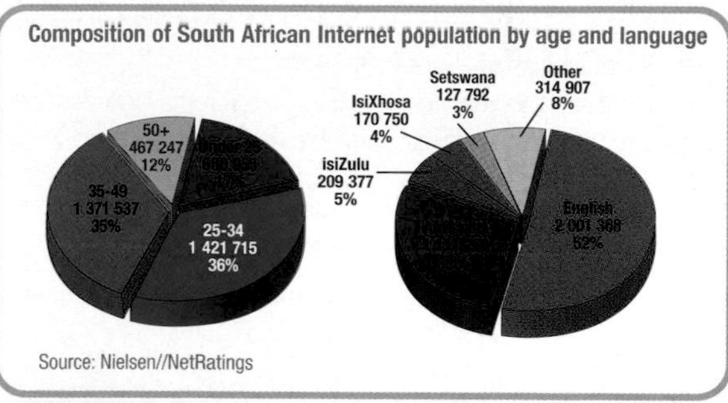

Source: Nielsen//NetRatings

State-owned signal-provider, Sentech, is on course to provide about 80% digital terrestrial transmission coverage by the start of the 2010 FIFA World Cup™ in South Africa.

Sentech intends to launch at least one high-definition television satellite channel in time for the World Cup.

In line with the Government's technology plan for 2010, the SABC also plans to have six more high-definition units in place by the end of 2009. Set-top boxes would enable South Africans to access digital signals using their analogue television sets.

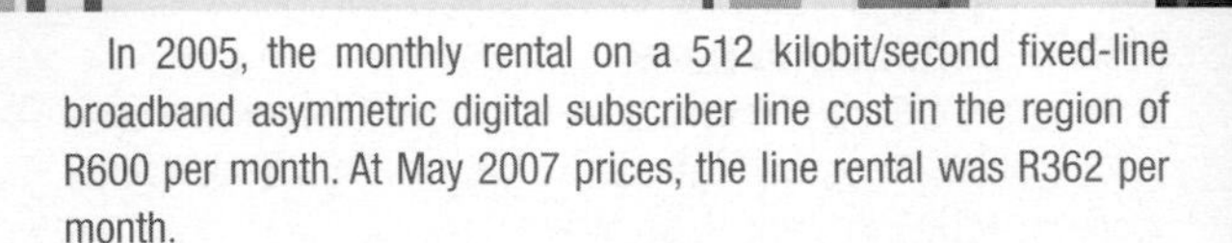

In 2005, the monthly rental on a 512 kilobit/second fixed-line broadband asymmetric digital subscriber line cost in the region of R600 per month. At May 2007 prices, the line rental was R362 per month.

Telkom

Telkom has been operating as a commercial company since October 1991 and is the largest provider of communications services in Africa, according to operating revenue and assets. The Telkom Group comprises the fixed-line company Telkom and a 50% shareholding in mobile telecommunications operator Vodacom. It was listed on the JSE Securities Exchange Limited and the New York Stock Exchange in March 2003.

Telkom's listing created meaningful value for Black Economic Empowerment (BEE) shareholders. Over 100 000 South African retail investors subscribed during Telkom's initial public offering, specifically targeted at historically disadvantaged individuals. In its first year as a listed company, the estimated value created for retail shareholders amounted to about R560 million.

For the financial year to 31 March 2007, the Telkom Group posted strong financial results. It declared a higher ordinary annual dividend of 600 cents (c) per share and a special dividend of 500 c per share in June 2007.

Telkom has until 1 November 2011 to unbundle the local loop which links the national telecommunications network to individual homes and businesses.

Postal sector

The Government-subsidised South African Post Office (Sapo) is required to provide a basic letter service that is reasonably accessible to all.

The first post office in South Africa was opened in the Castle in Cape Town in 1792.

The Post Office delivers almost six million letters per day to 10 million addresses in South Africa. It has 2 550 outlets covering the length and breadth of South Africa.

Annually, Sapo prints more than 384 million stamps and serves stamp collectors and dealers throughout the world.

As a preferred partner to government, the Post Office does pay-outs such as pension payments on behalf of the Department of Social Development. Its unequalled coverage of the country makes it particularly suited to this purpose. Motor-vehicle licences can also be paid at selected post offices.

The media

South Africa's Bill of Rights guarantees the freedom of the press and other media.

In 2007, South Africa was ranked as the 59th most free country in terms of press freedom in the world, sharing that position with Nauru, and beating Italy (61st) and Brazil (90th). Regarding press freedom in sub-Saharan Africa, South Africa ranked fourth, with only Mali, Ghana and Mauritius enjoying more press freedom.

Broadcasting

The independence of the public broadcaster, the South African Broadcasting Corporation (SABC), is guaranteed by legislation. The SABC is being corporatised and restructured to better fulfil its mandate.

Radio

In 2007, the SABC's national radio network comprised 18 stations broadcasting in 11 languages, which collectively reached an average daily adult audience of 19 million.

SABC News provides news and current affairs services to both SABC radio and television. For its domestic coverage, SABC News has 13 editorial offices, while world news is provided by strategically placed news bureaus, foreign correspondents and international news agencies.

Copy supplied to Radio News amounts to almost a million words a day, and is compiled around the clock into a weekly total of 1 568 bulletins and 190 current affairs programmes. Programmes are produced weekly in 13 languages on the SABC's radio services. There is a public broadcasting service radio station for each language group.

Channel Africa Network comprises four language services, reaching millions of listeners throughout Africa. Broadcasts are in English, French, Kiswahili and Portuguese. It targets audiences in Africa and the Indian Ocean islands, and concentrates on providing programmes with African content.

The Independent Communications Authority of South Africa has granted licences to the following private radio stations:

- Radio Algoa (ex-SABC)
- Classic FM (greenfield)
- Kaya FM (greenfield)
- YFM (greenfield)
- Highveld Stereo (ex-SABC)
- Radio 702
- Radio Jacaranda (ex-SABC)
- Radio Oranje (ex-SABC)
- East Coast Radio (ex-SABC)
- P4 (greenfield)
- Cape Talk MW (greenfield)
- Radio KFM (ex-SABC).

In March 2007, government announced the establishment of a new state-owned company that will provide long-distance connectivity to the country's telecommunications market on a cost basis.The new company, Infraco, will not be a fully fledged telecommunications company itself, but will act as a provider of broadband capacity through fibre-optic cables to other operators in the country.

The move forms part of South Africa's attempts to bring down the costs of telecommunications and Internet connectivity in the country.

Community radio stations have a huge potential for the support of, among other things, cultural and educational information exchange. These radio stations use all indigenous languages, ensuring that people receive information in languages they understand.

Television

South Africa has by far the largest television audience in Africa. There are more than four million licensed television households.

The SABC's national television network comprises three full-spectrum free-to-air channels and one satellite pay-TV channel aimed at audiences in Africa. Combined, the free-to-air sound broadcasting stations broadcast in 11 languages and reach a daily adult audience of almost 20 million people via the terrestrial signal distribution network and a satellite signal.

In October 1998, the country's first privately owned free-to-air television channel, e.tv, started operations.

M-Net became South Africa's first private subscription television service when it launched in 1986. Today, it broadcasts its array of general entertainment and niche channels to subscribers in more than 50 countries across the African continent and adjacent Indian Ocean islands.

MultiChoice Africa (MCA) was formed in 1995 to manage the subscriber services of its sister company, M-Net. It became the first African company on the continent to offer digital satellite broadcasting.

MCA is 100% owned by the MIH Group, which is listed on the JSE Limited, the Nasdaq in New York, and AEX in Amsterdam.

There are more than 1,2 million DStv subscribers in South Africa, and about 190 000 M-Net subscribers.

Print

Technically, the local print media rate among the best in the world. This is one reason why newspapers and magazines have held their

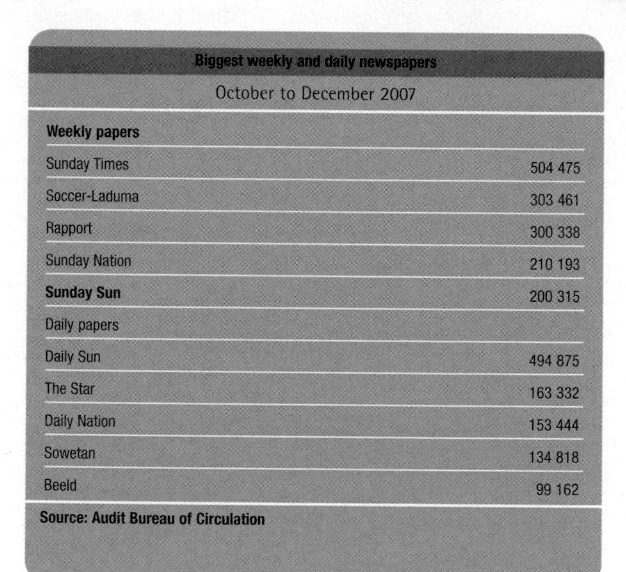

Biggest weekly and daily newspapers	
October to December 2007	
Weekly papers	
Sunday Times	504 475
Soccer-Laduma	303 461
Rapport	300 338
Sunday Nation	210 193
Sunday Sun	200 315
Daily papers	
Daily Sun	494 875
The Star	163 332
Daily Nation	153 444
Sowetan	134 818
Beeld	99 162

Source: Audit Bureau of Circulation

own in a volatile information era, identified by the vast development of various new forms of media-delivery platforms via the Internet.

South African newspapers and magazines are mainly organised into several major publishing houses: Media24 (part of Naspers, the largest media group in Africa), the Irish-based Independent News & Media (Pty) Limited group, Caxton Publishers & Printers Limited, Johnnic Communications and Associated Magazines. Other important media players include M & G Media Limited, the Natal Witness Printing & Publishing Company (Pty) Limited, Primedia Publishing Limited, Ramsay, Son and Parker (Pty) Limited, and Kagiso Media.

Since 1994, the major press groups have embarked on programmes to boost BBE in media ownership.

Top 20 magazines based on net sales, October to December 2006

1	Huisgenoot
2	You
3	TV Plus
4	Ideas/Idees
5	Sarie
6	Weg/Go
7	Cosmopolitan
8	People
9	Rooi Rose
10	True Love
11	Woman and Home
12	Move
13	Car
14	FHM
15	Finesse
16	Men's Health
17	Tuis/Home
18	Bona
19	SA Garden and Home
20	Fairlady

Source: Print Media South Africa

Newspapers

By mid-2007, the newspaper market consisted of:

- 22 dailies
- nine Sunday newspapers.

In July 2007, the SABC launched SABC News International, its 24-hour channel aimed at providing in-depth coverage of African stories. The channel will be structured in a similar way as other international news providers, such as the British Broadcasting Corporation.

In 2006, four of the daily newspapers had circulations over 100 000 and accounted for almost 50% of the total circulation in this category. They were *Beeld* (104 932), *Daily Sun* (467 681), *Sowetan* (133 195) and *The Star* (168 776) (Audit Bureau of Circulations, July to September 2006). The total circulation for these four grew by 3,3%, while the rest of the category only grew by 0,8%.

Almost 150 regional or country newspapers, most of which are weekly tabloids, serve particular towns or districts in the country by covering local affairs and carrying local advertising. Most are published in English or Afrikaans, and many are bilingual. The most popular publication day is Thursday, followed by Tuesday, and the bigger publications appear twice weekly.

The only truly national newspapers are the *Sunday Times*, *Rapport*, *Sunday Independent*, *Sunday Sun*, *City Press*, *Sunday World* and *Sunday Tribune*.

Magazines

The magazine industry in South Africa is fiercely competitive with new titles appearing all the time, despite the worldwide challenge from electronic and interactive media. Judging from the proliferation of titles on the shelves in supermarkets and bookstores, many readers are still attracted to print.

The trend to target certain niche markets with specialised publications is popular in the magazine industry and has led this section to grow with 40% more titles over the last 10 years. However, there is evidence to suggest that the overall reading population in South Africa is shrinking, which is a concern for the industry.

Weeklies *Huisgenoot* and *You* are the two biggest money-making magazines in South Africa.

Among the monthlies, women's magazines are still the most widely distributed despite declining sales. *Sarie*, *Rooi Rose*, *Cosmopolitan*, *Move*, *Ideas/Idees* and *True Love* are all in the top 10.

News agencies

The national news agency, the South African Press Association, is a co-operative, non-profit organisation.

The main foreign news agencies operating in South Africa are Reuters, *Agence France-Presse*, Associated Press, *Deutsche Presse-Agentur* and United Press International.

Media diversity

The independent Media Development and Diversity Agency (MDDA) is jointly funded by government, the media and other donors.

South Africa's top 20 advertising agencies – January to December 2006

Ranking 2006	Ranking 2007	Agency name	Income Rm	% Annual growth	No of staff	Staff to income R000s	Total no of clients	Equity ownership	Representivity
1	1	FCB SA (Johannesburg)	124,6	22,8	247	504	34	35,0%	40,9%
Five biggest accounts in 2006: Toyota, Vodacom, First National Bank, Uthingo, Tiger Brands									
2	2	Ogilvy Johannesburg	113,2	13,2	238	475	67	50,1%	45,8%
Five biggest accounts in 2006: KFC, Multichoice, SAB Miller, Sun International, SAA									
4	3	Ogilvy Cape	108,8	17,0	230	473	33	50,1%	44,8%
Five biggest accounts in 2006: VW/Audi, BP/Castrol, BAT, Old Mutual, SAB Miller/Sun International									
3	4	TBWA\Hunt\ Lascaris Johannesburg	104,9	7,0	127	825	22	30,0%	44,9%
Five biggest accounts in 2006: Standard Bank, Nissan, MTN Retail, Tiger Brands, Motorola									
5	5	Network BBDO	97,0	25,0	95	102	39	40,0%	44,2%
Five biggest accounts in 2006: Nedbank, Cell C, Frito Lay, SABC, Chicken Licken									

Source: Adex Nielsen Media Research/Media Inflation Watch

The 2007 Loerie Awards Ceremony was held in July in Margate, KwaZulu-Natal. TBWA\Hunt\Lascaris took most of the Loeries (61), including the Grand Prix Award for their Adcock Ingram advert.

Ogilvy South Africa revieved 54 Loeries, while Network BBDO took home 51 Loeries.

Headed by a nine-member board, the MDDA works to foster diversity, particularly in community and small commercial media, and to redress imbalances in the industry.

The MDDA awarded its first grants to community and small commercial media projects in January 2004.

In 2007/08, the agency received R11,9 million from government, R4,1 million from broadcasting partners and R3,6 million from print partners. The transfer from Government Communications was increased by R2,2 million for 2006/07 to expand the MDDA's operational activities, especially for additional personnel for monitoring funded projects, and also for the anticipated challenges that the Electronic Communication Act, 2005 is likely to pose for the agency.

At the end of November 2006, the MDDA had approved 114 projects to the value R27,9 million.

Advertising

Several South African agencies are active in Africa. The industry is self-regulated through the Advertising Standards Authority.

Adspend by medium – excluding self promotion					
	2005		2006		
	Rm	Share %	Rm	Share %	Rate inflation %
Print	6 804,1	39,7	8 018,8	39,9	6,9
TV	6 331,1	36,9	7 702,6	38,3	7,8
Radio	2 362,2	13,8	2 645,6	13,2	9,0
Outdoor	788,2	4,6	1 023,3	5,1	9,8
Cinema	591,2	3,4	393,3	2,0	137,3
Internet	140,7	0,9	174,1	0,9	n/a
Direct mail	121,5	0,7	136,3	0,7	n/a
Total	17 139	100	20 093,9	100	9,1

Source: Adex Nielsen Media Research/Media Inflation Watch

The aim of the Department of Transport is to lead the provision of an integrated, sustainable, reliable and safe transport system, by planning, developing, co-ordinating, promoting and implementing transport policies and strategies.

Public Transport Strategy (2007 – 2010)

In March 2007, Cabinet approved the Public Transport Strategy (2007 – 2020). This strategy aims to accelerate the improvement in public transport by establishing integrated rapid public transport networks (IRPTNs), which will introduce priority rail corridors and bus rapid transit (BRT) systems in cities.

The high-level Public Transport Action Plan supplements the Public Transport Strategy. It maps out phase one (2007 – 2010) to fast-track an implementation programme over the next four years that targets the initial development of high-quality IRPTNs in 2010 host cities.

The essential feature of the Public Transport Strategy is the phased extension of mode-based vehicle recapitalisation into IRPTNs. These networks comprise an integrated package of rapid rail, BRT and taxi and metered taxi priority networks, especially in major cities. The strategy is expected to improve public-transport services for over half the country's population.

The IRPTN package involves city-wide, transport-authority-controlled networks of rapid public transport corridors and feeder systems of smaller buses, taxis, bicycles, pedestrian access, as well as metered taxis and park-and-ride facilities.

Full special needs and wheelchair access for all trunk corridor rail and road vehicles will also be implemented.

By March 2007, the 2010 FIFA World Cup™ host cities had already submitted their phase-one network concepts on maximising alignment with 2010 legacy projects to the Department of Transport's Public Transport Infrastructure and Systems Fund. About R9 billion was allocated to improve public-transport infrastructure over the Medium Term

Expenditure Framework (MTEF) period. This includes R19,2 billion for airports, R5,5 billion for national roads, R8,5 billion for passenger rail and R9,2 billion for public transport for the 2010 World Cup.

Agencies

The four bodies tasked with commercialising certain elements of government's operational activities, are the South African National Roads Agency Limited (Sanral), the South African Maritime Safety Authority, the Cross-Border Road Transport Agency and the Civil Aviation Authority.

Transnet Limited

Transnet, which is transforming into a focused freight transport and logistics company, comprises the following operating divisions:

- Transnet Freight Rail (formerly Spoornet) – the freight rail division
- Transnet Rail Engineering (formerly Transwerk) – the rolling stock maintenance business
- Transnet National Ports Authority (TNPA) (formerly the National Ports Authority) – fulfils the landlord function for South Africa's port system
- Transnet Port Terminals (formerly South African Ports Authority) – manages port and cargo terminal operations in the nation's leading ports
- Transnet Pipelines (formerly Petronet) – the fuel and gas pipeline business, pumps and manages the storage of petroleum and gas products through its network of high-pressure, long-distance pipelines.

Transnet was set to spend about R17 billion in 2007/08 as part of its capital investment. Projects include:

- providing 110 locomotives for the coal line and 212 locomotives for the general freight business of Transnet Freight Rail

- widening and deepening the Durban Port's entrance channel
- constructing a new container terminal in Ngqura in the Eastern Cape
- expanding the Cape Town container terminal
- constructing a new multiproduct pipeline between Durban and Johannesburg to boost capacity from 2010.

Road transport

South Africa has the longest road network of any country in Africa. The Department of Transport continues to integrate and improve the road network by ensuring that it is well developed, well maintained and safe.

Sanral's main objectives are financing, managing control over, planning, developing, rehabilitating and maintaining the South African national roads network. It is responsible for the existing national road network of 16 750 kilometres (km) with an estimated asset value of over R40 billion. Over the MTEF period, transfers were expected to increase due to additional allocations of R350 million in 2007/08, R550 million in 2008/09 and R1,2 billion in 2009/10. The funding is for non-toll national-road infrastructure.

Minibus taxis are responsible for 65% of the 2,5 billion annual passenger trips in urban areas, as well as a high percentage of rural and intercity transport.

Buses and trains account for 21% and 14% respectively of all public transport.

According to the *National Household Travel Survey, 2003*, about 26% of households in South Africa have access to a motor car. At 108 cars per 1 000 of the population, car ownership in South Africa remains in its infancy.

Taxi Recapitalisation Programme (TRP)

Government's TRP strategy is underpinned by a strong desire to have an integrated public transport system.

Total motor-vehicle sales

Total market sales	Year	Sales
Total sales September	2007	49 996
Total sales September	2006	57 599
Total sales August	2007	57 970
Total sales August	2006	59 805
Total sales January – September	2007	468 652
Total sales January – September	2006	484 134

Source: National Association of Automobile Manufacturers of South Africa

The main objectives of the TRP are to have a taxi industry that supports a strong economy that puts the passenger first and that meets the country's socio-economic objectives.

Government recognises the critical role played by the industry, and endeavours to ensure its growth and sustainability. The TRP is not only about scrapping old taxi vehicles, but is also concerned with the sustainability and effective regulation of the industry. It is a direct response to the recommendations of the National Taxi Task Team to consider specific interventions to turn around the taxi industry.

Compliance with the necessary basic requirements include possession of legitimate documentation and securing the appropriate type of vehicles, specifically new taxi vehicles that comply with safety specifications.

A traffic-infringement management system, which includes a points-merit and -demerit system and a system of driver retraining and testing after serious crashes or repeat violations, will be introduced to deal with lawlessness on South Africa's roads and reduce road fatalities. The administrative adjudication of road-traffic offences was expected to be piloted in Pretoria in January 2007, which were to include the points-demerit system.

The TRP is part of government's broad, integrated public-transport network aimed at forming part of the larger public-transport feeder system.

By mid-2007, about 80 000 operating licences had been issued nationally. About 50 000 were uplifted by operators.

Nationally, more than 11 000 old and unroadworthy vehicles had been removed from the roads and over R600 million paid out as scrapping allowances.

Law enforcement is also one of the key pillars of implementing the TRP, and R2,2 billion has been set aside for this purpose. By mid-2007, the Road Traffic Management Corporation was developing a TRP law-enforcement strategy which would include the recruitment and training of staff for law-enforcement activities within the taxi industry. The strategy was expected to be completed by November 2007.

Goods transport

Eighty percent of all freight in South Africa is transported by road. Nearly 7% of gross domestic product is spent on freight transport.

About 69% of road-freight tonnage is carried by firms or operators transporting freight in the course of their business, and 29% by road haulage firms.

Construction of the Gautrain Rapid Rail Link commenced in September 2006. The project will comprise an 80-kilometre route and 10 new stations. By mid-2007, utilities such as water pipes, electricity and telecommunications cables had been removed in most areas and nearly 70% of affected properties along the proposed route had been handed over.

The train and bus depots were under construction in Midrand to stable and service Gautrain's 24 train sets and to station Gautrain's 150 commuter buses. About R8,8 billion had been expended on the project and the private sector was spending more than R3 billion.

South African Rail Commuter Corporation (SARCC)-Metrorail

The SARCC was established in 1990 to provide commuter rail services in South Africa. All the passenger rail entities in South Africa are being consolidated. The first phase of the consolidation has been concluded with Metrorail being transferred from Transnet to the SARCC with effect from 1 May 2006. The second phase will see the Shosholoza Meyl transferred to the Department of Transport.

The corporation's role as concessionaire is to establish and monitor service standards, safety and security levels, and operating efficiencies. Up to 1,7 million people use the commuter rail service daily.

The SARCC infrastructure and assets comprise 478 stations, some 2 240 km of electrified single-rail track and 4 564 coaches.

Investment for passenger rail has more than doubled since 1994 to over R16 billion in 2007.

Transnet Freight Rail has a 20 247-km rail network, of which approximately 1 500 km comprises heavy haul lines. The network connects the ports and hinterland of South Africa as well as the rail networks of the sub-Saharan region. Transnet Freight Rail infrastructure represents about 80% of Africa's rail infrastructure.

It operates freight trains, serving customers in the following major segments:

- mining: coal, iron ore, manganese, granite, asbestos, chrome and non-ferrous metals
- manufacturing: chemicals, fuel and petroleum, fertiliser, cement, lime, iron steel and scrap
- agriculture and forestry: grain, stockfeed and milling, timber, paper and publishing, and fast-moving consumer goods
- containers and automotive: intermodal wholesale, automotive and industrial.

Transnet Freight Rail offers freight logistics solutions to customers in all industries countrywide.

Civil aviation

The Airports Company of South Africa (Acsa) owns and operates the 10 principal airports, including the three major international airports in Johannesburg, Cape Town and Durban. The others are domestic airports in Bloemfontein, Port Elizabeth, East London, George, Kimberley, Upington and Pilanesberg. Other airports in South Africa include Lanseria (Midrand), Gateway (Polokwane), Nelspruit and Kruger (Mpumalanga).

By January 2007, Acsa had begun its five-year investment programme in all major airports in the country.

About R5,2 billion will be spent over five years to accommodate the 2010 World Cup. Some R492 million was spent at the Johannesburg, Cape Town and Durban international airports, and R46 million was invested at the Port Elizabeth, East London, George, Bloemfontein, Kimberley, Upington and Pilansberg national airports. It is projected that Acsa will handle more than 31 million passengers by 2012.

By October 2007, there were 10 067 aircraft on the South Africa's register. Air travel in South Africa has grown above 10% per year over the past three years, largely due to the proliferation of low-cost airlines following the deregulation of the industry in the early 1990s and the increased volume of international traffic flowing into the country. This can be evidenced by the fact that, in 1993, fewer than 12 international airlines flew into South Africa. However, this number increased to 20 by 1995 and by mid-2007, more than 70 international airlines were flying into the country regularly.

South African Airways (SAA)

SAA is Africa's leading airline. In April 2006, it became a member of the worldwide Star Alliance, the first African airline to join the elite international network.

SAA's membership added 25 new African routes and destinations to the Star Alliance Network. Other members of the network include Air Canada, Lufthansa and United Airlines.

The Airports Company of South Africa plans to handle 31 million passengers by 2012. Its infrastructure upgrading has been boosted by R19,3 billion for the next three years, as part of expanding airport capacity ahead of the 2010 FIFA World Cup™.

South Africa has a number of airlines flying between its major cities, and to some of its smaller ones, with fares ranging from first-class to cut-price economy. Flights can be booked online from anywhere in the world.

Eight major domestic airlines operate in the country, as well as a number of smaller charter airline companies.

Ports

The TNPA is the largest port authority on the continent. It owns and manages South Africa's ports at Richards Bay, Durban, East London, Port Elizabeth, Mossel Bay, Cape Town, Saldanha and Ngqura.

The TNPA provides suitable infrastructure as a conduit for the country's imports and exports. As port landlord, it is responsible for:

- developing and managing port properties
- developing, advising and implementing national port policies
- providing and maintaining port infrastructure (i.e. breakwaters, seawalls, channels, basins, quay walls and jetties), and the sustainability of ports and their environments
- co-ordinating marketing and promotional ativities for each port.

The TNPA also has a control function, which includes:

- providing vessel-traffic control and navigational aids
- licensing and leasing terminals to operators
- monitoring the performance of port operators
- ensuring the orderly, efficient and reliable transfer of cargo and passengers between sea and land.

Facts and figures about South African Airways (SAA):

- SAA serves more than 700 destinations throughout the world.
- It carries more than seven million passengers each year and serves 34 cities in 26 countries on six continents.
- It employs close to 10 000 people worldwide, including 3 000 at SAA Technical. Staff include about 2 800 flight attendants and more than 800 pilots.

Commercial ports play a crucial role in South Africa's transport, logistics and socio-economic development. About 98% of South Africa's exports are conveyed by sea.

In April 2007, the Minister of Transport, Mr Jeff Radebe, appointed board members to the National Ports Regulator, which was established in terms of the National Ports Act, 2005.

Its primary function will be the economic regulation of the ports system, in line with government's strategic objectives to promote equity of access to ports and to monitor the activities of the TNPA. The regulator will also promote regulated competiton, hear appeals and complaints, and investigate such complaints.

The adoption and implementation of measures to enhance maritime security has resulted in South Africa being fully compliant with the International Ships and Ports Security Code since July 2004.

As of 1 June 2007, international travellers using South Africa's airports are prohibited from carrying hand luggage containing liquids, aerosols and gels (LAGs) exceeding 100 millilitres (ml). These include perfume, shampoo, suntan lotion, creams, toothpaste and hair gel.

The new security measures are in line with the International Civil Aviation Organisation's standards.

Hand luggage with LAGs exceeding 100 ml is confiscated, while passengers are only allowed to carry one parcel on board.

International travellers are required to place essential liquids to be carried on board in a resealable clear, plastic bag with a capacity of not more than one litre and a total diameter of 80 centimetres.

With prior arrangement, permission is granted to people with medical problems to carry more LAGs if they produce a doctor's prescription to that effect.

Items carried on board that need to be placed in bags include formula milk and food for babies, prescription medicine in liquid and gel form, essential non-prescription medication, eyecare products, and other liquids and gels, including juice needed by diabetic passengers.

Lipsticks in tubes, solid deodorant, lip balm and similar solids are allowed on board.

AGRICULTURE, FORESTRY AND LAND

South Africa has a dual agricultural economy: a well-developed commercial sector and a predominant subsistence sector. About 12% of the country can be used for crop production. High-potential arable land comprises only 22% of total arable land. Some 1,3 million hectares (ha) are under irrigation.

Agricultural activities range from intensive crop production and mixed farming to cattle-ranching in the bushveld, and sheep-farming in the more arid regions.

Economic contribution

Primary agriculture contributes about 2,5% to the gross domestic product (GDP) of South Africa and about 8% to formal employment. However, there are strong linkages into the economy, so that the agro-industrial sector comprises about 15% of GDP.

South Africa is self-sufficient in virtually all major agricultural products, and in a normal year is a net food exporter. However, the country remains vulnerable to drought.

Production

Producer prices of agricultural products increased, on average, by 18,2% from 2005 to 2006, compared with a decrease of 7,5% during the previous year.

In 2006, the producer prices of field crops rose by 31,8%, against a decrease of 18% the previous year. This increase was mainly the result of a 50% increase in the price of summer grains and increases of 33,7% and 39,1% in the prices of winter cereals and dry beans, respectively.

Producer prices of horticultural products increased by 4,7% in 2006 compared with 2005. Prices of vegetables increased, on average, by 12,8% during 2006, while the prices of fresh fruit decreased by 0,8%.

The producer prices of animal products were 23,2% higher in 2006 than in 2005. Prices received for slaughtered stock increased by 5,3%. The price of beef increased by 26,7%, while that of mutton increased by 19,6%. Prices received for pastoral products increased by 22,5%. The price farmers received for milk was 6,1% higher. Prices received for poultry products rose by 7,4%.

Gross value of agricultural production, 2006	
Field crops	
Maize	6 760 352
Wheat	2 993 449
Hay	2 228 198
Grain sorghum	119 425
Sugar cane	2 268 719
Ground-nuts	233 648
Tobacco	262 787
Sunflower seed	987 446
Cotton	90 251
Other	1 654 116
Total	17 598 391
Horticulture	
Viticulture	2 783 216
Citrus fruit	3 132 249
Subtropical fruit	1 513 233
Deciduous and other fruit	4 538 608
Vegetables	4 608 090
Potatoes	2 961 671
Other	1 211 532
Total	20 748 590
Animal products	
Wool	886 754
Poultry and poultry products	15 729 909
Cattle and cattle products	11 331 213
Sheep and goats slaughtered	2 198 484
Pigs slaughtered	1 427 699
Milk	5 114 218
Other	1 916 505
Total	38 604 782
Grand total	76 951 763

Source: Directorate: Agricultural Statistics, Department of Agriculture

AGRICULTURE, FORESTRY AND LAND

Field crops and horticulture

- Maize is the largest locally produced field crop, and the most important source of carbohydrates in the Southern African Development Community (SADC) for animal and human consumption.
  South Africa is the main maize producer in the SADC, with an average production of about 8,9 million tons (Mt) a year over the past 10 years.
  It is estimated that more than 8 000 commercial maize producers are responsible for the major part of the South African crop, while the rest is produced by thousands of smallscale producers.
  Maize is produced mainly in North West, the Free State and Mpumalanga.
  A total of 6,9 Mt of maize was produced in 2005/06 on two million hectares of land (developing agriculture included).
- Wheat is produced in the Western Cape and the Free State. Average wheat production has been about 2 Mt a year over the past 10 years.
- South Africa is the world's 12th-largest producer of sunflower seed. An area of 472 480 ha was planted in 2005/06, producing 520 000 tons (t).
- Some 2,5 Mt of sugar are produced per season. About 50% of this is marketed in southern Africa, while the rest is exported to markets in Africa, the Middle East, North America and Asia.
- South Africa is the leading exporter of protea cut flowers,

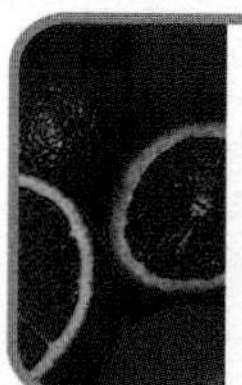

The Comprehensive Agricultural Support Programme focuses on on-and-off farm infrastructure, information and knowledge management, financial assistance, technical and advisory services, training and capacity-building, and marketing and business development.

Between 2004/05 and 2006/07, the Government successfully rolled out almost 2 500 projects supporting over 167 000 beneficiaries.

In 2007/08, 786 projects were expected to be rolled out to benefit an additional 60 000 farmers.

In December 2007, Cabinet approved the Biofuels Industrial Strategy. It will be implemented in phases with the first phases of development being from 2008 to 2013, a five-year period. The strategy proposes a 2% biofuels production by 2013, which is a revised target from the initial 4,5% target proposed in the draft strategy. The revision on the target is in consideration of the agricultural concerns.

The strategy further proposes that the use of maize be excluded in the development of the biofuels in the initial stages of this industry development. This is largely due to food-security concerns, fears around price increases, and the fact that maize is a staple food source for the majority of the poor in the country.

which account for more than half of proteas sold on the world market.

Some other crops:

- The area planted to lucerne totals about 30 000 ha.
- Deciduous fruit is grown mainly in the Western Cape and in the Langkloof Valley in the Eastern Cape. Smaller production areas are found along the Orange River and in the Free State, Mpumalanga and Gauteng.

  In 2005/06, apples made up the largest percentage of the crop (39%), while grapes totalled 25% and pears 19%. About 73% of the total crop was produced in the Western Cape, 12% in the Northern Cape, 11% in the Eastern Cape and 2% in Limpopo.
- Internationally, South Africa's wines are highly competitive, with the industry showing a sustainable and increasingly positive trend over recent years. The wine industry contributes some R163 billion a year to South Africa's GDP and employs 257 000 people directly and indirectly, while an additional R4,2 billion is generated annually through wine tourism.
- Citrus production is largely limited to irrigation areas and takes place in Limpopo (16 255 ha), Mpumalanga (11 681 ha), the Eastern Cape (12 923 ha), KwaZulu-Natal (4 004 ha), the Western Cape (9 524 ha) and Northern Cape (639 ha).

Total agricultural exports					
	2002	2003	2004	2005	2006
Average: five years					
Total South African products					
R millions	314 927	273 127	292 079	327 125	393 047
Total agriculture products					
R millions	25 460	22 794	22 074	25 458	26 978
Agriculture as % of total exports	8,1	8,3	7,6	7,8	6,9

Source: Agricultural Statistics, Department of Agriculture

A total of 2,2 Mt of citrus were produced in 2006/07, which was a 10% increase compared with 2005/06.

- Pineapples are grown in the Eastern Cape and northern KwaZulu-Natal. Other subtropical crops such as avocados, mangoes, bananas, litchis, guavas, papayas, granadillas, and macadamia and pecan nuts are produced mainly in Mpumalanga and Limpopo and in subtropical coastal areas of KwaZulu-Natal and the Eastern Cape.
- In 2006, South Africa produced 686 582 t of subtropical fruit, which was 81 585 t or 10,6% less than in 2005.

Livestock

About 80% of agricultural land in South Africa is mainly suitable for extensive livestock-farming. Livestock are also kept in other areas, usually in combination with other farming enterprises. Numbers vary according to weather conditions. Stockbreeders concentrate mainly on developing breeds that are well-adapted to diverse weather and environmental conditions.

By mid-2007, there were 13,5 million cattle, 24,9 million sheep and 6,4 milion goats. South Africa normally produces 85% of its meat requirements, while 15% is imported from Namibia, Botswana, Swaziland, Australia, New Zealand and Europe.

Rooibos tea is grown only in the Cedarberg area of the Western Cape, about 200 kilometres north of Cape Town. There is no alternative source of supply anywhere in the world.

Food security

The Integrated Food Security and Nutrition Programme, adopted in July 2002, aims to eradicate hunger, malnutrition and food insecurity by 2015.

By May 2007, more than six million learners in public primary schools had access to quality meals. Some 6 000 food-production projects and 7 429 vegetable gardens were in place in nodal schools.

The agricultural production packages, which are aimed at improving food security among vulnerable communities in all nine provinces, had reached over 66 000 beneficiaries. By May 2007, more than 5 000 small and micro agro-enterprises had received financial assistance amounting to R41 million.

Production of important field crops and horticultural products, 2006 ('000 t)	
Maize	6 923
Wheat	2 172
Sugar cane	20 275
Grain sorghum	110
Ground-nuts	84
Sunflower seed	541
Deciduous and other soft fruit	1 536
Citrus fruit	1 945
Subtropical fruit	684
Vegetables	2 151
Potatoes	1 854

Source: Directorate: Agricultural Statistics, Department of Agriculture

Livestock (million)	2005	2006
Cattle	13,8	13,5
Sheep	25,3	25,0
Pigs	1,7	1,6
Goats	6,4	6,4

Source: Directorate: Agricultural Statistics, Department of Agriculture

Land and Agricultural Development Bank of South Africa (Land Bank)

The bank provides a comprehensive range of retail and wholesale financial products and services designed to meet the needs of commercial and developing farmers and agriculture-related businesses.

The Land Bank, through its Corporate Social Investment Section, has partnered with Roundabout (Pty) Ltd to provide safe drinking water to previously disadvantaged schools and communities in outlying areas.

Forestry

South Africa has developed one of the largest planted forests in the world.

Plantations cover about 1,3 million ha of South Africa's land surface. Production from these plantations amounted to more than 22 million m^3 of commercial roundwood, valued at almost R5,1 billion. Together with processed wood products, total turnover for the industry was about R15 billion in 2006, including R6,8 billion worth of wood-pulp.

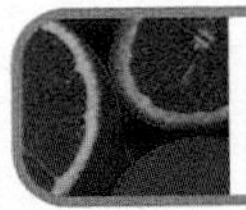

South Africa's national tree, the yellowwood tree (*Podacarpus*), can grow to a height of more than 40 m with a girth of 8 m, and can live for up to 800 years.

The forestry sector employs close to 170 000 people and contributes more than R16 billion to the South African economy. The impact of the sector is felt in rural areas and there is significant scope for forestry to expand and contribute towards uplifting those in the second economy.

Indigenous forests

There are about 530 000 ha of indigenous or natural forests in the country, which occur mainly along the southern and eastern escarpment, the coastal belt and in sheltered kloofs or ravines.

There has been an increase in the use of natural forests as sources of medicine, building material, fuel, wood and food. It is estimated that around 80% of South Africa's population still uses medicinal plants, most of which are sourced from natural habitats.

For the first time, South Africa has a detailed inventory of all its natural forests, which is used to accurately monitor changes in forest areas. The Department of Water Affairs and Forestry has completed a classification of natural forests, represented by 24 broad forest types. The Natural Forests Protected Areas System guides the setting aside and redemarcation of natural forests as protected areas.

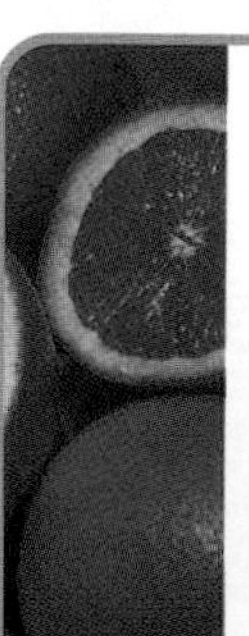

The Minister of Water Affairs and Forestry, Mrs Lindiwe Hendricks, proclaimed the first 21 champion trees as protected under the National Forests Act, 1998 in the *Government Gazette* of December 2006. These are individual trees and groups of trees shortlisted by a panel of experts considered to be of national conservation importance. This declaration comes a year after an initial list of trees was published for comment.

Among the listed trees are:

- the famous Tsitsikamma Big Tree along the Garden Route
- the Post Office Milkwood Tree of Mossel Bay
- Sagole Baobab in Limpopo province (largest tree in South Africa)
- Camphor trees planted at Vergelegen Estate three centuries ago.

Guidelines have been developed for the use of these trees to ensure the continued benefits they offer the people of the country, both economically and ecologically.

The Champion Tree Project also entered an exciting phase with new discoveries of exceptionally large trees.

Restructuring forests

The Department of Water Affairs and Forestry is pursuing a restructuring programme in the forestry sector, which will eventually see the department becoming a sector leader and regulator of forestry in South Africa.

Land affairs

The Department of Land Affairs' responsibilities include deeds registration, surveys and mapping, cadastral surveys, spatial planning and land reform.

A project to upgrade townships surveyed under the apartheid government has made it possible for thousands of people to register properties as freehold where previously they held lesser rights.

The Chief Directorate: Surveys and Mapping manages the national control survey network, which provides a unique, highly accurate positioning system across South Africa.

The 1:50 000 topographical map series is the largest scale map series, providing full coverage of South Africa.

The popular large-scale 1:10 000 orthophoto map series provides coverage of predominantly built-up areas, areas of economic importance and areas experiencing rapid development.

The Chief Directorate: Deeds Registration aims to maintain a public register of land, as well as an efficient system of registration aimed at affording security of title to land and rights to land.

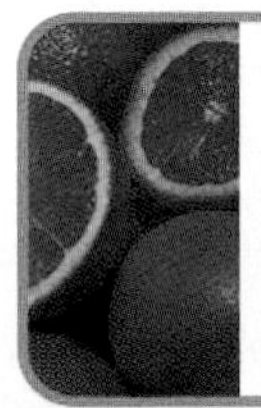

South Africa has 211 primary wood-processing plants, 206 of which are owned by the private sector and only five of which are owned by local and state authorities. Of these, some 115 are sawmills; 16 mining-timber sawmills; 49 pole-treating plants; 25 pulp, paper and board mills; one match factory; and five charcoal plants. The total roundwood intake into these processing plants in 2005 was 236 million m^3 valued at R5 billion. The value of sales of timber products produced by these primary processing plants totalled R15 025 billion.

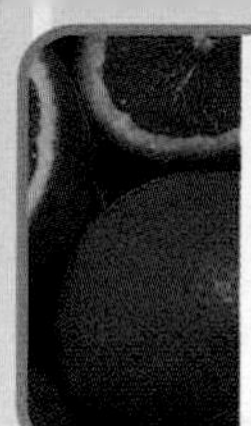

The Commission on the Restitution of Land Rights has delivered on the biggest land claim ever settled in South Africa, Tenbosch Properties with a total value of R1,1 billion involving 32 387 hectares (ha) of land. Most of the land is used for commercial farming.

Another significant land claim is the St Lucia Wetland Park, a world heritage site. The settlement comprises seven land-restitution claims by the local communities of 1 825 families on the 22 908 ha of land.

Government has committed R89 million towards the finalisation of this claim. Twenty-five percent of this amount will be allocated to the claimants for development.

Land reform

The Department of Land Affairs aims to be a global leader in the creation and maintenance of an equitable and sustainable land dispensation that results in social and economic development for all South Africans.

The department's key focus is on providing enhanced land rights to all South Africans, with particular emphasis on previously disadvantaged individuals, that would result in increased income levels and job opportunities, productive land use and well-planned human settlements.

South Africa's land reform is premised on three programmes: land-tenure reform, redistribution and restitution. While the Department of Land Affairs implements land-tenure reform and redistribution, the Commission on the Restitution of Land Rights (CRLR) implements the restitution programme.

The department has four branches, namely Land and Tenure Reform, Restitution, Land Planning and Information, and Financial Management and Corporate Services.

Land restitution

The CRLR is a statutory body set up in terms of the Restitution of Land Rights Act, 1994, as amended. The role of the commission is to provide redress to victims of dispossession of rights in land, as a result of racially discriminatory laws and practices that took place after 1913.

The commission is led by the Chief Land Claims Commissioner and has nine regional offices headed by regional land claims commissioners.

Across the country, out of a total of 79 696 claims lodged, 74 417 claims had been settled by 31 March 2007 (93% of the total number of claims).

The success of mining in South Africa is also measured by its long-term impact on the quality of life of affected communities and the environment.

Some of the country's most important minerals are:

- gold – the unique Witwatersrand Basin yields some 96% of South Africa's gold output
- diamonds – the country is among the world's top producers
- titanium – heavy mineral-sand occurrences containing titanium minerals are found along the coasts
- manganese – enormous reserves of manganese are found in the sedimentary rocks of the Transvaal Supergroup
- platinum-group metals (PGMs), chrome and vanadium – more than half of the world's reserves occur in the Bushveld Complex in Mpumalanga, Limpopo and North West
- bituminous coal and anthracite – seam beds occur in the Karoo Basin, in Mpumalanga, KwaZulu-Natal, Limpopo, Free State and the Eastern Cape
- copper phosphate, titanium, iron, vermiculite and zirconium – found in the Phalaborwa Igneous Complex in Limpopo.

Reserves

South Africa's reserves of the following commodities are the highest in the world:

- manganese
- PGMs
- vanadium
- chromium
- gold
- alumino-silicates.

Gold

South African gold output fell by 7,6% to 2,02 million ounces (62 807 kg) in the first three months of 2007, compared with the same period in 2006. South Africa's gold production tumbled by 3,1% in the fourth quarter of 2006 to 68 118 kg, compared with the previous quarter.

South Africa's mineral production, 2006				
Commodity	Unit	Reserves	%	World ranking
Aluminium	Kt	846	2,7	9
Alumino-silicates	Kt	228	36,4	1
Antimony	t	5 979	3,2	7
Chrome ore	Kt	7 494	38,7	1
Coal	Mt	245	4,9	5
Copper	Kt	97	0,7	16
Fluorspar	Mt	n/a	n/a	n/a
Gold	t	295	11,7	1
Iron ore	Mt	40	3	7
Lead	Mt	42,2	1,2	13
Manganese ore	Kt	4 612	13,3	2
Nickel	Kt	42,4	3,1	9
Phosphate rock	Kt	2 577	1,7	10
Platinum-group metals	Kg	303	56,7	1
Silver	t	88	0,4	17
Titanium minerals	Mt	952	19,8	2
Uranium	t	795	1,6	11
Vanadium	Kt	23	48	1
Vermiculite	Kt	210	39,6	1
Zinc metal	Kt	32,1	0,3	22
Zirconium minerals	Kt	n/a	n/a	n/a

Mt=megaton, Kt=kiloton, t=ton, n/a=not available, Kg=kilogram

Source: Minerals Bureau

The lowest levels of gold production since 1922 occurred in 2006, despite gold prices reaching multi-year record highs then.

On a year-on-year basis, the rate of decline rose to 9,3% in the fourth quarter compared with the 2,9% decline recorded in the third quarter of 2006.

The Chamber of Mine's gold-mine members reported a quarter-on-quarter decline in production of 2,6% to 58 342 kg in the fourth quarter of 2006.

On a year-on-year basis, gold production declined by 10% in the last quarter of 2006, as the 4,9% increase in tons of ore milled was not sufficient to compensate for the 14,2% decline in the average grade mined.

The year-on-year decline in the average grade mined was facilitated by the 41,7% increase in the gold price to an average of R143 929/kg which, in turn, allowed mining companies to mine lower-grade ores that had previously been uneconomic to mine.

The year-on-year increase in cash production costs of 16,3% eroded some of the grade flexibility that higher prices gave the mines.

However, on 6 November 2007, the gold price rose to its highest level in nearly three decades after crude oil rose more than a dollar due to supply concerns, and safe-haven buying possibly occuring due to concerns about the United States of America's credit market.

In February 2007, the Department of Minerals and Energy and mining group De Beers announced an agreement aimed at creating an even more empowered and sustainable diamond mining and exploration industry in South Africa.

In terms of this agreement, the West Coast operations of Alexkor and De Beers Consolidated Mines' Namaqualand mines will be amalgamated into a new, stand-alone diamond mining company.

This independent and empowered company will, among other things, realise the full economic potential of the West Coast diamond mining industry. As a first step in this process, De Beers issued a 20% stake in its Namaqualand Mines to the department.

South Africa's mineral reserves, 2006				
Commodity	**Unit**	**Reserves**	**%**	**World ranking**
Alumino-silicates	Kt	51	n/a	n/a
Antimony	t	200	6,4	4
Chrome ore	Kt	5 500	72,4	1
Coal	Mt	31 022	3,5	8
Copper	Kt	13	1,4	14
Fluorspar	Mt	80	16,7	2
Gold	t	36 000	40,1	1
Iron ore	Mt	1 500	0,9	9
Lead	Mt	3 000	2	7
Manganese ore	Kt	4 000	80	1
Phosphate rock	Kt	2 500	5	4
Platinum-group metals	Kg	70 000	87,7	1
Silver	t	n/a	n/a	n/a
Titanium minerals	Mt	220	18,3	2
Uranium	t	341	7,2	5
Vanadium	Kt	12 000	31	1
Vermiculite	Kt	80	40	2
Zinc metal	Kt	15	3,3	8
Zirconium	Kt	14	19,4	2

Mt=megaton, Kt=kiloton, t=ton, n/a=not available, Kg=kilogram

Source: Minerals Bureau

Silver

On 6 November 2007, silver reached its best level in almost 18 months to track gold's strength. It reached an intraday high of US$14,84 an ounce early in November 2007, its highest level since mid-May 2006, before easing to US$14,83/14,88.

Coal

Coal is South Africa's major indigenous energy resource, and is relied on for the generation of most of the country's electricity and a significant proportion of its liquid fuels. It supplies about 88% of South Africa's primary energy needs. It is mined at collieries, some of which are among the largest in the world. In 2006, operating collieries dropped to 60. Of these, a relatively small number of large-scale producers supply coal primarily to electricity and synthetic fuel producers. About 46,5% of coal mining is done underground and about 53,5% is produced in opencast mines. South Africa has about 31 billion tons of recoverable coal reserves, making it the sixth-largest holder of coal reserves in the world.

In 2006, South African mines produced 246 million tons (Mt) of coal. Of this figure, 177 Mt was used locally, at a value of

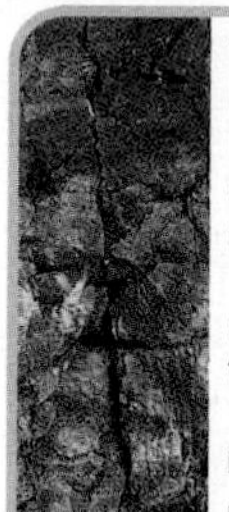

The Mining Qualifications Authority (MQA) Graduate Development Programme was introduced to help unemployed graduates from universities and universities of technology, who had obtained qualifications that had been identified as scarce and critical skills according to the Minerals Sector Skills Plan.

The programme aims to provide experience to these unemployed graduates so that they may become employed in their respective professions.

By July 2007, 103 candidates had completed the MQA's Executive Preparation Progamme, with 26 candidates waiting to receive their certificates.

The Department of Minerals and Energy continues to support the development of small-scale mining, including jewellery-making projects.

With an annual budget of R21 million in 2007, the department supported four projects in Limpopo to the tune of R14,6 million and three in KwaZulu-Natal at R7,2 million.

In 2006, the department received more than 80 applications for financial assistance and the figure was expected to double in 2007.

R16,2 billion, with export sales totalling about 68,8 Mt at a value of R21,2 billion.

The companies that dominate the coal industry are Anglo Coal, BHP Billiton, Sasol Mining, Eyesizwe Coal, Kumba Coal and Xstrata, accounting for 90% of saleable coal production. The eight largest mines contribute 61% of total output.

Diversifying the primary energy mix is especially challenging. South Africa has an abundance of low-cost coal, which means that reliable and inexpensive supplies are at hand. On the face of it, this facilitates Eskom's mandate of providing South Africa with affordable and reliable electricity. Yet, Eskom also has a duty to manage environmental impacts and has a responsibility to combat climate change.

Platinum-group metals

South Africa's PGM production increased by 9,6% to 302,9 tons (t) in 2005, while PGM revenue increased by 16,8% to US$6,04 billion. The average platinum price for 2005 was 6% higher at US$897/oz, while the average palladium price was 12,6% lower at US$201/oz. World demand for platinum increased by 1,8% to 208,7 t in 2005.

On 6 November 2007, platinum inched up to US$1 460/1 465 an ounce from US$1 459/1 463 in New York. Palladium rose to US$372/376 an ounce from US$371/375 in New York.

Non-ferrous minerals

Refined copper, nickel, cobalt, titanium and zirconium concentrates dominate this sector, with support from zinc, lead and arsenic concentrates. The sector contributes some 12% and 4% respectively to total primary local sales and total primary export sales. About 44% of total revenue is from local sales for further value-adding operations.

Ferrous minerals

This sector consists of manganese and chrome, and is dominated by iron ore. It has been a leading performer in the primary minerals industry in recent years, with revenue in dollar terms growing at about 10,3% annually. Demand depends on the fortune of the world's steel and stainless steel industries.

Export earnings from ferrous minerals increased by 70,45% from R4,84 billion in 2004 to R8,25 billion in 2005, despite the fact that higher dollar earnings were severely discounted by a much higher average rand-dollar exchange rate ratio for 2005. Higher prices also affected total ferrous sales, which rose by 45,2% to R11,63 billion.

Industrial minerals

This sector comprises a wide variety of mineral products, with over 85% of revenue being from local sales. In dollar terms, domestic total sales increased by 19% to US$ 925 million. In rand terms, local sales increased by 17% to R6 billion and export sales decreased by 5% to R1 billion.

During 2005, 83% of local sales comprised aggregate and sand (38%), limestone and lime (22%), phosphate rock concentrate and sulphur (4%).

Exports were dominated by dimension stone (26%), vermiculite (19%), andalusite (19%), fluorspar (22%) and phosphate rock concentrate.

Processed minerals

Ferro-alloys and aluminium dominate this sector, with solid support from titanium slag, phosphoric acid, vanadium, zinc metal and low-manganese pig-iron. Through investment in beneficiation, it has been the outstanding performer in the mineral industry over the last 20 years, with revenue in dollar terms growing by 6,3% annually.

International prices of processed minerals surged strongly during 2004 on the back of vigorous growth in demand in China and the East. As a result, export sales earnings were at an all-time high of US$4,096 billion in 2004, up 48% from US$2,762 billion in 2003.

Other minerals

This sector is dominated by diamonds, with support from hydrocarbon fuel, uranium oxide and silver.

The industry

The commodities boom of 2005 continued into 2006, and preliminary figures for 2006 indicated that mineral sales grew by 36,7% to R195,2 billion and those of processed minerals grew at a moderate 14,5%. Unlike in other mining countries, this strong growth in mineral sales was initially not matched by any meaningful fixed capital investment. A marked improvement has been noted in this area.

New Black Economic Empowerment-compliant mines opened, especially in Limpopo and North West. Near Brits in the North West, International Ferrometal South Africa was officially opened, which is a sign of confidence in the regulatory environment.

Over the last few years, South African mining houses have transformed into large, focused mining companies that include Anglo Platinum, AngloGold, De Beers, Implats and Iscor. The Chamber of Mines represents 85% of mining production.

Including suppliers and considering the multiplier effect, many millions of people rely on the industry for their livelihood.

Policy

The Mineral and Petroleum Resources Development Act (MPRDA), 2002 aims to:

- recognise that mineral resources are the common heritage of all South Africans
- promote the beneficiation of minerals
- guarantee security of tenure for existing prospecting and mining operations
- ensure that historically disadvantaged people (HDP) participate more meaningfully
- promote junior and small-scale mining.

In terms of the Act, new-order rights may be registered, transferred and traded, while existing operators are guaranteed security of tenure. Mining rights are valid for a maximum of 30 years and renewable for another 30 years, while prospecting rights are valid for up to five years and renewable for another three.

An empowerment charter for the industry, which is supported by mining houses and labour, targets:

- 15% ownership of mines by HDP within five years
- HDP holding 40% of junior and senior management positions within five years
- 26% HDP shareholding within 10 years
- 10% participation by women within five years.

Government is committed to helping junior and small-scale miners upgrade their operations into economically viable units. The first step is to legalise these mines.

The South African Small-Scale Mining Chamber was launched in July 2005 in Kimberley in the Northern Cape.

By April 2007, the department had received 11 447 applications for various types of rights since the promulgation of the MPRDA 2002. The number of applications received is unprecedented in the history of mining in South Africa. All applications are expected to be finalised within the timeframes prescribed in the Act.

ENERGY AND WATER

Putting clean and affordable water and energy within everyone's reach is a key national goal. At the same time, planning ensures that these key drivers of economic growth are delivered reliably and cost-effectively to industry, commerce and agriculture.

The Department of Minerals and Energy's Energy Policy is based on the following key objectives:

- attaining universal access to energy by 2012
- ensuring accessible, affordable and reliable energy, especially for the poor
- diversifying primary energy sources and reducing dependency on coal
- practicing good governance, which must also facilitate and encourage private-sector investments in the energy sector
- providing environmentally responsible energy.

Current estimates suggest that R107 billion will be needed between 2005 and 2009 to meet the country's growing energy needs. Eskom will invest R150 billion over the next five years. Some R23 billion is reserved for independent power-producer entrants.

The refurbishment of three power stations – Camden in Ermelo, Grootvlei in Balfour and Komati in Middelburg – will add 3 800 megawatts (MW) to the system.

In August 2007, Cabinet approved the Energy Security Strategy, a policy document that will change South Africa's approach to the security of energy.

The fuel shortages of 2005 and projected challenges as well as the blackouts and brownouts that hit the electricity supply industry in 2006 and 2007 have raised the need for the strategy to be devised.

Phase one of the strategy focuses on liquid-fuels issues, an energy security framework and the proposed energy-planning approach. Phase two will address electricity-related issues.

The approved strategy seeks to:

- secure adequate supplies of affordable energy for continued economic growth and development in the short term
- enable policy- and decision-makers to make informed decisions on these complex interdependent energy outcomes in the medium term
- ensure that strategic planning and subsequent growth and development are sustainable in the long term.

Key elements of the policy include:

- Implementing an integrated energy modelling and planning approach to ensure co-ordination and enhanced integration of planning in dealing with future energy policy in support of achieving energy security.
- Improving Transnet Freight Services' operational efficiencies in servicing the liquid-fuels sector, by focusing on routes that allow for block trains/block loads, and allocating additional capacity to the Durban-Gauteng Corridor.
- Improving operational efficiencies at ports, especially during periods of increased demand for imported crude oil or refined products in South Africa. This includes ensuring that back-of-port facilities are not used as part of refining operations.

The Energy Efficiency Strategy, which was approved in March 2005, sets a national target for improving energy efficiency by 12% by 2015.

On 1 June 2007, the Department of Minerals and Energy, in partnership with the Department of Public Enterprises, Eskom and other state organs, launched an intensive multimedia energy efficiency campaign, targeting ordinary households and industrial consumers. The campaign sought to encourage prudent consumer behaviour without negatively affecting the economy.

This intervention was expected to yield enormous benefits by reducing overall energy demand, promoting energy security, and making a contribution towards environmental conservation and savings for individual households.

- Promoting local refining as far as possible, with a particular preference for production from local resources, including those from South Africa's neighbouring states.
- Developing Transnet Pipelines' new multiproducts pipeline, which is necessary to alleviate the identified capacity constraints in the petroleum supply chain by 2010.
- Promoting energy efficiency and other demand-side initiatives in all sectors of the economy. This should be complemented by measures aimed at effectively managing interaction with the natural environment.

Energy in South Africa

Energy comprises about 15% of South Africa's gross domestic product, creating employment for about 250 000 people. Eskom's total electricity sales grew to 218 120 gigawatt/hour by March 2007. High liquid-fuel sales figures demonstrate the growth of the South African economy and the importance of energy as a key driver of the country's economy, especially the large-scale energy-intensive primary mineral beneficiation and mining industries that dominate the economy.

This energy intensity is above average, with only 10 other countries having higher commercial primary energy intensities.

Eskom is launching a demand-side management programme to reduce demand by about 3 000 megawatts (MW) by 2012 and a further 5 000 MW in the next 13 years. The programme intends to alleviate imminent supply constraints and obviate the need for more costly supply options that are under consideration. Eskom will pursue energy-saving measures nationally, following the success of a campaign that saved about 500 MW a day during power shortages in the winter of 2006 in the Western Cape.

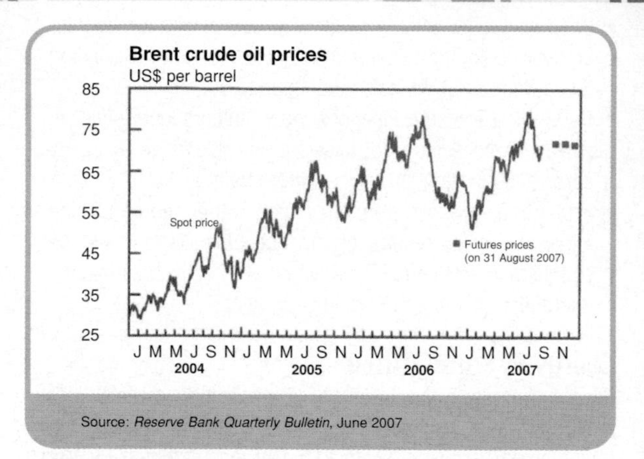

Source: *Reserve Bank Quarterly Bulletin*, June 2007

Power sources

Coal

In 2006, South African mines produced 246 million tons (Mt) of coal. Of this figure, 177 Mt worth R16,2 billion was used locally, with export sales to the value of R21,2 billion, totalling 68,8 Mt. South Africa has about 31 billion tons of recoverable coal reserves, making it the sixth-largest holder of coal reserves in the world.

Nuclear

Approval of the Nuclear Energy Policy and Strategy is expected to create many jobs and boost the economy. The document proposes the increased use of nuclear energy to supplement current energy sources.

Nuclear energy is likely to contribute 15% of South Africa's energy in the next 30 years. If the strategy is approved, an extra 10 000 MW could be added to the current 39 000 MW within 10 years. This would entail recapitalising certain nuclear agencies, financing others and setting up new ones.

The Pebble-Bed Modular Reactor was transferred to the Department of Public Enterprises in March 2006.

Given the increasing demand for energy and the need to combat global warming, nuclear energy is re-emerging as an attractive alternative. There are 30 nuclear plants being built in 12 countries and over 50 more being planned.

The Department of Minerals and Energy will support the construction of a demonstration power plant and pilot fuel plant, and facilitate the timely processing of the environmental impact assessment.

The draft document sets out a phased approach to creating a nuclear industry. Infrastructure would be maintained and upgraded until 2010. Thereafter, up to 2015, new nuclear power plants would be constructed. These would be operational in 2025. According to the Department of Minerals and Energy, the country's abundance of uranium cannot be ignored as an alternative energy source, nor can the economic benefits thereof.

The document also proposes that enriched uranium be sold internationally, allowing the country to compete in the global nuclear market.

Eskom Koeberg Nuclear Power Station's two reactors outside Cape Town supply 1 800 MW to the national grid when both operate at full power, thus providing about 6,5% of South Africa's electricity.

The National Nuclear Regulator is the prime safety regulator and is responsible for protecting persons, property and the environment against nuclear damage by establishing safety standards and regulatory practices. It exercises safety-related regulatory control over the siting, design, construction and operation of nuclear installations and other actions.

The Nuclear Energy Corporation of South Africa (Necsa) undertakes and promotes research and development in the field of nuclear energy, radiation sciences and technology, medical isotope manufacturing, nuclear liabilities management, waste

The Integrated National Electrification Programme (INEP) remains the flagship of the Department of Minerals and Energy. The department began funding the INEP in April 2001. Eskom is responsible for implementing the programme in its licensed areas of supply on the department's behalf.

Eskom continues to exceed its electrification targets. The target for 2006 was 141 578 connections – the actual number connected was 152 125. Since the inception of the electrification programme in 1991, more than 3 469 650 homes have been electrified, including subsequent in-fill connections.

management and decommissioning. It is a public entity reporting to the Minister of Minerals and Energy.

Necsa's reactor-produced radioisotopes are exported to more than 50 countries.

The research reactor at Pelindaba, Safari-1, is the most commercialised reactor of its kind in the world with International Organisation for Standardisation 9001-accreditation. It earns South Africa foreign revenue worth millions of rands.

Liquid fuels

The South African Petroleum Industry Association announced strong growth in petroleum product sales in the first quarter of 2007.

Aggregate sales of major petroleum products showed a strong increase of 7,3% in the first quarter of 2007, compared with the first quarter of 2006. The most significant increases were in diesel (13,1%) bitumen (36,3%) and liquid petroleum gas (LPG) (15%).

Petrol sales grew by 4,4% and jet fuel sales by 4,6%.

Sales of paraffin, a source of household energy, dropped by 13,4%.

In the first quarter, the percentage split of petrol sales between unleaded petrol (ULP) and lead-replacement petrol (LRP) was 64% and 36% respectively. This represents a significant increase in the penetration of ULP from the level of 43% that prevailed in May 2006 and indicates lower demand for LRP.

The petrol price in South Africa is linked to certain international petrol markets in United States dollar. This means that supply and demand for petroleum products in the international markets, combined with the Rand-Dollar exchange rate, influence the domestic price.

The National Petroleum Gas and Oil Corporation of South Africa (PetroSA) is responsible for exploring and exploiting oil and natural gas, as well as producing and marketing synthetic fuels produced from offshore gas at the world's largest commercial gas-to-liquids plant in Mossel Bay, about 400 km east of Cape Town.

Sasol

The Sasol group of companies comprises diversified fuel, chemical and related manufacturing and marketing operations, complemented by interests in technology development, oil and gas exploration, and production.

Its principal feedstocks are obtained from coal, which the company converts into value-added hydrocarbons through Fischer-Tropsch-process technologies.

Oil and gas

South Africa has very limited oil reserves and imports from the Middle East and Africa (Saudi Arabia, Iran, Kuwait, the United Arab Emirates, Yemen, Qatar, Iraq, Nigeria, Egypt and Angola) meet about 95% of South Africa's crude oil requirements.

Refined petroleum products such as petrol, diesel, residual fuel oil, paraffin, jet fuel, aviation gasoline, LPG and refinery gas are produced by:

- refining crude oil (oil refineries)
- converting coal to liquid fuels and gas to liquid fuels (Sasol)
- turning natural gas into liquid fuels (PetroSA)

Another major role-player in South Africa's liquid fuels industry is the Central Energy Fund (CEF). It's state-granted mandate is to engage in acquiring, exploring, generating, manufacturing, marketing and distributing any energy form, especially oil and gas. It also engages in research relating to the energy sector. The CEF's diversified portfolio of activities is housed in the following active subsidiaries:

- The Strategic Fuel Fund Association that was established to procure and store crude oil and manage strategic crude oil stocks for South Africa. It trades and leases spare storage ullage and is involved in oil pollution control.
- PetroSA owns and operates the world's largest gas-to-liquids plant at Mossel Bay. PetroSA is also involved in oil and gas exploration and production, and its offshore production platform supplies gas and condensates by gas pipeline to its onshore plant for conversion into a range of environmentally friendly transportation fuels and associated products for the domestic and international markets.
- The Petroleum Agency South Africa promotes and markets exploration in South African territory (both offshore and onshore for oil and gas), negotiates and monitors concessions and licences on behalf of the Government, and is the custodian of geological and geophysical data.
- iGas is a state-owned entity for the development of gas infrastructure in South Africa. iGas partnered Sasol and ENH of Mozambique in establishing the natural gas pipeline from Mozambique to South Africa. The Mozambique-South Africa gas transmission pipeline started operating officially in March 2004.

The wholesale and retail markets for petroleum products in South Africa are subject to a set of government controls. The Government regulates wholesale margins and controls the retail price of petrol. The industry has entered into product exchange agreements to serve different markets. Together, these controls provide for access to fuel throughout the counrty and protect consumers, while providing a reasonable return on investment to the oil industry and enhancing opportunities for employment.

The refiners and wholesale marketers move products from the refineries by coastal barge, rail, truck and pipeline to roughly 200 depots. From these, aboout 4 600 service stations and 100 000 direct consumers (mostly farmers) are served.

Refineries and Sasol produce LPG and illuminating paraffin (kerosene). Most LPG is used by consumers and the rest is used in refineries as fuel and/or exported to neighbouring countries.

Limited natural gas reserves exist around the South African coast. PetroSA exploits the reserves off the coast of Mossel Bay, where the gas is converted at the Mossgas plant Into liquid fuels.

Sasol produces gas from coal and has built a gas pipeline to import gas from Mozambique. Prospects to import gas from Namibia to South Africa are being researched.

Although gas usage has increased in recent years, the importance of gas in the South African energy economy is still small compared to other countries. Industry remains the largest customer by far.

Electricity

South Africa supplies two thirds of Africa's electricity and is one of the four cheapest electricity producers in the world. About 88% of South Africa's electricity is generated in coal-fired power stations. Koeberg, a large nuclear station near Cape Town, provides about 6,5% of capacity. A further 2,3% is provided by hydroelectric and pumped storage schemes.

In South Africa there are few, if any, new hydro sites that could be developed to deliver significant amounts of power, due to water scarcity. Eskom, the national state-owned utility, which also owns and operates the national electricity grid, dominates the generation of electricity, supplying about 95% of South Africa's electricity.

Energy and the environment

The Electricity Distribution Industry (EDI) Restructuring Bill was expected to be presented to Parliament before the end of 2007. This corresponds with Cabinet's decision to restructure the EDI into six wall-to-wall regional electricity distributors (Reds) as public entities managed through the Public Finance Management Act, 1999 and regulated by the National Energy Regulator of South Africa.

By August 2007, EDI Holdings and the South African Local Government Association were working to re-establish Red1 in line with Cabinet's decision.

Water

South Africa is largely a semi-arid, water-stressed country. The country's average rainfall of about 450 mm a year is well below the world average of about 860 mm a year. To overcome the problem of variable river flows, many large storage dams have been built.

The available water supply is reduced by evaporation from dams, and by commercial afforestation and sugar-cane farming.

The total net abstraction of water from surface-water resources amounts to about 10 200 million m^3 a year for the whole country, after allowing for the re-use of return flows. This represents about 20% of the total mean annual run-off of 49, 2 billion m^3 per year (all standardised to 98% assurance of supply).

A further 8% is estimated to be lost through evaporation from storage and conveyance along rivers, and 6% through land-use activities. As a national average, about 66% of the natural river flow (mean annual run-off) therefore still remains in the country's rivers.

Water policy

Cabinet approved the first edition of the National Water Resource Strategy (NWRS) in September 2004. The NWRS describes how

Major dams in South Africa

Dam	Full supply capacity (10 m³)	River
Gariep	5 341	Orange
Vanderkloof	3 171	Orange
Sterkfontein	2 616	Nuwejaarspruit
Nuwejaarspruit Vaal	2 603	Vaal
Pongolapoort	2 445	Pongola

Source: Department of Water Affairs and Forestry

South Africa's water resources will be protected, used, developed, conserved, managed and controlled in accordance with the requirements of the National Water Policy, 1997 and the National Water Act, 1998. These documents are based on government's vision of a transformed South African society in which every person has the opportunity to participate in productive economic activity and lead a dignified and healthy life.

One of the most ambitious binational water projects ever is the Lesotho Highlands Water Project between South Africa and Lesotho.

The first phase, which was completed in 1998, consisted of the construction of three dams, various tunnels and a hydroelectric plant.

Since its inception, the Working for Water Programme has invested more than R2,5 million to clear invasive alien vegetation and establish programmes in over 300 areas.

About 20 000 short-term jobs have been created annually in the process, providing employment opportunities for local community members, with a special focus on securing opportunities for the marginalised, such as women, the youth and people with disabilities.

By participating in the programme, workers are not only given the opportunity to develop new skills, but also have access to HIV and AIDS projects, childcare facilities and primary healthcare initiatives.

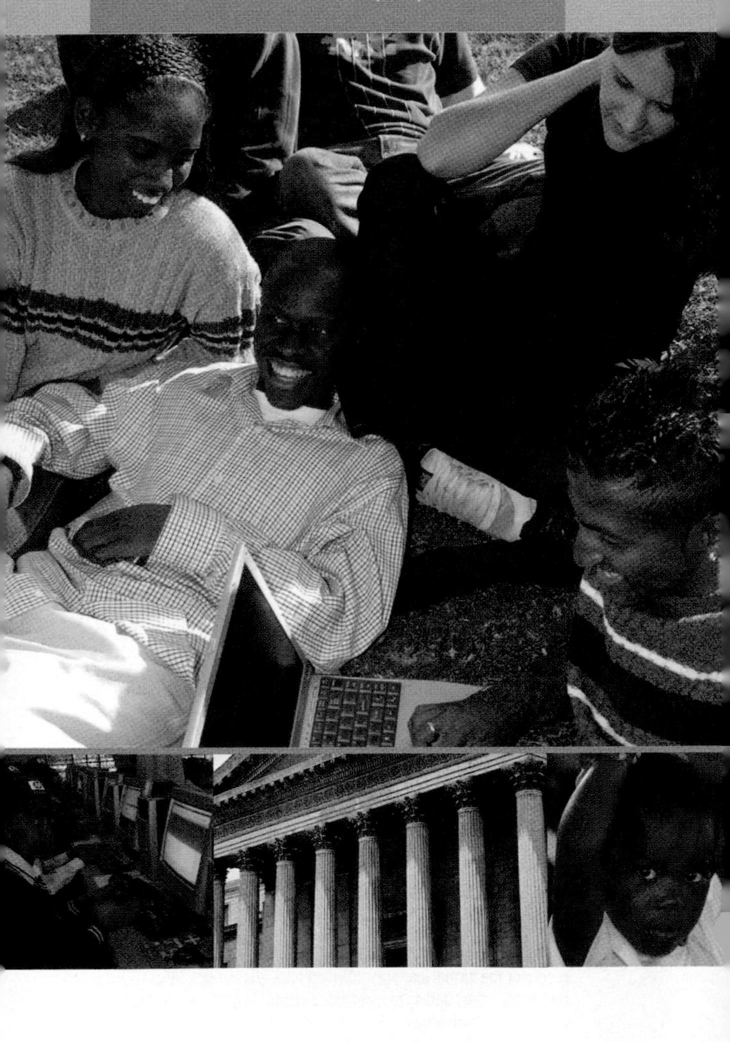

The right to education is enshrined in South Africa's Bill of Rights; not only for children but also for adults.

Formal education in South Africa is categorised according to three levels – General Education and Training (GET), Further Education and Training (FET) and Higher Education (HE)

Structures

South Africa has a single national education system, which is organised and managed by the national Department of Education and the nine provincial departments.

Statutory bodies include the Council of Education Ministers, heads of the Education Department's Committee, General and FET Quality Assurance Council, South African Qualifications Authority, Council on HE, South African Council for Educators, National Board for FET, Education Labour Relations Council and the National Student Financial Aid Scheme.

Quality Improvement and Development Strategy

Government plans to invest some R12,5 billion over the next five years to improve and develop education by means of a

In June 2007, the Minister of Education, Ms Naledi Pandor, launched the second *Trends in Public Higher Education* report, which analysed the South African Qualifications Authority's National Learners' Record Database.

The database informs governmental research and decision-making in terms of the labour market, and education and training. It enables individual learners to verify their own achievements, or to request their verification by potential/current employers and/or employment agencies. It also provides unemployed graduates with a portal through which they can access and disseminate their own achievements in a regulated manner.

The database is expected to eventually contain a complete record of the formal learning achievements of all South Africans. By mid-2007, the database contained information on 20 million learning achievements of 7,5 million students, and a register of about 8 000 qualifications and 10 000 unit standards.

Seventy-six percent of the 597 schools targeted for the provision of water during the 2006/07 financial year were provided for, and more than 50% of 2 409 schools received sanitation.

programme that will concentrate on addressing apartheid's legacy in education.

Five thousand schools that do not perform well and are located in the least able districts will be identified and provided with resources such as libraries, laboratories and teaching material. Their teachers will get support in the form of high-quality school-based education development programmes, and better district development teams.

Teaching and learning will focus on the acquisition of important content and academic skills, and on equipping learners with literacy and numeracy skills.

The progress made by learners and their schools will be monitored and assessed regularly.

Policy

Schooling is compulsory between the ages of seven and 15. All learners are guaranteed access to quality learning. There are two types of schools: independent (private) and public.

At public schools, parents vote on the level of school fees. Poor parents are given exemption or reductions.

In 2007, there were five million learners in 13 912 no-fee schools.

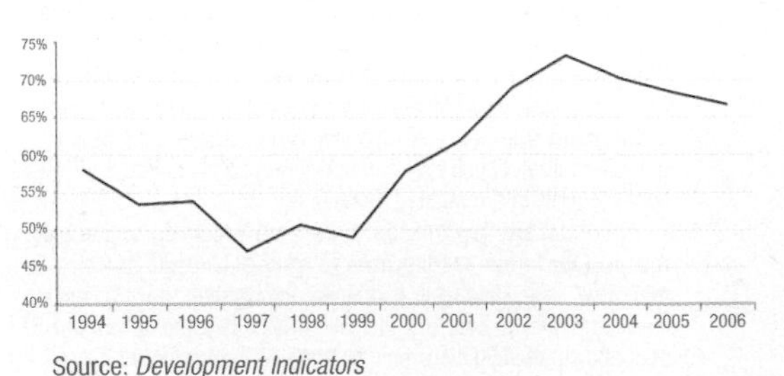

Source: *Development Indicators*

Learners

By mid-2007, the South African public education system had 12,3 million learners, 387 000 educators and about 26 592 schools, including 400 special-needs schools and 1 000 registered private schools. Of all schools, 6 000 were secondary schools (grades 8 to 12) and the rest were primary (grades 1 to 7) schools.

Learners attend school for 13 years. The first year of education, Grade R or reception year, and the last three years are not compulsory. Many primary schools offer Grade R, which can also be completed at nursery school.

The matric exam pass rate in 2006 was 67%. Although this represented a slight decrease, the number of learners writing and passing the Senior Certificate increased substantially.

A total of 351 503 learners passed the Senior Certificate in 2006, which was 4 419 more than in 2005. In 2006, 85 830 candidates achieved university exemption compared with 86 531 in 2005.

A total of 25 217 learners passed Mathematics on the Higher Grade (HG) and 29 781 passed Physical Science HG.

Curriculum development

The National Curriculum Statement (NCS) aims to develop the full potential of all learners as citizens of a democratic South Africa.

It seeks to create a lifelong learner who is confident and independent; literate, numerate and multiskilled; compassionate, with a respect for the environment and the ability to participate in society as a critical and active citizen.

The NCS (grades R to 9) were implemented in the Foundation Phase (grades R to 3) in 2004, the Intermediate Phase (grades 4 to 6) in 2005 and in grades 7 to 10 in 2006. Grades 8 and 9 were implemented in 2007.

The NCS is available in all 11 official languages and in Braille, in keeping with the Constitution, which grants parity of esteem to all languages.

The South African Council for Educators has a register of approximately 495 000 educators, of which 19 000 are registered provisionally.

It requires learners in grades 10 to 12 to do four compulsory subjects, namely two official languages, Mathematical Literacy or Mathematics and Life Orientation. In addition, a learner must select three approved subjects.

The department also developed the guidelines for teaching and assessment that were distributed to schools in 2005. Provincial departments of education ran one-week workshops to orientate Grade 10 educators.

Further Education and Training

In 2002/03, the FET college sector saw the merger of 152 technical colleges into 50 multisite-campus FET colleges.

Each new college operates under a single governing council appointed to oversee effective and accountable management across and within the various FET college campuses and sites. The recorded increase in student intake, the development of new programmes and increased participation in learnerships bear testimony to the potential for growth in this sector.

From 2006/07 to 2008/09, government is expected to invest R1,9 billion in the recapitalisation of the 50 public FET colleges.

FET provides learning and training from National Qualifications Framework (NQF) levels 2 to 4, or the equivalent of grades 10 to 12 in the school system, and a FET Certificate (FETC) in General Vocational and in Trade Occupational, on NQF levels 2 to 4 in FET colleges. The FETC will replace the current Senior Certificate in 2008.

Higher Education transformation

According to a strategic plan for HE, enrolment at HE institutions will rise from 15% to 20% of school leavers within 15 years. Within five years, enrolments in the humanities will decline, while those in Business and Commerce, and Science, Engineering and Technology will rise.

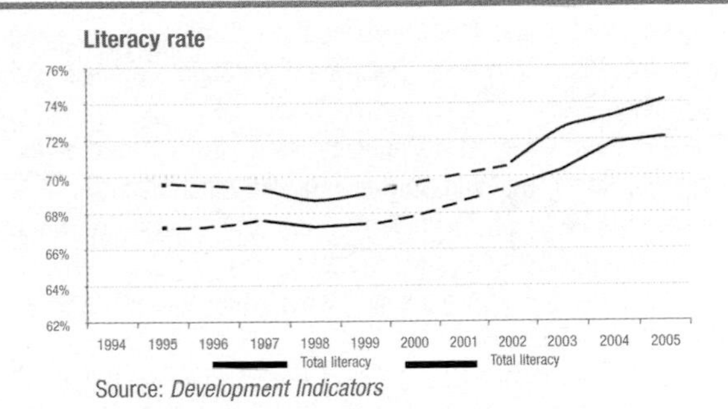

Source: *Development Indicators*

The 2001 National Plan for HE also envisaged:

- research being funded through a separate formula based on research output
- targets being set to increase the numbers of black and female students and academic staff.

The total cost for the restructuring of the HE system was estimated at R1,9 billion for the period 2001/02 to 2006/07.

The HE landscape consists of the following institutions:

- University of the Witwatersrand
- University of Cape Town
- University of Stellenbosch
- Rhodes University
- University of the Western Cape (which incorporated the Dental Faculty of Stellenbosch University)
- University of Zululand
- University of Venda
- University of the Free State (which incorporated the QwaQwa Campus of the University of the North and the Bloemfontein Campus of Vista)
- North West University (which incorporated the Potchefstroom University for Christian Higher Education and Vista Sebokeng Campus)
- University of Pretoria (retained its name after incorporating the Mamelodi Campus of Vista University)

- University of South Africa (retained its name after merging with the Vista University Distance Education Campus and Technikon SA)
- Tshwane University of Technology (from the merger of the Pretoria, North West and Northern Gauteng technikons)
- Durban Institute of Technology (from the merger of Natal Technikon and Technikon ML Sultan)
- Central University of Technology (formerly Technikon Free State)
- Mangosuthu Technikon
- University of Johannesburg (from the merger of the Rand Afrikaans University with Technikon Witwatersrand, which incorporated the Soweto and East Rand campuses of Vista University)
- University of Limpopo (from the merger of the Medical University of South Africa and the University of the North)
- Nelson Mandela Metropolitan University (from the merger of the University of Port Elizabeth, Port Elizabeth Technikon and Port Elizabeth Campus of Vista)
- University of Fort Hare (which incorporated the East London Campus of Rhodes University)
- Cape Peninsula University of Technology (from the merger of the Cape Technikon and Peninsula Technikon)
- Vaal University of Technology (formerly Vaal Triangle Technicon)
- Walter Sisulu University for Technology and Science (from the merger of the University of Transkei, Border Technikon and Eastern Cape Technikon)
- National Institute for Higher Education, Northern Cape
- National Institute for Higher Education, Mpumalanga.

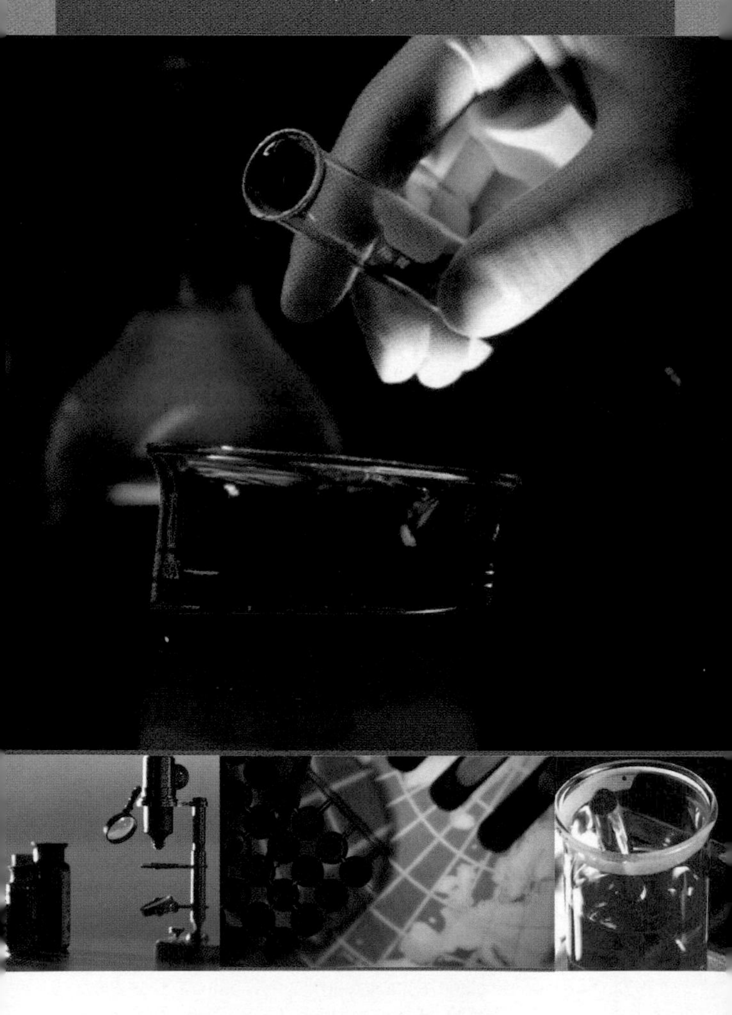

SCIENCE AND TECHNOLOGY

South Africa's science and research are world-class. The Department of Science and Technology seeks to realise the full potential of science and technology (S&T) in social and economic development, through the development of human resources (HR), research and innovation.

Expenditure is expected to continue to increase rapidly, rising from R1,4 billion in 2003/04 to an expected R4,1 billion in 2009/10, an average annual increase of 20%. Most of this expenditure is made up of transfers to public entities for S&T initiatives.

Strategies

The Department of Science and Technology primarily focuses on implementing the National Research and Development Strategy, which provides for an integrated approach to HR development, knowledge generation, investment in infrastructure and improving the strategic management of the public S&T system.

Government has recommitted itself to the Research and Development (R&D) Strategy of 1% of gross domestic product (GDP) to be invested by both public and private sectors by 2008. This implies an additional R2-billion investment across both sectors.

The department continues to develop strategies in new areas of knowledge and technology. Strategies for indigenous knowledge, nanotechnology, astronomy and intellectual property, derived from publicly funded research, have been developed.

Biotechnology innovation centres (Brics)

The National Biotechnology Strategy (NBS), which was launched in 2001, sets the agenda for the development of South Africa's biotechnology industry.

Other initiatives include establishing regional Brics, namely: BioPAD, Cape Biotech, LIFElab and the Plant Biotechnology

In March 2007, the Deputy Minister of Science and Technology, Mr Derek Hanekom, launched the National Fish Collection.

Completed in 2006, the facility stores close to a million marine, estuarine and freshwater fish specimens, collected during field trips, or received as gifts and exchanges from other research organisations and museums around the world.

Unique to the National Fish Collection, the South African Institute for Aquatic Biodiversity also boasts an unusual albino great white shark caught by fisherfolk off the Eastern Cape coast.

The development of modern facilities, such as the National Fish Collection, is expected to play a critical role in shaping the future of research on aquatic biodiversity in South Africa.

Innovation Centre. Brics were created to act as instruments for the implementation of the NBS.

The Brics' focus areas cover a wide spectrum of the subdisciplines in biotechnology. These include human and animal health, biopharmaceuticals, industrial bioprocessing, mining biotechnology, bioinformatics and plant biotechnology. One of the challenges facing the South African biotechnology sector is the public's lack of understanding and knowledge of biotechnology applications and benefits.

A programme initiated as a result of this is the Public Understanding of Biotechnology Programme, which provides the South African public with factual information, enabling them to participate meaningfully in debates about biotechnology and make informed decisions.

Advanced Manufacturing Technology Strategy (AMTS)

The AMTS guides efforts in the manufacturing sector, including the aerospace industry. It strives to:

- develop technology platforms that increase current and create new competitive advantages
- establish partnerships and human-capital development.

The aim is to enhance the knowledge base and the knowledge intensity of South Africa's manufacturing sector.

In 2006, the Department of Trade and Industry launched the National Aerospace Centre of Excellence located at the University of Witwatersrand. This centre aims to upgrade and reposition the country's aerospace industry.

Nanotechnology

South Africa's National Nanotechnology Strategy recognises the needs of local industry and focuses on the essential building blocks of nanoscience, namely synthesis, characterisation and fabrication. The strategy is aimed at increasing the number of nanotechnology characterisation centres in South Africa. In 2007, National Treasury allocated R450 million to implement the strategy.

Known as "the technology of the very small" (i.e. about 1/80 000 of the diameter of a human hair), nanotechnology comprises a wide range of technologies, techniques and multidisciplinary research efforts, for application in a range of cross-cutting industries and activities. These include aerospace, manufacturing and automotive industries; energy conversion, storage and distribution; the hydrogen economy; chemicals; electronics and information processing; as well as biotechnology and medicines, among other things.

The Centre for High Performance Computing (CHPC) is the first of its kind in South Africa. Initiated by the Department of Science and Technology, hosted by the University of Cape Town and managed by the Meraka Institute of the Council for Scientific and Industrial Research, the CHPC is making scientific "supercomputing" a reality for South Africa.

The Minister of Science and Technology, Mr Mosibudi Mangena, officially opened the facility in Cape Town in May 2007.

The CHPC supports a diverse base of researchers and scientists, and facilitates the collaboration and multidisciplinary approach needed to solve complex computational problems.

The centre will advance South Africa's research capabilities in areas such as advanced manufacturing, space science and research into infectious diseases.

South Africa has been shortlisted as one of two sites to host the ambitious Square Kilometre Array (SKA) radio telescope, which will have multiple receiving surfaces and will provide radio astronomers with one million square metres of collecting area. The Northern Cape is an ideal location for the SKA's core array.

The Southern African Large Telescope at Sutherland in the Northern Cape is one of South Africa's flagship scientific projects. It is the largest single optical telescope in the southern hemisphere.

South African industry and researchers have been key players in nanotechnology and the practical application of nanoscience for a number of years, for example, Sasol's chemical processing by catalysis.

Indigenous Knowledge System (IKS)

Since government launched the IKS Policy in 2004, a number of successes has been achieved on key cross-cutting issues, including the timely establishment of a ministerial advisory committee. The committee will assist in the establishment of IKS chairs located within higher education institutions, based on nationally prioritised areas such as traditional medicines, knowledge studies and indigenous food security.

In March 2007, South Africa and Zambia hosted the second Southern African Development Community workshop on IKS policy development in the region. The workshop recommended to member states, among other things, the need to harmonise the region's policy framework within the next two years.

Early in 2007, the Human Sciences Research Council (HSRC) released the results of the first official *South African Innovation Survey* – modelled on the survey used in all European Union countries in 2005/06 – showing that more than half of South Africa's companies engaged in the development of new products and processes between 2002 and 2004.

South Africa's rate of innovation is well above that of the European average of 42% for 2004. According to the survey, South African companies spent about R27,8 billion on innovative activities in 2004, representing about 2,4% of the total turnover of all business covered in the industrial and service sectors.

While the bulk of this expenditure was devoted to the acquisition of new machinery, equipment and software, in-house research and development expenditure accounted for about 20% of total innovation expenditure. Ten percent of successful innovators in industry received public funding for innovation activities.

Government plans to start developing IKS databases. A hardware multimedia recordal system to capture synchrotextual documentation, such as the registration of holders of indigenous knowledge, interviews and satellite-information linkages, was expected to be developed.

By mid-2007, the first pilot IKS centre was being established at the University of Zululand. It will support the IKS Laboratory on Traditional Medicines at the Medical Research Council (MRC).

Supporting innovators

Technology for Human Resources for Industry Programme (Thrip)

The programme aims to increase participation by small, medium and micro-enterprises (SMMEs), Black Economic Empowerment entities, black and female researchers and students, as well as to increase the share of the Thrip budget allocation to historically disadvantaged individuals and universities of technology.

Thrip supports, on average, 2 400 tertiary students each year.

Innovation Fund (IF)

The IF was created to promote technological innovation, increase networking and cross-sectoral collaboration, increase competitiveness, improve quality of life, ensure environmental sustainability and harness information technology (IT).

Tshumisano

The Tshumisano Technology Station Programme is advancing technology transfer and skills development to enhance equitable economic development. In this regard, the HE sector has a vital role in supporting SMMEs to become engines of growth. The Tshumisano Trust is collaborating with universities of technology in particular to promote the development of industries in manufacturing, chemicals and textiles, and by supporting innovation within SMMEs and student skills development.

The Department of Science and Technology launched a database that is aimed at quantifying and monitoring the levels of unemployment among Science, Engineering and Technology (SET) graduates in South Africa. This is aimed at addressing the challenge of unemployment among graduates in this sector.

The Minister of Science and Technology, Mr Mosibudi Mangena, launched the Database Management System of unemployed SET graduates in Pretoria in May 2007.

The database will be used by job seekers, potential employers, prospective candidates for postgraduate studies, institutions for higher learning and other stakeholders to improve the rate of human-capital development, especially in SET.

Technology stations are the:

- Tshwane University of Technology (TUT): Electronics and Electrical Engineering, complemented by IT
- Central University of Technology: Metals Value-Adding and Product Development
- TUT: Chemistry and Chemical Engineering
- Mangosuthu Technikon: Chemistry and Chemical Engineering
- Vaal University of Technology: Materials and Processing Technologies
- Nelson Mandela Metropolitan University: Automotive Components
- Nelson Mandela Metropolitan University: Downstream Chemicals
- Cape Peninsula University of Technology: Clothing and Textile
- University of Johannesburg: Metal-Casting Technology
- Durban Institute of Technology: Reinforced and Moulded Plastics
- Cape Peninsula University of Technology: Agrifood Processing Technologies.

National Science Week (NSW) is an annual week-long event aimed at encouraging the youth to pursue careers in science and technology, and highlighting the importance of science in everyday life. NSW 2007 was held from 12 to 19 May and the theme was *Tomorrow's Science and Technology are in our Youth's Hands.*

National research facilities

The National Research Foundation (NRF) manages South Africa's national research facilities. It promotes and supports basic and applied research. The NRF oversees the following national research facilities:

- South African Astronomical Observatory
- Hartebeesthoek Radio Astronomy Observatory
- Hermanus Magnetic Observatory
- South African Institute for Aquatic Biodiversity
- South African Environmental Observation Network
- National Zoological Gardens
- iThemba Laboratory for Accelerator-Based Sciences (iThemba Labs).

Science councils

Council for Scientific and Industrial Research (CSIR)

The CSIR is one of the largest scientific and technology research, development and implementation organisations in Africa. The organisation undertakes and applies directed research and innovation in S&T to improve the quality of life of South Africans.

Mintek

Mintek, South Africa's national mineral-research organisation, is one of the world's leading technology organisations specialising in mineral processing, extractive metallurgy and related areas. Collaborating with industry and other R&D institutions, Mintek provides service testwork, process development, consulting and innovative products to clients worldwide.

Mintek is an autonomous statutory organisation and reports to the Minister of Minerals and Energy. About 30% of the annual budget of R350 million is funded by the State Science Vote, with the balance provided by contract R&D, sales of services and products, technology licensing agreements and joint-venture operating companies.

The Department of Science and Technology and the National Research Foundation have jointly implemented and are managing the Internship Programme to provide work experience for unemployed graduates and empower them with practical and accelerated learning programmes towards building workplace competencies.

Human Sciences Research Council (HSRC)

The HSRC is South Africa's statutory research agency and conducts research that generates critical and independent knowledge, relative to all aspects of human and social development. Alleviating poverty and developing and implementing policy are central to its research activities. The HSRC's research also extends beyond South Africa through projects and collaborations in other African countries.

Medical Research Council

The MRC conducts research through six national programmes, and collaborates with most of the world's top health-research agencies to improve the nation's health status and quality of life.

The MRC disseminates research information through the National Health Knowledge Network. The council has established the African Biotechnology Information Centre in co-operation with various universities.

The MRC's National HIV and AIDS Lead Programme co-ordinates the South African AIDS Vaccine Initiative.

Agricultural Research Council (ARC)

The ARC is committed to promoting agriculture, and related sectors, through research and technology development and transfer.

Council of Geoscience (CGS)

The CGS supplies the country with geoscience data to establish a safe and cost-effective physical infrastructure.

South African Bureau of Standards (SABS)

The SABS produces, maintains and disseminates standards. It promotes standardisation in business and government, and administers compulsory standards on behalf of the State. It also certifies international quality standards.

Other important research bodies and areas

The National Institute for Tropical Diseases in Tzaneen, Limpopo, continually assesses various malaria-control programmes.

The South African National Antarctic Programme manages three bases, one at Vesleskarvet, Antarctica; a second on Marion Island in the south Indian Ocean; and a third on Gough Island, a British territory in the South Atlantic Ocean.

South Africa is the only African country with a presence in Antarctica, and which is also conducting research there in physics, engineering, Earth sciences, and biological and oceanographic sciences.

The South African base, Sanae IV, is one of few country bases built on hard rock, as opposed to the ice shelf, and is regarded as one of the more modern bases on Antarctica. The Department of Science and Technology has finalised the Antarctic Research Strategy for South Africa.

Mine-safety research

The Safety in Mines Research Advisory Committee aims to advance mineworkers' safety. It has a permanent research-management office overseeing research in rock engineering, engineering and occupational health.

Energy research

The Chief Directorate: Energy of the Department of Minerals and Energy manages a policy-directed research programme. This

The Youth into Science Programme's primary objective is to contribute towards the development of the priority skills base. Through this programme, the Department of Science and Technology will be recruiting young people to pursue careers in areas of scarce skills. Its targets include doubling science and technology literacy among the youth and nurturing more than 5 000 young people with talent and potential in Science, Engineering and Technology by 2010.

includes transport energy, renewable energy and energy for developing areas, coal, electricity, energy efficiency, energy economy and integrated energy-policy formulation.

Agricultural research

Agricultural research is conducted by the ARC, several universities and the private sector.

Water research

Water research in South Africa is co-ordinated and funded by the Water Research Commission in Pretoria.

The organisation's most active partners in water research are:

- universities and universities of technology
- professional consultants
- science councils
- water and waste utilities
- non-governmental organisations.

By mid-2007, a brand new research base worth R200 million was being built to replace the existing one on Marion Island. The building was expected to be ready for occupation by May 2008.

It will house 80 people and include laboratories, office space, a jacuzzi, an operation centre, two helicopter decks, a technical centre with a workshop, a gymnasium, storage space, a conference room and a medical centre.

The research base on Marion Island is the home of a team of researchers that focuses on the unique wildlife on the island. The researchers also gather important weather data at a weather station. The South African National Antarctic Programme operates the research base.

Coastal and marine research

The Chief Directorate: Marine and Coastal Management advises on the use of marine living resources and the conservation of marine ecosystems, by conducting and supporting relevant multidisciplinary scientific research and monitoring the marine environment.

Environmental research

The Chief Directorate: Environmental Management of the Department of Environmental Affairs and Tourism annually finances several research and monitoring programmes.

The programmes focus on waste management and pollution, nature conservation, river management, the coastline and marine environment, and the atmosphere, among other things.

Access to housing and secure accommodation is integral to government's commitment to reducing poverty and improving the quality of people's lives.

Funding

Between 2005 and June 2007, government produced 2,4 million houses, benefiting more than nine million people. The housing backlog was decreased from 2,4 million to 2,2 million. Annual production grew from 252 000 to 272 000 a year.

The Department of Housing was allocated R45,3 billion in 2007/08.

Comprehensive Housing Plan

The Minister of Housing, Dr Lindiwe Sisulu, announced the Comprehensive Housing Plan for the Development of Integrated Sustainable Human Settlements in September 2004.

Cabinet approved the plan as a framework for housing programmes in the next five years, which aims to eradicate informal settlements in South Africa in as short a period as is physically possible.

It provides for comprehensive oversight by government in promoting the residential property market. This includes:

- developing low-cost housing
- providing medium-density accommodation and rental housing
- providing establishing stronger partnerships with the private sector
- providing social infrastructure and amenities.

The N2 Gateway Pilot Project in Cape Town is the biggest housing project yet undertaken by government. It will see the development of about 30 000 dignified dwellings at sites along a 30-kilometre stretch of the N2 Highway.

The Comprehensive Housing Plan is being implemented through a pilot project in each province that will improve the living conditions of 103 000 households in informal settlements.

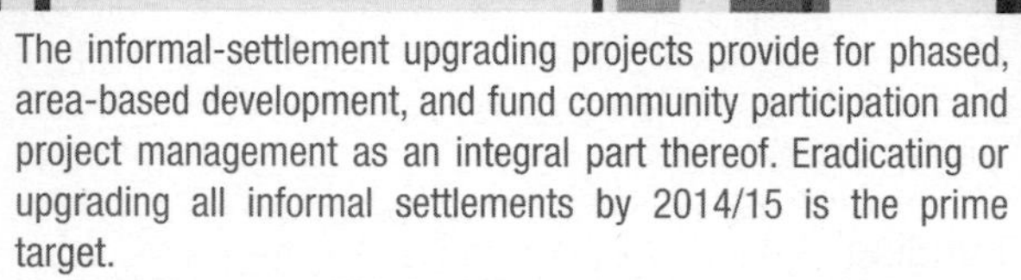

The informal-settlement upgrading projects provide for phased, area-based development, and fund community participation and project management as an integral part thereof. Eradicating or upgrading all informal settlements by 2014/15 is the prime target.

Key focus areas identified by the Comprehensive Housing Plan include:

- accelerating housing delivery as a key strategy for poverty alleviation
- using housing provision as a major job-creation strategy
- ensuring that property can be accessed by all as an asset for wealth creation and empowerment
- leveraging growth in the economy, combating crime and promoting social cohesion
- using housing development to break barriers between the First-Economy residential property boom and the Second-Economy slump
- using housing as an instrument for developing sustainable human settlements in support of spatial restructuring
- diversifying housing products by emphasising rental stock.

Rental housing for the poor

About 1,8 million South African households in the middle- to lower-income groups live in rented accommodation as opposed to about 5,2 million households that own property. At national level, 45% of households earn between R0 to R800 per month, while 45% of households at metropolitan level fall within the R801 to R3 200 income bracket.

There is a dire need for public rental housing for the poor, which the department aims to address by means of various options.

The department has formulated an affordable rental-housing programme for people in the low-income bracket who may live in housing stock arising out of:

- public-sector hostels provided for the purposes of housing migratory labour in the previous dispensation
- municipal rental stock which has not been transferred to the households who inhabit these units and that will continue to be used as rental accommodation because of the low economic status of the households
- new high-rise housing stock that will be built for the specific purpose of accommodating low-income households in rental accommodation.

Policy now exists that will allow for the increased allocation of housing units to ex-combatants and for Truth and Reconcilliation Commission reparations on a preferential basis. Over the next five years, an average of 30% of subsidised units are expected to be allocated to this target group.

Breaking New Ground (BNG) Programme

The BNG Programme is aimed at improving overall housing delivery.

A typical BNG starter house comprises a minimum of two bedrooms, a living area and inside bathroom.

Community Residential Unit Programme

The Public Sector Hostels Upgrading Programme, which was used to effect cosmetic improvements to dilapidated hostels only, has been revised and is now called the Community Residential Unit Programme. The programme provides a holistic and integrated development approach towards residential units, as well as a more appropriate funding mechanism and tenure arrangements for renovating hostels.

Capacity-building

The Department of Housing has undertaken several initiatives to support small housing enterprises and promote Black Economic Empowerment and gender mainstreaming.

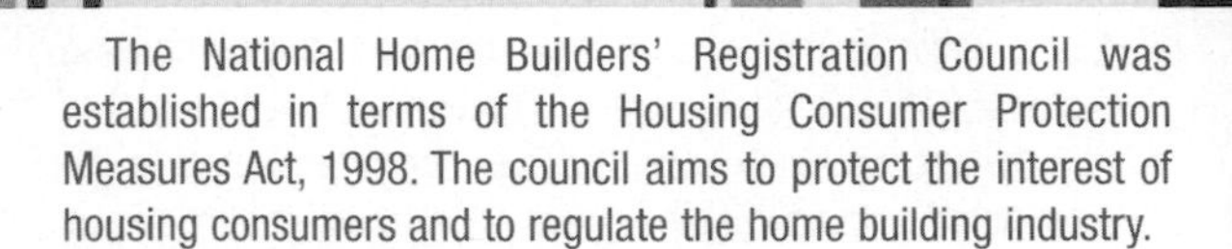

The National Home Builders' Registration Council was established in terms of the Housing Consumer Protection Measures Act, 1998. The council aims to protect the interest of housing consumers and to regulate the home building industry.

Delivery partners

The Department of Housing collaborates with various organisations towards breaking new ground in housing delivery.

The revenue of the National Housing Finance Corporation (NHFC) is derived from interest and service charges for its wholesale lending and financial services.

The NHFC's mandate has been expanded to enable the institution to directly lend to low- and medium-income end users. A new business model for the corporation has been developed and approved for implementation. The process to operationalise all the components of the models is under way and has been piloted as from May 2007 through the Postbank with a view of a full roll-out towards the end of 2007/08. The pilots were taking place in Johannesburg, Soweto and Pretoria central:

Approved projects per province, March 2007	
Eastern Cape	480
Free State	724
Gauteng	1 188
KwaZulu-Natal	603
Limpopo	602
Mpumulanga	56
Northern Cape	277
North West	277
Western Cape	607
Total	**5 321**

Source: Department of Housing

- By September 2006, the NHFC had acheived R24 million in revenue against a target of 33 million, with a profit of R22 million.
- By September 2006, the institution had signed three rental housing contracts with a loan value of R56 million, 24 credit-linked loan contracts with a loan value of R92 million, 11 infrastructure and community facility contracts with a loan value of R80 million, and 51 subsidy housing loans with a value of R217 million.
- In 2007/08, the National Urban Reconstruction and Housing Agency was expected to continue financing contractors in the subsidy housing, credit-linked housing and community infrastructure subsectors.
- Servcon Housing Solutions (Pty) Ltd is a private company established in terms of the Companies Act, 1973, as a product of the Record of Understanding between government (Department of Housing), the Banking Association of South Africa and participating financial

Approved subsidies per province, March 2007	(R)'000
Eastern Cape	302 729
Free State	169 350
Gauteng	1 191 754
KwaZulu-Natal	387 297
Limpopo	208 081
Mpumulanga	185 712
Northern Cape	54 949
North West	212 049
Western Cape	331 979
Total	**3 043 900**

Source: Department of Housing

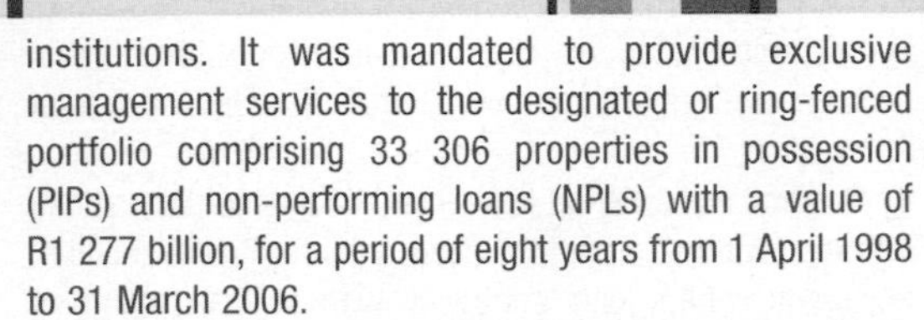

institutions. It was mandated to provide exclusive management services to the designated or ring-fenced portfolio comprising 33 306 properties in possession (PIPs) and non-performing loans (NPLs) with a value of R1 277 billion, for a period of eight years from 1 April 1998 to 31 March 2006.

- Thubelisha Homes, a not-for-profit company, helps the owners of PIPs or NPLs to relocate to more affordable homes. Thubelisha was appointed project manager and implementing agent of the N2 Gateway Project.
- Another not-for-profit company, the Social Housing Foundation, aims to build capacity for social-housing institutions.
- The Rural Housing Loan Fund's main purpose, as a wholesale lending institution, is to enable retail institutions to provide loans to low-income earners to finance housing in rural areas.

Subsidies

A government housing subsidy is a grant provided by government to qualifying beneficiaries for housing purposes. Government does not give beneficiaries cash. The grant is used only for acquiring housing goods and services or the provision of complete houses that comply with the minimum technical and environmental norms and standards. The following subsidies exist:

- Consolidation Subsidy
- Individual Subsidy
- Project-Linked Subsidy
- Institutional Subsidy
- Relocation Assistance
- Discount Benefit Scheme
- Rural subsidies
- People's Housing Process.

The South African Housing Subsidy Scheme subsidised quantum amounts for the period 1 April 2007 to 31 March 2008 in respect of a 40 m^2 house.

Individual and project-linked subsidies	Top structure funding	Own contribution	Product price
R0 – R1 500 R1 501 – R3 500	R38 984 R36 505	None R2 479	R38 984 R38 984
Indigent: Aged, disabled and health-stricken R0 – R3 500	R38 984	None	R38 984
Institutional subsidies			
R0 – R3 500	R36 505	Institution must add capital	At least R38 984
Consolidation subsidies			
R0 – R1 500 R1 501 – R3 500	R38 984 R36 505	None R2 479	R46 484 R46 484
Indigent: Aged, disabled and health-stricken R0 – R3 500	R38 984	None	R46 484
Rural subsidies			
R0 – R3 500	R38 984	None	R38 984
People's Housing Process			
R0 – R3 500	R38 984	None	R38 984

Cabinet's Justice, Crime Prevention and Security (JCPS) Cluster focuses on reducing serious and violent crime by 7% to 10% anually. The JCPS Cluster is following a two-pronged crime-fighting strategy that confirms the central role of law-enforcement agencies, and acknowledges the principle of community involvement and establishing partnerships as primary instruments in preventing and combating crime.

The policy documents governing policing in South Africa include the South African Police Service (SAPS) Act, 1995 and the 1996

National Crime-Prevention Strategy.

The operational priorities of the department's strategic plan for 2005 to 2010 are:

- combating organised crime
- fighting serious and violent crime
- addressing crime against women and children
- improving on other SAPS priorities that affect basic service delivery.

Reducing crime

Crime prevention in South Africa is based on the principles of community policing, that is, partnerships between the community and the SAPS. Partnerships between police officers (who are appointed as sector managers) and communities strengthen existing community policing forums (CPFs), which have been in place since 1993.

Sector policing was introduced in 2002/03 to increase the visibility and accessibility of police officers, particularly in areas that have limited infrastructure and high crime levels. It is implemented continually.

By mid-2007, sector policing had been introduced in 169 priority areas; 35 285 additional reservists had been recruited and 1 064 CPFs were operating well at 1 115 police stations. The CPFs are actively involved in crime-prevention and awareness programmes, allowing the police to mobilise and involve communities in the fight against crime, as well as forming partnerships with business and

The budget allocation for the police service in the 2003/04 financial year was R22,7 billion, which increased to R25,4 billion in 2004/05, R29,3 billion in 2005/06 and R32,5 billion in 2006/07.

The 2007/08 budget allocation is R35,9 billion and is expected to reach R43,6 billion in three years. The personnel numbers in the service rose from 140 560 in 2003/04 to 149 060 in 2004/05. By the end of 2009/10, the numbers are expected to be 193 240.

By May 2007, there were 1 115 fully fledged police stations in the country.

other stakeholders in communities to address concerns about crime.

Meetings were held with the National Community Policing Consultative Forum (NCPCF), which represents the CPFs across the country. Among the things discussed were:

- reshaping the CPFs to give them more powers and resources
- recasting the CPFs as the co-ordinators of the partnership between communities and the police
- properly defining the programme to mobilise communities to participate fully in community policing.

The NCPCF has drafted a document that seeks to improve community involvement. The CPFs will be empowered to help the police become known among their people, identify trustworthy and capable persons within the communities to be recruited into the police reservist service, and also mobilise volunteers who can assist the police in certain areas of policing, including trauma counselling for victims of domestic violence, and abused women and children. In 2006/07, 7 665 new reservists were recruited, thus raising the number of police reservists to more than 45 000.

The new recruits included 80 former commando members. At least 12 536 reservists were called up for crime-fighting operations during 2006/07.

Firearms control

The Firearms Control Act, 2000 and the Firearms Control Amendment Act, 2003 aim to assist the SAPS in preventing the proliferation of illegal firearms and removing them from society, and controlling legally owned firearms.

To get a firearm licence, applicants must pass a competency test and obtain a competency certificate.

Between July 2004 and March 2007, 103 541 licensed firearms were handed to the police voluntarlly, together with 1 468 840 rounds of ammunition. During the same period, the police confiscated 73 132 illegal firearms and 1 125 666 rounds of ammunition. Between 2002 and 2006, police destroyed 415 351 firearms. By mid-2007, 13 sports-shooting organisations, five hunting associations, 14 collectors' associations, 292 businesses in hunting, 439 training-providers and 298 shooting ranges had been licensed. The SAPS had received 286 094 competency certificates and 408 114 renewal applications, respectively.

Some 120 121 competency certificates were finalised and 84 885 renewals of firearm licences processed.

Forensic Science Laboratory (FSL)

The FSL in Pretoria is implementing revolutionary new technology that will quadruple its capacity to process DNA samples.

Previously, some 200 samples were processed manually daily, but implementing the Automated Genetic Sample Processing System is expected to ensure that 800 samples are processed daily. The system is the only one of its kind in the world and is a robotic system that combines engineering and science.

In 2006/07, the FSL finalised 48 670 biology cases and the Integrated Ballistics Information System received 168 732 cases.

The FSL has acquired an infrared device to assist in differentiating between inks and documents, and detecting alterations or additions to documents. It has also gained gas chromatograph mass spectrometers for analysing drug-related cases. The Craig Micro Spectrometer was obtained for analysing colour in such things as fibres and paint samples.

Criminal Record Centre

The Automated Fingerprint Information System palm-print extension and matcher upgrade was successfully implemented in December 2004 and operational by January 2005. The palm-print extension contributes to crime-solving.

During the 2006/07 financial year, over a million crime-related fingerprint enquiries were received by the CRC, as well as 912 710 non-crime-related enquiries.

Detective Service

The Detective Service is responsible for maintaining an effective crime-investigation service. It investigates crimes and gathers all related evidence required by the prosecuting authority to redress crime.

The Detective Service consists of the following components:

- General Investigations
- Organised Crime
- Commercial Crime
- Serious and Violent Crime.

Visible Policing

Visible Policing is responsible for providing a proactive and reactive policing service. It is regarded as a line function and its components are visible policing, social-crime prevention, police emergency services, specialised operations, firearm and liquor control, borderline operations and crime-combating operations.

Visible Policing is responsible for combating crime through anti-crime operations, activities at police stations, maintaining high visibility and the availability of police officials at grassroots level. It also oversees sector policing, reservists, municipal police services and closed-circuit television surveillance.

Social-Crime Prevention deals with crimes affecting the social fabric of society, including crimes against women and children. Through its Victim-Empowerment Programme (VEP), 594 stations have victim-friendly facilities.

During 2006/07, 11 victim-friendly facilities were upgraded. The VEP has the Safe Schools Programme and launched the Drug-Reduction-in-Schools pilot at 11 schools in the Pretoria, Gauteng. An action plan for school safety developed by the national Department of Education was expected to be implemented in 2007/08. It aims to address issues ranging from reducing behavioural and social challenges such as bullying, the use of weapons, child abuse and gangsterism to strengthening infrastructure and environmental issues that contribute to crime in schools.

The unit's Children Living in Streets Programme facilitates protective safety nets for children living on the streets by mobilising a network of service-providers to reunite children with their communities and reintegrate them into families.

Two pilot programmes are running in Sunnyside and Hillbrow, Gauteng.

The Police Emergency Services responds to crimes in progress, and provides dog and mounted services. Hostage and suicide negotiators and police divers, and uniformed units such as the 10111 emergency centres and the Flying Squad, provide specialised services.

The Police Emergency Services is also responsible for optimising the Integrated Crime-Prevention Road Policing Strategy, which aims to improve safety and order in the road environment by preventing and combating criminality and lawlessness.

In April 2007, President Thabo Mbeki met with the Big Business Working Group in Pretoria. The Joint Government/Business Team tackling crime-fighting explained the initiatives that they had taken as well as their "Step Change" crime-fighting initiative that involved close collaboration between government and business. The group had teams dealing with reducing violent organised crime, improving the criminal justive system's effectiveness, mobilising society and enhancing overall service delivery. They would focus on house robberies, vehicle robbery, cash-in-transit and business heists in the short term.

Firearms and Liquor Control eradicates the proliferation of firearms for use in crime and violence in South Africa. The component also ensures compliance with and effective enforcement of liquor-control legislation to address serious, violent and contact crime in South Africa.

Specialised Operations provides a rapid-response capacity for intervening in extreme situations where normal policing is ineffective, including combating public violence; stabilising serious and violent crime incidents; policing public gatherings; rendering specialised operational support (including the Air Wing and Special Task Force); and handling high-risk operations.

The Air Wing has received an additional helicopter for each province. A second air wing unit, which was established at Bulembu in the Eastern Cape, will serve the East London, Bhisho and Mthatha areas. Two newly-acquired Squirrel helicopters with spray equipment allow for regular dagga-spraying operations in the Eastern Cape and KwaZulu-Natal.

Borderline Operations combats transnational crimes at air, sea and land borderlines. Air Borderline Control includes policing more than 1 000 smaller airfields and airstrips. Sea Borderline Control is responsible for policing smaller sea harbours and slipways, including the South African ocean up to the 300 Nautical Mile Zone.

Land Borderline Control polices the South African land borderline. The SAPS is taking over the borderline control function from the South African National Defence Force (SANDF). This will be finalised in 2009.

Preparations for the 2010 Soccer Cup

South Africa is expected to deploy 30 000 police officers specifically to ensure the safety of visitors to the country during the 2010 FIFA World Cup™. There is likely to be one police officer for every 10 foreign tourists for the duration of the event.

The Government plans to increase the number of police officers in the country from the current 156 000 to more than 190 000 officers over the next three years.

These numbers will be increased by South Africa's police reservist (volunteer) service, and is expected to grow to 80 000 by 2009, supported by an additional government budget of R260 million.

By mid-2007, the SAPS was strengthening its partnerships with the country's 300 000-strong private security industry, as well as with local communities.

The SAPS has been allocated a further R600 million to prepare for the World Cup, mostly to purchase equipment ranging from light aircraft to retractable fencing.

Other equipment needed includes mobile command centres, water cannons, crime-scene trailers, new armour for vehicles, new tools for bomb squads, and light aircraft equipped with video cameras for sending live footage to officers on the ground, to patrol the skies above World Cup venues.

Each stadium will have one or two mobile police centres with high-tech monitoring equipment for them to perform functions such as identity checks.

In addition, every host city will have a dedicated 2010 police station with separate holding cells, a courtroom for speedy judgments and a home affairs office for possible deportations. International police officers from every country playing in the event will also be present, wearing their own uniforms, to assist the public and the SAPS.

Defence

The mission of the Department of Defence is to defend and protect South Africa, its territorial integrity and its people.

The department, under the auspices of the New Partnership for Africa's Development, participates in various initiatives to secure peace and stability on the continent.

Bubele Kitie Mhlana, popularly known as "Bravo", is the captain of *SAS Isandlwana*, making him the first African commander of a frigate. The process of qualifying as a naval commander of a frigate is long and arduous, and demands considerable intellectual growth and development.

The SANDF is an all-volunteer force consisting of a regular core force and a reserve force. In addition to military matters, the Department of Defence is involved in search-and-rescue operations, hydrography and securing national key points.

Uniformed members of the SANDF have the right to join trade unions, but may not go on strike or picket.

Peace support

Based on the *White Paper on South African Participation in International Peace Missions*, the SANDF continues to participate in peace missions, for which various members of the Department of Defence have been trained. By September 2007, external deployments included Burundi, the Democratic Republic of Congo, the Sudan, Ethiopia and Eritrea.

Acquisition of weapon systems

The Directorate: Army Acquisition is engaged in various capital projects at various stages of execution. The projects include upgrades of existing equipment and several major new systems.

The focus is on the South African Army's combat-vehicle capability. This includes the Mamba, Casspir, Olifant Mk II main battle tank, Rooikat armoured car and GV6 self-propelled gun systems that are being upgraded to extend their duration, while the new infantry combat-vehicle and supply-support vehicle programmes are close to being contracted.

Armaments Corporation of South Africa (Armscor)

Armscor's primary function is to acquire defence products and services for the SANDF, and to co-manage, with the Department

Lieutenant (Lt) Phetogo Molawa, 21, is the South African National Defence Force's (SANDF) first black female helicopter pilot.

Lt Molawa, from the Free State, recently completed her initial helicopter training in the SANDF and is one of only a few female helicopter pilots in the South African Air Force (SAAF). She displayed her flying prowess in an SAAF Oryx helicopter to delegates attending the third Women's Conference in Defence in Centurion outside Pretoria in August 2007.

The SANDF has set itself the target of 30% representation by women in all its decision-making structures by 2009. In 2007, the Minister of Defence, Mr Mosiuoa Lekota, announced the appointment of 11 new brigadier-generals and two new rear admirals. Eight of the new brigadier-generals were women, bringing the total number of female generals in the SANDF to 25.

of Defence, the development of technologies for future weapon systems and products.

It also manages the disposal of excess, forfeited, redundant or surplus defence material for the SANDF and subsidiary companies that directly support defence technology and acquisition strategies.

Armscor provides the department with tender-board functions, project security and arms-control compliance assurance.

Denel Group of South Africa

Denel is a profit-driven company wholly owned by the State. However, France's Turbomeca owns 51% of is airmotive division. It is recognised as a world leader in artillery systems.

Through offset deals, Denel supplies aerostructures for Gripen and Hawk aircraft to BAE Systems and Saab. It has started licensed manufacturing of the Agusta A119 Koala helicopters for AgustaWestland and provides parts to the Boeing Company.

Intelligence services

South Africa has two civilian intelligence structures: the National Intelligence Agency (NIA) and the South African Secret Service (SASS).

Denel, under the political direction of the Ministry of Public Enterprises, has been restructured and reorganised. Armscor, under the political direction of the Ministry of Defence, was being streamlined by mid-2007 as an acquisition division of the Department of Defence. The research divisions of both Denel and Armscor will be located in a new body called the Defence Evaluation and Research Institute.

The NIA's mission is to provide government with domestic intelligence and counter-intelligence. The NIA's mandate has been divided into seven areas of interest: counter-intelligence, political, economic and border intelligence, terrorism, organised crime and corruption.

The SASS is South Africa's foreign-intelligence capacity. A civilian ministry and a Cabinet committee exercise executive control.

The SASS' objective is to forewarn, inform and advise government on real and potential threats to South Africa's security, and on socio-economic opportunities for the country.

Judicial authority is vested in the courts, which are independent and subject only to the Constitution of South Africa, 1996 and the law. No person or organ of state may interfere with the functioning of the courts.

The courts

Constitutional Court

This is the highest court in all constitutional matters and deals only with constitutional issues. The court's work includes deciding whether Acts of Parliament and the conduct of the President and executive are consistent with the Constitution, including the Bill of Rights.

The court's decisions are binding on all persons, including organs of state, and on all other courts. It consists of the Chief Justice of South Africa, the Deputy Chief Justice and 11 Constitutional Court judges.

Supreme Court of Appeal (SCA)

The SCA is the highest court in respect of all other matters. The court has jurisdiction to hear and determine an appeal against any decision of a high court. Decisions of the SCA are binding on all courts of a lower order.

It consists of the President and Deputy President of the SCA and a number of judges of appeal determined by an Act of Parliament.

High courts

There are 10 court divisions and three local divisions, which judges of the provincial courts concerned preside over.

A provincial or local division has jurisdiction in its own area over all persons in that area. These divisions hear matters that are of such a serious nature that the lower courts would not be competent to make an appropriate judgment or impose a penalty. Except where minimum or maximum sentences are prescribed

The Department of Justice and Constitutional Development's budget allocation for 2006/07 was R7,3 billion, of which R1,5 billion was for the National Prosecuting Authority, R2,4 billion for the court-services programme and R986 million for chapter nine institutions. Chapter nine institutions are established by the Constitution and have as their general mandate the strengthening of constitutional democracy in South Africa.

by law, their penal jurisdiction is unlimited and includes life imprisonment.

The Land Claims Court and the Labour Court have the same status as the High Court. In the case of labour disputes, appeals are made to the Labour Appeal Court.

Regional courts

Regional courts established in each regional division have jurisdiction over all offences, except treason. Unlike the High Court, the penal jurisdiction of the regional courts is limited.

Magistrates' courts

By mid-2007, there were 1 912 magistrates in the country (including regional court magistrates). A magistrate's court has jurisdiction over all offences except treason, murder and rape.

Small claims courts

A commissioner in the Small Claims Court hears cases involving civil claims not exceeding R7 000.

By July 2007, there were 156 such courts throughout the country. The commissioner is usually a practising advocate or attorney, a legal academic or another competent person who offers his or her services free of charge. Neither the plaintiff nor the defendant may be represented or assisted by counsel at the hearing. There is no appeal to a higher court.

There is a national programme that aims to strengthen and roll out small claims courts to rural and peri-urban areas by pursuing the strategic objectives of:

- providing access for all, especially the poor and the vulnerable
- establishing systems and rules of court that are accessible and easy to understand
- providing trained administrative support staff
- attracting and retaining commissioners.

Sexual offences courts

These specialised courts allow sexual offences cases to be handled with sensitivity to avoid secondary victimisation of traumatised victims.

Equality courts

By the end of 2006/07, 220 magisterial courts had courts designated as equality courts and the remaining 146 magisterial districts were expected to be designated in the first quarter of 2007/08. Section 16(1)(a) of the Promotion of Equality and Prevention of Discrimination Act, 2000 provides that every high court is an equality court for its area of jurisdiction. To support the effective functioning of equality courts, 139 permanent equality clerk posts were created, half a million rand was spent on promotional material and over 1 290 magistrates and 300 clerks of court were trained in equality matters.

Community courts

Community courts, like the Hatfield Community Court in Pretoria, are normal district magistrates' courts that assist in dealing with matters in partnership with the community and business. These courts focus on restorative justice processes, such as diverting young offenders into suitable programmes.

Thirteen community courts have been established. By mid-2007, four had been formally launched and were fully operational in Hatfield, Fezeka (Gugulethu), Mitchell's Plain and Cape Town. Another nine pilot sites commenced in Durban (Point), KwaMashu, Mthatha, Bloemfontein, Thohoyandou, Kimberley, Phuthaditjaba, Hillbrow and Protea (Lenasia).

Court for Income Tax Offenders

In October 1999, the South African Revenue Service (Sars) opened a criminal courtroom at the Johannesburg Magistrate's Office dedicated to the prosecution of tax offenders. The court deals only

Operation Isondlo, initiated by the Department of Justice and Constitutional Development in 2006/07, led to many children's maintenance defaulters being traced, appearing in court and paying maintenance. As a result, many new applications were received countrywide and the number of children receiving maintenance increased. Between January and February 2007 alone, 865 beneficiaries and defaulters were traced.

with cases concerning failure to submit tax returns or failure to provide information requested by Sars officials. It does not deal with bigger cases such as tax fraud.

Chief's courts

An authorised African headman or his deputy may hear and determine civil claims arising from indigenous law and custom, brought before him by an African against another African within his area of jurisdiction.

Litigants have the right to choose whether to institute an action in a chief's court or in a magistrate's court. Proceedings in a chief's court are informal. An appeal against a judgment of a chief's court is heard in a magistrate's court.

National Prosecuting Authority (NPA)

The NPA structure includes the National Prosecutions Service (NPS), the Directorate: Special Operations, the Witness-Protection Programme, the Asset Forfeiture Unit (AFU) and units such as the Sexual Offences and Community Affairs (Soca) Unit, the Specialised Commercial Crime Unit (SCCU) and the Priority Crimes Litigation Unit (PCLU).

From 30 July to 3 August 2007, ordinary South Africans were given free access to legal services from hundreds of female lawyers countrywide, as part of the Department of Justice and Constitutional Development's and the South African Women Lawyers' Association's "Access to Justice Week" initiative.

The initiative aimed to provide free legal advice and services to the people, especially those who could not afford to pay private law firms for such services.

Services that were provided included the drafting of wills, securing maintenance, administrating estates, child custody and rights in marriage, foster parenting and guardianship, domestic violence and providing information regarding the National Credit Act, 2005.

Asset Forfeiture Unit

The AFU was created in 1999 in terms of the Prevention of Organised Crime Act, 1998. The AFU can seize and forfeit property that was bought from the proceeds of crime, or property that was used to commit a crime.

The AFU has two major strategic objectives, namely to:

- develop the law by taking test cases to court and creating the legal precedents necessary to allow for the effective use of the law
- build capacity to ensure that asset forfeiture is used as widely as possible to aid in the fight against crime significantly.

The AFU deposited some R120 million in the special account for fighting crime, with R77 million paid out in 2006 to centres for battered women and to boost the capacity of the South African Police Service (SAPS), the NPA and Sars to deal with crime.

Special Investigating Unit (SIU)

The SIU works closely with government departments to deal with fraud, corruption and serious maladministration in state institutions. It was established in terms of the SIU and Special Tribunals Act, 1996 and investigates cases referred to it by the President. It is the only institution that can conduct forensic investigations and consequently institute civil litigation to recover state assets or public money.

Sexual Offences and Community Affairs Unit

Various concrete steps have been taken to give effect to the national crackdown on sexual offences:

- Multidisciplinary rape-care centres, known as Thuthuzela care centres, have been established. Here rape investigations are accelerated and humanised. The Thuthuzela care centres are 24-hour, one-stop service centres where victims have access to all services, including police, counselling, doctors, court preparation and prosecutors. The main objectives of these centres are to eliminate secondary victimisation, reduce case cycle times and increase convictions. By mid-2007 there were 10 centres.

- New child-witness rooms have one-way glass partitions enabling child witnesses to testify in a friendly and secure environment without the risk of being intimidated.

Through Project Ndabezitha, Soca successfully trained 104 traditional leaders from five provinces on managing domestic violence in rural areas.

Priority Crimes Litigation Unit

The PCLU manages and directs investigations and prosecutions of priority crimes, including contraventions of nuclear, chemical/biological and conventional-arms control legislation; and tracing missing persons arising from the Truth and Reconcilition Commission (TRC).

National Prosecutions Service

The NPS performs the core function of the NPA, namely, instituting criminal proceedings on behalf of the State, and carrying out any necessary functions incidental to instituting and conducting criminal proceedings.

Specialised Commercial Crime Unit

The Pretoria-based SCCU brings specialisation to the investigation and prosecution of commercial crimes emanating from the commercial branches of the SAPS in Pretoria and Johannesburg.

Three new courts and offices have been established in the Johannesburg and Pretoria central business districts for specialised commercial-crime cases.

Similar courts were established during 2004/05 in Durban and Port Elizabeth.

The SCCU continues to achieve an above-average conviction rate.

Integrated Justice System

This system aims to use technology to improve the co-ordination of the activities of departments in government's Justice, Crime Prevention and Security Cluster.

The system entails, among other things:

- a virtual private network
- an automated fingerprint identification system and DNA database
- an integrated case-flow management system, including case, person (offender, victim and witness) and exhibits
- better tracking of people, including inmates.

Access to justice

The department continues to prioritise access to justice for vulnerable groups, including:

- implementing relevant legislation and enabling policy, for example, the Sexual Offences Bill that Parliament passed in May 2007
- ensuring assistance from prosecutors and public defenders for child maintenance
- enforcing the right of children to receive support from earning parents
- prioritising child justice and all cases involving children, especially those in prison awaiting trial.

Public Protector

The Public Protector investigates complaints from the public or on own initiatives against government at any level, its officials, persons performing public functions, corporations or companies where the State and statutory councils are involved.The Public Protector's services are free and available to everyone. Complainants' names are kept confidential as far as possible.

The President appoints the Public Protector on recommendation of the National Assembly and in terms of the Constitution, for a non-renewable period of seven years.

The Legal Aid Board and South African Police Service are working on systems that will allow legal-aid applications to be submitted electronically from police stations, to facilitate access to legal representation and ensure that arrested people have legal representation when they first appear in court. This is expected to reduce delays caused by accused people having to find attorneys.

The Public Protector is subject only to the Constitution and the law, and functions independently from government and any political party.

No person or organ of state may interfere with the functioning of the Public Protector.

The Public Protector has the power to report a matter to Parliament, which will debate it and ensure that the Public Protector's recommendations are followed.

Victims' charter

The Service Charter for Victims of Crime in South Africa and minimum standards for services for victims of crime, are important instruments elaborating and consolidating rights and obligations relating to services applicable to victims and survivors of crime in the country.

The charter identifies the following rights of crime victims:

- to be treated with fairness, respect, dignity and privacy
- to offer information
- to receive information
- protection
- assistance
- compensation
- restitution.

Truth and Reconciliation Commission Unit

The TRC was dissolved in March 2002 by way of proclamation in the *Government Gazette*. The TRC handed its final report to the President in March 2003.

The TRC made recommendations to government in respect of reparations to victims and measures to prevent the future violation of human rights. In keeping with the presidential mandate given in April 2003, the TRC Unit was established in the Department of Justice and Constitutional Development in September 2005, to audit, monitor and co-ordinate the

Sentence length breakdown as at 31 August 2007

Sentence length	Number
<6 months	4 572
>6 – 12 months	4 046
>12 – 24 months	4 012
2 – 3 years	13 081
3 – 5 years	10 975
5 – 7 years	7 614
7 – 10 years	15 278
10 – 15 years	23 117
15 – 20 years	11 731
>20 years	9 747
Life	7 640
Death	6
Other sentenced	977
Total sentenced	**112 796**

Source: Department of Correctional Services

implementation of the TRC recommendations and render victim-support services.

The TRC Unit works closely with the President's Fund, which is located in the Office of the Chief Financial Officer in the Department of Justice and Constitutional Development. The President's Fund has been giving effect to the payment of both urgent interim reparations and once-off individual grants of R30 000 each to the 16 837 victims who applied for reparations and were approved by the TRC.

By March 2007, 15 610 beneficiaries had been paid reparations. By March 2007, R50 million had been paid in respect of urgent interim reparations and R469 million in respect of the once-off individual grants, amounting to a total of R519 million.

The Department of Correctional Services has firm working relations with, among other things, the American Correctional Association and the International Corrections and Prisons Association.

Participation in bilateral commissions and joint commissions of co-operation has resulted in the department hosting several delegations from various countries, as well as the Commission on Human and Peoples' Rights under the African Union.

Efforts to trace individuals have included awareness campaigns via the print and electronic media. The Government Communication and Information System also conducted door-to-door campaigns via its regional structures.

Correctional services

The Department of Correctional Services strives to provide adequate correctional-centre accommodation that complies with accepted standards. By March 2007, offenders were housed in 238 correctional centres countrywide, including:

- eight correctional centres for female offenders only
- 13 youth correctional facilities
- 131 correctional centres for male offenders only
- 867 correctional centres for both male and female offenders.

Three correctional centres were closed for renovations.

In centres where male, female and juvenile offenders are accommodated, female and juvenile offenders are housed in separate designated sections.

Overcrowding in prisons

To alleviate overcrowding, unsentenced juveniles have been transferred to places of secure care, some sentences have been converted to correctional supervision, and facilities have been renovated or upgraded.

National and provincial action plans to fast-track all children awaiting trial from prisons and police cells since October 2004 have led to a reduction in the number of children awaiting trial.

No prisoners may be released before they have served at least half their sentence. The Criminal Law Amendment Act, 1997 provides for much harsher sentences for serious crimes. These changes are expected to place an even greater burden on prisons.

An independent judicial inspectorate regularly visits all prisons to report on conditions and prisoners' treatment.

The building of four new-generation prisons in Kimberley, Klerksdorp, Leeukop and Nigel got under way and is expected to be completed in November 2008.

By mid-2007, construction at Klerksdorp and Nigel was expected to start. Similar facilities are to be built in the Eastern Cape, Western Cape and KwaZulu-Natal. Construction of another three new-generation correctional centres in Paarl, East London and Port Shepstone, announced in 2006, is expected to start in 2008. The five new-generation correctional centres will have 3 000 beds each. South Africa's correctional centres can house 115 327 inmates.

By March 2007 they held 161 023 inmates. There was some 40% overcrowding (45 696 people), making the country's correctional centres 140% full. Of the total offender population, 48 228 inmates were awaiting trial. The average cost of incarceration was about R123,37 a day.

Interventions included the increase of available bed spaces by nearly 15% through renovations, limited expansions and the recommissioning of old prisons, thus reducing awaiting trail detainees by 22% through greater integration of the whole criminal justice system, and progressively optimising the use of legal instruments at the department's disposal.

Mother-and-child units have been established in eight female correctional centres countrywide. By March 2007, there were 154 infants under the age of five in these units. This shows a reduction from the previous year.

Inmates per security category as at 31 August 2007

Sentence categories	Women	Men	Total
Maximum security	184	28 052	28 236
Medium security	1 474	60 314	61 788
Minimum security	52	2 134	2 186
Total	**1 710**	**90 500**	**92 210**

Source: Department of Correctional Services

community

SOCIAL DEVELOPMENT

The Department of Social Development aims to ensure the provision of comprehensive, integrated, sustainable and quality social-development services that address vulnerability and poverty, and to create an enabling environment for sustainable development in partnership with those committed to building a caring society.

Legislation

President Thabo Mbeki signed the Children's Act, 2005 in June 2006. In July 2007, the National Assembly passed the Children's Amendment Bill and referred it to the National Council of Provinces to be ratified. However, until Parliament passes the Children's Amendment Bill, and the Children's Act, 2005 and the Amendment Bill become a single comprehensive Act, the Child Care Act, 1983 will remain in effect.

The Children's Act, 2005 provides for the establishment of the National Child Protection Register that will record all persons found unsuitable to work with children. It will also list any person found through the Children's Court and criminal courts to be unsuitable to work with children.

In terms of this new law, childcare facilities, including welfare organisations offering foster care and adoption, will be able to check prospective employees, foster parents and adoptive parents against the register.

The Older Persons Act, 2006 contains provisions to improve the lives of older South Africans. The main objectives of the Act are to:

Number of social development beneficiaries as at April 2007:
Old-Age Grant: 2 194 066
War Veterans' Grant: 2 317
Disability Grant: 1 425 105
Foster Care Grant: 405 813
Care Dependency Grant: 98 690
Child Support Grant: 7 910 748
Grant-in-Aid: 32 280.

- maintain and promote the status, well-being, safety and security of older persons
- recognise the skills and wisdom of older persons
- encourage older persons' participation in community activities to promote them as people.

Payment of social grants

Beneficiaries of social grants increased from 3,8 million people in April 2001 to more than 12,8 million in September 2007.

Research studies have consistently confirmed that these grants not only reduce the occurrence of hunger and extreme poverty, but that they also facilitate household access to basic services and economic opportunities. Social assistance increased from 2,9% of gross domestic product in 2003/04 to 3,3% in 2006/07. Social grants contribute more than half of the income of the poorest 20% of households and have doubled in real terms over the past five years.

In 2007, the South African Social Security Agency was officially launched.

Poverty relief

Eradicating poverty is the highest priority in government's efforts to build a better life for all. In this regard, the Department of Social Development manages the Sustainable Livelihoods Programme. This programme aims to assist communities in a range of developmental projects and to develop best practices to link social grants to the livelihood strategies of direct and indirect beneficiaries and income-generating vehicles such as co-operatives.

By mid-2007, the first phase of a four-phased pilot project was implemented in the Eastern Cape. The objective of this pilot project is to restore the poor and vulnerable as quickly as possible to self-reliance. The pilot project introduced the "sweat equity" principle, which provides beneficiaries with an opportunity to invest-in-kind in their own development initiatives.

This process ensures that beneficiaries are not passive onlookers but rather become active partners in the development process.

It also ensures ownership, commitment and accountability on the side of beneficiaries, which are critical and necessary ingredients for sustainability. Through this process, government supports beneficiary-driven initiatives and is therefore perceived not just as a provider, but as an enabler.

The department is, in addition to lending social assistance, implementing poverty-relief initiatives. The department will hand over to the provinces all the projects that were implemented by the national department and supported by the Independent Development Trust.

Home- and community-based care (HCBC)

HCBC is based on the premise that vulnerable children and their families are better protected and supported within the context of their communities. As a result, this programme informs one of the main development strategies presently implemented by the department to enable communities and people affected by HIV

Amounts of grants per month as at 1 April 2007

Grant type	Amount
Old-Age Grant	R870
Disability Grant	R870
War Veterans' Grant	R890
Foster Care Grant	R620
Care Dependency Grant	R870
Child Support Grant	R200
Grant-in-Aid	R200

Source: Department of Social Development

South Africa is signatory to various international declarations on the promotion and protection of the rights of women and children, such as the Convention on the Rights of the Child, the Convention on the Elimination of All Forms of Discrimination Against Women, and the Declaration on the Elimination of Violence Against Women.

Percentage of registered non-profit organisations per province

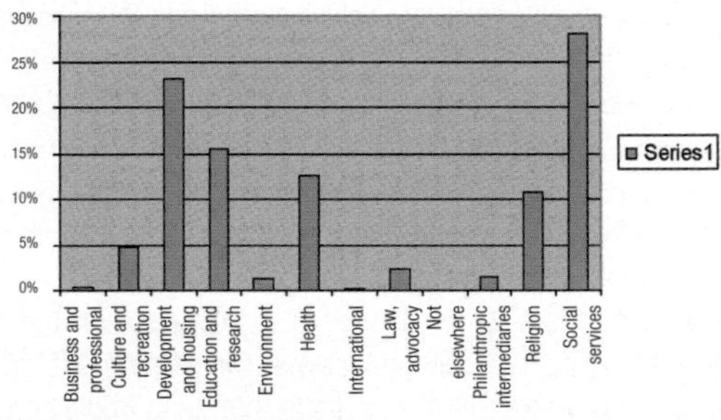

Source: Department of Social Development

and AIDS to access social-development services. Norms and standards for the implementation of HCBC and support has been developed to ensure the good quality of services and to provide a minimum package of services to be rendered. The norms and standards were based on the evaluation of costs and process indicators for HCBC done in three provinces.

In 2006/07, the programme:

- identified 206 889 orphans and vulnerable children and extended appropriate services to them
- assisted 34 025 child-headed households by providing access to counselling and support services
- assisted 356 073 affected families and distributed 155 754 food parcels
- established 611 childcare forums nationwide to identify orphans and vulnerable children
- distributed 47 607 school uniforms
- provided stipends to 11 059 caregivers
- funded 750 non-governmental organisations and faith-based organisations
- provided cooked meals to 102 723 children through various community multipurpose centres.

National councils

The department strives to strengthen the capacity of civil society to actively engage in social and economic development, by supporting the following national councils:

- National Council for Persons with Physical Disabilities
- Deaf Federation of South Africa
- South African National Epilepsy League
- South African Federation for Mental Health
- Cancer Association of South Africa.

Statutory bodies include the National Development Agency (NDA), relief boards and the Central Drug Authority.

Services to orphans made vulnerable by HIV and AIDS

The department provides care and support to orphans and other children made vulnerable by HIV and AIDS and other circumstances. The child-care forums work hand-in-hand with social workers, welfare organisations and other structures in the community to ensure that the identified children get access to appropriate services.

The department has established a number of community-based drop-in centres where children are provided with meals before they go to school and are also given lunch boxes. The caregivers at the drop-in centres also assist children from child-headed households with homework, and involve them in life-skills programmes.

National Development Agency

The NDA is a statutory funding agency that aims to contribute to the alleviation of poverty, address its causes, and strengthen the capacity of civil-society organisations to combat poverty.

The key strategic objectives of the NDA are, among other things, to grant funds to civil-society organisations to meet the development needs of poor communities; proactively strengthen

In August 2007, Cabinet approved the Prevention and Treatment of Substance Abuse Bill. The new legislation promotes more community-based services, and will be more sensitive towards the needs of children.

organisations' institutional capacity for long-term sustainability; source funds for the NDA; and promote consultation, dialogue and the sharing of development experiences.

Non-Profit Organisations (NPOs)

The NPO Act, 1997 mandates the Department of Social Development to contribute towards creating an enabling environment within which NPOs can flourish. The Directorate: NPOs was established in terms of this legislation to manage the registration facility and increase public access to information on registered organisations. The legal mandate requires that the directorate registers organisations within two months after receipt of a complete application and provide support for organisations to register and meet reporting requirements.

The registration and reporting of organisations has increased substantially since the inception of the Act in 1998. By mid-2007, 44 062 organisations had registered.

Social assistance and security fraud

An employment-assistance directorate has been established to link social-grant beneficiaries with economic activities and poverty-alleviation strategies, for the possible exit from the social-grants system. In line with this thinking, Cabinet approved, in principle, a proposal to explore possible economic activities and poverty-alleviation strategies for the same purpose.

The department's national facilities to combat fraud and corruption in the social-security system consist of:

- a toll-free national security fraud hotline (0800 60 10 11) that operates 24 hours a day, seven days a week
- an e-mail address (*fraud@socdev.gov.za*) and a free-call fax service number (0800 61 10 11).

As part of the Anti-Corruption and Fraud Prevention Strategy, internal-control systems have been improved and forensic and investigating teams deployed in all provinces.

The investigation has achieved the following results:

- Some 21 588 government employees were found to be on the system irregularly and have since been removed, and 3 657 have already been referred for disciplinary action ranging from warnings to dismissals.
- A total of 5 656 people have been arrested and taken to court. The convicton rate exceeds 80%.
- By mid-2007, R63 million had been recovered from disentitled beneficiaries.
- Altogether 143 485 people have been recommended for removal from the system and 21 587 civil-servant grants have been stopped.
- The pay-out of 123 610 beneficiaries have been cancelled due to non-collection or direct requests from beneficiaries.
- The investigation saved the Government R7,7 billion.

By May 2007, more than 86 000 beneficiaries had applied for indemnity and their grants were suspended. This saved the department investigation costs of an estimated R400 million.

The department, in collaboration with all national and provincial law-enforcement agencies, including the South African Police Service and the Special Investigation Unit was expected to establish the Inspectorate for Social Security by the end of 2007.

ENVIRONMENT

In terms of its biological heritage, South Africa is recognised as one of the richest nations in the world. The overarching vision of the Department of Environmental Affairs and Tourism is a prosperous and equitable society living in harmony with its natural resources.

Government leads protection of the environment by example. At regional level, the provincial conservation agencies are major role-players, and independent statutory organisations such as South African National Parks (SANParks) and the South African National Biodiversity Institute (Sanbi) are valuable partners in the country's total conservation effort.

South Africa has taken several concrete steps to implement the United Nations' (UN) Agenda 21 on Sustainable Development. These include reforming environmental policies, ratifying international agreements and participating in many global and regional sustainable-development initiatives.

Environmental heritage

South Africa enjoys the third-highest level of biodiversity in the world. It has between 250 000 and a million species of organisms, much of which occur nowhere else in the world.

While South Africa occupies about 2% of the world's land area, it is estimated that the country is home to 10% of the world's plants and 7% of the reptiles, birds and mammals. The southern African coast is home to almost 15% of known coastal marine species, providing a rich source of nutrition and supporting livelihoods of coastal communities.

World Wetlands Day: 2 February
National Water Week: 19 to 25 March
Earth Day: 20 March
World Water Day: 22 March
World Meteorological Day: 23 March
World Environment Day: 5 June
World Oceans Day: 8 June
World Desertification Day: 17 June
National Arbour Week: 1 to 7 September
International Day for the Protection of the Ozone Layer: 16 September
World Tourism Day: 27 September
World Habitat Day: 4 October
National Marine Day: 20 October

South Africa's second *National State of Environment Report*, released in June 2007, includes a number of new components, such as a section on human vulnerability to environmental change, alternative environmental futures, and recommendations for action.

Specialist studies focusing on a number of themes include atmosphere and climate, land, waste, biodiversity, inland water, marine and coastal ecosystems, human settlements, energy, environmental governance and human vulnerability to environmental change.

The publication in 2006 of the *National Spatial Biodiversity Assessment* by the Department of Environmental Affairs and Tourism and Sanbi revealed that 34% of South Africa's ecosystems were threatened, with 5% critically endangered; while 82% of the 120 main rivers were threatened and 44% critically endangered. Of the 13 groups of estuarine biodiversity, three were in critical danger and 12% of marine biozones were under serious threat.

The Minister of Environmental Affairs and Tourism, Mr Marthinus van Schalkwyk, launched South Africa's National Biodiversity Strategy and Action Plan in June 2006. It aims to guide conservation and the management of biodiversity to ensure sustainable and equitable benefits for all communities.

The country's three globally recognised biodiversity hotspots include the Cape Floral Region, which falls entirely within South African boundaries; the Succulent Karoo, which South Africa shares with Namibia; and Maputaland-Pondoland, which South Africa shares with Mozambique and Swaziland.

The coastline meets the Atlantic, Indian and Southern oceans, which that provide exceptional habitats ranging from cool water kelp forests to tropical coral reefs.

The Cape Floral Kingdom has the highest recorded species diversity for any similar-sized temperate or tropical region in the world. It is a world heritage site.

Biodiversity is protected and promoted through institutions and initiatives such as the:

- South African Biodiversity Facility
- South African Biosystematics Initiative
- South African Environmental Observation Network
- Biobank South Africa.

Biomes

There are eight major terrestrial biomes, or habitat types, in South Africa. These biomes can, in turn, be divided into 70 veld types. The biomes are savanna, Nama-Karoo, succulent Karoo, grassland, fynbos, forest, thicket and desert. The fynbos biome is one of only six floral kingdoms worldwide.

Conservation areas

South Africa is committed to meeting the World Conservation Union (IUCN) target of 10% of land area being under protection. There is a number of management categories of protected areas in South Africa, which conform to the accepted categories of the IUCN.

Scientific reserves

These are sensitive, undisturbed areas managed for research, monitoring and the maintenance of genetic sources. Access is limited. Examples are Marion Island and the Prince Edward islands near Antarctica.

Wilderness areas

These areas are extensive in size, uninhabited, underdeveloped, and access is strictly controlled. Examples are the Cederberg Wilderness Area and Dassen Island in the Western Cape.

National parks and equivalent reserves

SANParks manages several national parks throughout South Africa, excluding in Gauteng, North West and KwaZulu-Natal. The system of national parks is representative of the country's important ecosystems and unique natural features.

Commercial and tourism-conservation development and the involvement of local communities are regarded as performance indicators. These areas include national parks proclaimed in terms of the National Environment Management: Protected Areas Act, 2003, provincial parks, nature reserves and indigenous state forests.

A transfrontier conservation area (TFCA) is a cross-border region. The conservation status of the areas within it varies from national parks, private game reserves, and communal natural-resource management areas to hunting concession areas. Though fences, highways, railway lines or other barriers separating the constituent areas, they are managed jointly for long-term sustainable use of natural resources. Unlike transfrontier parks, free movement of animals between the components of a TFCA is not always possible.

TFCAs aim to facilitate and promote regional peace, co-operation and socio-economic development. The success of TFCAs depends on community involvement. In turn, TFCAs are likely to provide local communities with opportunities to generate revenue.

TFCAs are expected to allow tourists easy movement across international boundaries into adjoining conservation areas.

The six identified TFCAs are the:

- Ais-Ais/Richtersveld Transfrontier Conservation Park
- Kgalagadi Transfrontier Park
- Limpopo-Shashe TFCA
- Great Limpopo Transfrontier Park
- Lubombo Transfrontier Conservation and Resource Area
- Maloti-Drakensberg Transfrontier Conservation and Development Area.

The National Environmental Management: Protected Areas Amendment Act, 2004 protects South Africa's biosphere reserves, which are generally formed around existing core conservation areas.

Biosphere reserves include outstanding natural beauty and biological diversity, exist in partnership with a range of interested land owners and can incorporate development, as long as it is sustainable, while still protecting terrestrial or coastal ecosystems.

National and cultural monuments

These are natural or cultural features, or both, and may include botanical gardens, zoological gardens, natural heritage sites and sites of conservation significance.

In December 1999, Robben Island, the iSimangaliso Wetlands Park (formerly the Greater St Lucia Wetlands Park) and the Cradle of Humankind were proclaimed world heritage sites by the United Nations Educational, Science and Cultural Organisation (Unesco).

The Ukhahlamba-Drakensberg Park was nominated as a mixed site. In July 2003, the site of the Mapungubwe civilisation became

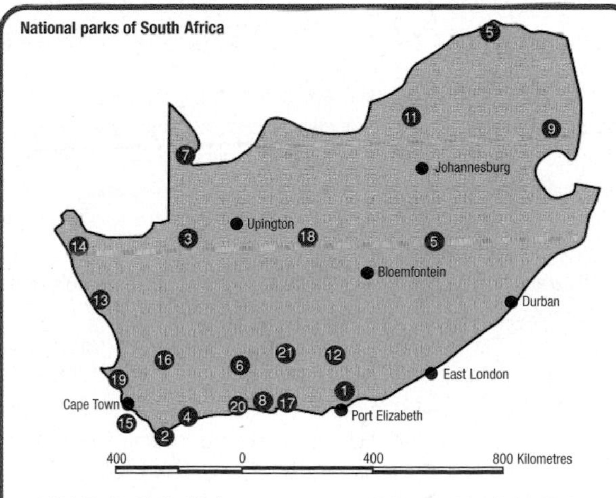

1. Addo Elephant National Park
2. Agulhas National Park
3. Augrabies Falls National Park
4. Bontebok National Park
5. Golden Gate Highlands National Park
6. Karoo National Park
7. Kgalagadi Transfrontier Park
8. Knysna National Park
9. Kruger National Park
10. Mapungubwe National Park
11. Marakele National Park
12. Mountain Zebra National Park
13. Namaqua National Park
14. Ais-Ais/Richtersveld National Park
15. Table Mountain National Park
16. Tankwa Karoo National Park
17. Tsitsikamma National Park
18. Vaalbos National Park
19. West Coast National Park
20. Wilderness National Park
21. Camdeboo National Park

the fifth heritage site. The Cape Floral Region also became a world heritage site at the end of June 2004.

The Vredefort Dome in the Free State was declared South Africa's seventh world heritage site at the 29th session of the Unesco World Heritage Conference held in Durban in July 2005, when the body met in sub-Saharan Africa for the first time.

Makapan Valley in Limpopo and the Taung Cave in North West were declared extensions of the Cradle of Humankind.

The Richtersveld Cultural and Botanical Landscape was declared in 2007 and covers an area of 160 000 hectares (ha) of dramatic mountainous desert in the north-western part of South Africa.

Habitat and wildlife management areas

These areas include conservancies; provincial, regional or private reserves created for the conservation of species, habitats or biotic communities; marshes; lakes; and nesting and feeding areas.

Sustainable-use areas

These areas emphasise the sustainable use of products in protected areas such as the Kosi Bay Lake System in KwaZulu-Natal.

Wetlands

Wetlands include a wide range of inland and coastal habitats – from mountain bogs, fens and midland marshes to swamp forests and estuaries, linked by green corridors of streambank wetlands.

The Working for Wetlands Programme focuses on wetland restoration, while maximising employment creation, support for small, medium and micro-enterprises and skills transfer.

Botanical gardens

Sanbi manages eight national botanical gardens in five of South Africa's nine provinces. The gardens collectively attract over 1,25 million visitors a year, are signatories to the International

Agenda for Botanic Gardens in Conservation, and are founding members of the African Botanic Gardens Network.

The largest garden is Kirstenbosch, situated on the eastern slopes of Table Mountain in Cape Town. It displays 5 300 indigenous plant species, and was voted one of the top seven botanical gardens in the world at the International Botanical Congress held in Missouri, United States of America, in 1999.

The other gardens in the national network are the Karoo Desert in Worcester, Harold Porter in Betty's Bay, Free State in Bloemfontein, KwaZulu-Natal in Pietermaritzburg, Lowveld in Nelspruit, Walter Sisulu in Roodepoort/Mogale City, and the Pretoria National Botanical Garden.

The Pretoria National Botanical Garden houses the National Herbarium of South Africa, the largest in the southern hemisphere.

Zoos

There are a number of zoological gardens in South Africa. The 85-ha National Zoological Gardens (NZG) of South Africa in Pretoria is one of the world's 10 best. It attracted more than 600 000 visitors in 2006. The national zoo is responsible for the biodiversity conservation centres in Lichtenburg and Mokopane, and the satellite zoo and animal park at the Emerald Animal World complex in Vanderbijlpark.

In June 2007, the Minister of Environmental Affairs and Forestry, Mr Marthinus van Schalkwyk, announced that South African National Parks (SANParks) had been allocated R574,9 million for infrastructure development and to improve facilities in the country's nature reserves, in preparation for the 2010 Soccer World Cup and beyond. Coupled with the R600 million that is being spent on the infrastructure component of the Expanded Public Works Programme, total expenditure on upgrading, as well as new rest camps, roads, fences and other infrastructure, will have exceeded R1 billion by 2010.

SANParks signed an agreement with FIFA accommodation and ticketing company, Match, providing football fans with the chance to have a truly unique African experience during the 2010 World Cup.

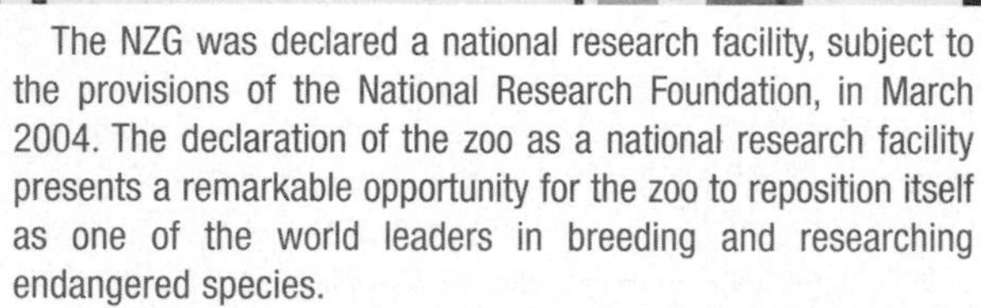

The NZG was declared a national research facility, subject to the provisions of the National Research Foundation, in March 2004. The declaration of the zoo as a national research facility presents a remarkable opportunity for the zoo to reposition itself as one of the world leaders in breeding and researching endangered species.

On 1 April 2006, the zoo's collection included 2 889 specimens of 213 mammal species, 1 418 specimens of 221 bird species, 4 639 specimens of 217 fish species, 118 specimens of 12 invertebrate species, 529 specimens of 113 reptile species, and 88 specimens of five amphibian species.

Marine protected areas (MPAs)

The MPAs are modelled on the success of the Isimangaliso Wetlands Park – with strict zoning of both marine and coastal protected areas. The four MPAs are Aliwal Shoal on the south coast of KwaZulu-Natal, the coastal and marine environment next to Pondoland in the Eastern Cape, Bird Island at Algoa Bay, and the Cape Peninsula in the Western Cape.

Some of the protection measures to be implemented in the MPAs are restrictions for people who want to fish, as well as restrictions for stowing fishing gear when fishing from a vessel.

Marine resources

The sustainable exploitation of marine resources on the one hand and the demand for fish products from local and foreign consumers on the other, pose a growing challenge globally, and South Africa, with its 3 000 km-long coastline, is no exception. The Marine Living Resources Act, 1998 sets out the broad objectives of fishery management and access rights. It also sets empowerment and broad transformation objectives for the fishing industry.

South Africa's fisheries are among the best-managed in the world.

In September 2007, South African National Parks (SANParks), announced the launch of the first South African National Parks Week.

This inaugural event, which was held from 18 to 24 September, was supported by First National Bank (funding patron).

The theme was *Know Your National Parks* and the main objectives of the week were to create awareness; instil a sense of pride in South Africa's natural, cultural and historical heritage; educate the public on the importance of nature and biodiversity; and give the public a broader understanding of the custodianship role played by SANParks in conservation issues. This initiative is in line with the organisation's conservation efforts to bring national parks closer to the people. Some of the preceding initiatives were the Kids in Parks, Kruger to Kasie and Imbewu programmes, which all aim at developing a strong stakeholder base for national parks through awareness and education.

The public had free access to all national parks during the week. Events included career-guidance exhibitions, hiking trails, photography competitions, exhibitions on various activities around the parks, game drives, evening boma braais, storytelling sessions and sports activities.

The highlight of the week's activities was the 75th anniversary celebration of the former Kalahari Gemsbok National Park, which now forms part of the Kgalagadi Transfrontier Park with Botswana.

In September 2005, South Africa took delivery of the last of four environmental-protection vessels, the *Victoria Mxenge*. The other three vessels, *Lilian Ngoyi*, *Sarah Baartman* and *Ruth First*, were received in September 2004, January 2005 and May 2005, respectively.

The patrol vessels – all named after women who showed courage, dedication and commitment to the struggle for freedom – are used in assisting with high-speed disaster relief, search and rescue, evacuations, firefighting, pollution control, towing and other emergency operations. The *Florence Mkhize* speed vessel was introduced in June 2006 to assist in combating poaching.

South African beaches participate in the Blue Flag Campaign, which works towards sustainable development at beaches and marinas. This include environmental education and information for the public, decision-makers and tourism operators.

In September 2007, the Minister of Environmental Affairs and Tourism, Mr Marthinus van Schalkwyk, published the Policy for the Development of a Sustainable Marine Aquaculture Sector in South Africa, following the completion of a two-year intensive stakeholder engagement process. The main purpose of the policy is to encourage acceleration of the development of the marine aquaculture industry.

South Africa's coastal-management policy is one of the best in the world, with the country being the first outside Europe to gain Blue Flag status for coastal management.

Some of the most popular beaches in South Africa are:

- Dolphin Beach, Jeffrey's Bay
- Humewood Beach, Port Elizabeth
- Kelly's Beach, Port Alfred
- Kings Beach, Port Elizabeth
- Wells Estate, north of Port Elizabeth
- Addington Beach, Durban
- Hibberdene Beach, south coast, KwaZulu-Natal
- Margate Main Beach, south coast, KwaZulu-Natal
- Marina/San Lameer Beach, south coast, KwaZulu-Natal
- North Beach, Durban
- Ramsgate Main Beach, south coast, KwaZulu-Natal
- Bikini Beach, Gordon's Bay
- Clifton 4th Beach, Cape Town
- Grotto Beach, Hermanus
- Hawston Beach, near Hermanus
- Kleinmond Beach, near Hermanus
- Lappiesbaai Beach, Stilbaai
- Mnandi Beach, Strandfontein.

ARTS AND CULTURE

The Department of Arts and Culture is the custodian of South Africa's diverse cultural, artistic and linguistic heritage. It is directly responsible for several public entities, including museums, art galleries, the National Archives and six playhouses.

A large proportion of the department's budget is dedicated to supporting and developing institutional infrastructure to showcase, restore and preserve South Africa's heritage for future generations.

Arts and culture initiatives

Investing in Culture

Investing in Culture is the department's flagship programme to eradicate poverty, providing the necessary skills to enable people to assume greater responsibility for their future.

The Investing in Culture Programme aims to provide access to skills and markets as a tool for urban regeneration, rural development and job creation.

Over 5 000 jobs were directly created, with 62% of the beneficiaries being women, 53% youth, and 8,5% people with disabilities. Forty percent of the funds for this programme is invested in nodal municipalities in support of integrated sustainable rural development and urban renewal programmes. Some R96,3 million went towards Investing in Culture in 2007.

National coat of arms

South Africa's coat of arms was adopted in 2000.

Symbolism

Rising sun: a life-giving force

Protea: beauty and the flowering of the nation

Ears of wheat: fertility of the land

Elephant tusks: wisdom, steadfastness and strength

Knobkierie and spear: defence of peace

Drum: love of culture

The motto, *!Ke e:/xarra//ke,* written in the Khoisan language of the !Xam people, means "diverse people unite".

Legacy projects

Monuments, museums, plaques, outdoor art, heritage trails and other symbolic representations create visible reminders of, and commemorate, the many aspects of South Africa's past.

Government has initiated several national legacy projects to establish commemorative symbols of South Africa's history and celebrate its heritage.

The legacy projects include the:

- Women's Monument
- Chief Albert Luthuli's house in KwaDukuza, KwaZulu-Natal
- Battle of Blood River/Ncome Project
- Samora Machel Project
- Nelson Mandela Museum
- Constitution Hill Project
- Sarah Baartman Monument and the Khoisan Legacy Project
- Freedom Park Project.

Construction of the Freedom Park Project, a memorial to the anti-apartheid struggle at Salvokop in Pretoria, began in 2002. It is expected to be completed in 2010.

The first phase of the R560-million memorial site was handed over to government in March 2004. This phase, costing R45 million, involved the design and construction of the Garden of Remembrance in honour of the country's departed freedom

The first-ever auction devoted exclusively to South African visual art, held in 2007 at Bonhams in London, raised about R20 million.

It comprised paintings by Irma Stern, Gerard Sekoto, Alexis Preller and Jacob Hendrik Pierneef, and all were sold well above their reserve prices.

At an earlier auction at Bonhams, paintings by Sekoto fetched a record price. Among them were nine water-colours depicting scenes inspired by the Sharpeville Massacre of 1960, a watershed moment in the South African liberation struggle, which is now annually commemorated as Human Rights Day.

The Department of Arts and Culture acquired *Recollections of Sharpeville* and *The Round Up* by Sekoto on behalf of the nation. They are on permanent loan to the South African National Gallery.

fighters. The intermediate phase commenced in October 2005 with the development of sikhumbuto and moshate. The construction of the second phase, namely a //hapo museum, the Pan African Archives (a living archive), an administration block and tiva, is planned for 2010. Other initiatives include:
- Living Heritage/Intangible Cultural Heritage: indigenous music and oral history project
- Heritage Month celebrations
- Mosadi wa Konokono (Women of Substance).

Arts and culture organisations

The following organisations play an active role in preserving and promoting South Africa's arts and culture:
- National Heritage Council
- South African Heritage Resources Agency
- South African Geographic Names Council
- National Arts Council of South Africa (NAC)
- arts institutions such as the State Theatre in Pretoria, Playhouse Company in Durban, Artscape in Cape Town, Market Theatre in Johannesburg, Performing Arts Centre of the Free State in Bloemfontein and the Windybrow Theatre in Johannesburg
- Business and Arts South Africa
- Arts and Culture Trust.

Cultural industries

The Cultural Industries Growth Strategy capitalises on the economic potential of the craft, music, film, publishing and design industries. The Department of Arts and Culture provides support in the form of financing, management capacity, advocacy and networking, by developing public-private partnerships and other initiatives that use culture as a tool for urban regeneration.

South Africa's entertainment industry is valued at about R7,4 billion. According to the *Creative Research Education and*

2007 South African Music Awards (Samas)
The 13th annual Sama ceremony took place in April 2007. Among the winners were:
- Best Female Artist: Simphiwe Dana – *The One Love*
- Best Male Artist: Vusi Mahlasela – *Naledi Ya Tsela*
- Best Duo/Group: Mafikizolo – *Six Mabone*
- Best Newcomer: Siphokazi – *Ubuntu Bam*
- Album of the Year: Simphiwe Dana – *The One Love*
- Song Of The Year: DJ Sbu – *Remember when it Rained.*

Training Enterprise South Africa Report, it employs an estimated 20 525 people. Film and television alone are worth R5,8 billion and have a strong technical base of skills and infrastructure. More than 100 000 people are employed within the music, film and television industries. A further 1,2 million people earn their living through crafts and related trade sectors.

Worldwide, the turnover of cultural industries makes it the fifth-largest economic sector, comprising design, performing arts, dance, film, television, multimedia, cultural heritage, cultural tourism, visual arts, crafts, music and publishing.

Cultural tourism

Cultural festivals, African-cuisine projects, cultural villages, heritage routes and story-telling are areas that can benefit from South Africa's booming tourism industry.

Arts festivals

In 2006, the Department of Arts and Culture provided financial support to 27 arts and culture festivals.

The National Arts Festival, held annually in July in Grahamstown, Eastern Cape, is one of the largest and most diverse arts gatherings in Africa. Other major festivals are held in Oudtshoorn, Johannesburg, Durban, Cape Town, Potchefstroom and Bloemfontein.

Theatre

South African theatre is internationally acclaimed as being unique and of top quality.

The theatre scene in South Africa is vibrant, with many active spaces across the country offering everything from indigenous drama, music, dance, cabaret and satire, to West End and Broadway hits, classical music, opera and ballet.

Music

While local music styles such as South African jazz have influenced African and world music for decades, gospel and kwaito are the most popular and most recorded styles today. Kwaito combines elements of rap, reggae, hip-hop and other styles into a distinctly South African sound.

Orchestras

The NAC is responsible for the funding of the KwaZulu-Natal, Cape and Gauteng orchestras as well as the Cape Town Jazz Orchestra.

Dance

Contemporary work ranges from normal preconceptions of movement and performance art or performance theatre, to the completely unconventional. Added to this is the African experience, which includes traditional dance inspired by wedding ceremonies, battles, rituals and everyday life.

The Dance Factory in Johannesburg provides a permanent platform for all kinds of dance and movement groups, while the Wits (University) Theatre is home to the annual Dance Umbrella, a showcase for new work.

The Cape Town City Ballet is the oldest ballet company in the country.

Ivan Vladislavic's novel, *Portrait with Keys*, was shortlisted for the prestigious Royal Society of Literature Ondaatje Prize. The R140 000-prize is awarded annually to a book of the highest literary merit – fiction, non-fiction or poetry, best evoking the spirit of a place. *Portrait with Keys* was published by Umuzi in South Africa and was expected to be published by Portobello in the United Kingdom in 2007.

Visual arts

South Africa has a range of art galleries that showcase collections of indigenous, historical and contemporary works.

Universities also play an important role in acquiring artwork of national interest. These include, among other things, collections housed in the Gertrude Posel Gallery of the University of the Witwatersrand, the University of South Africa Gallery in Pretoria, the Edoardo Villa Museum and other galleries at the University of Pretoria and a collection of contemporary Indian art at the University of Durban-Westville.

The department funded the Cape Africa initiative, which included a conference on contemporary art in Africa and the diaspora and an exhibition. Trans Cape was the first in a series of large-scale arts events organised by the Cape Africa Platform. The exhibition brought some of the most innovative and challenging contemporary African art to Cape Town. Exhibitions were held in over 20 venues and sites along a cultural route that spanned the Cape metropolitan area.

Crafts

The development of South Africa's crafts industry is an ongoing priority for government, through the Department of Arts and Culture. Numerous stakeholders are involved in various initiatives to develop this sector. The development policy focuses on addressing the co-ordination of the sector; preserving indigenous knowledge

The Department of Arts and Culture hosted the inaugural Beautiful Things Crafts Supermarket as part of the 50th anniversary of the Women's March celebrations. The event was held at the Bryntirion Estate in Pretoria, from 29 November to 3 December 2006. South Africa's first lady, Mrs Zanele Mbeki, is the patron of the exhibition. The theme for the exhibition was *Women Participation and Empowerment in the South African Craft Sector*.

The event was the culmination of selection processes that took place across the country to identify high-quality and marketable crafts products.

The craft supermarket highlighted training, business and career opportunities in the craft sector. A crafted dialogue mapped out a strategic direction of the sector in line with the Government's Programme of Action and the Accelerated and Shared Growth Initiative for South Africa.

The Lion King, the musical which has been seen by more than 52 million people across the globe, showed in South Africa in 2007 and early 2008.

A 1 900-seat theatre, specially constructed at Montecasino to accommodate the enormity of the show, is now one of 10 lyric theatres in the world.

Bringing the show to South Africa was the dream of composer and singer, Lebo M, who performed and composed songs in the first production on Broadway in 1997.

The Lion King opened in June 2007 with an entirely local cast of 53 and a 20-member orchestra backed by a technical crew of 40.

systems; acknowledging living treasures, product development and training; skills development; market access; access to information; raw material; and funding. The Department of Arts and Culture is working towards the launch of a fully functional national representative body as a one-stop service facility for South African crafters, which can also provide a networking forum.

By mid-2007, plans were under way to establish a crafts emporium to increase market access. A nationally recognised award for master crafters and a skills transfer programme will help preserve indigenous knowledge.

Film

The film and video sector generates around R518 million a year. Film production is actively supported by government; just one initiative is the Film and Television Production Rebate introduced by the Department of Trade and Industry.

South Africa offers foreign producers world-class film facilitation, logistics, facilities, talent and administration-management services.

Television production accounts for more than a third of total film/television revenue, with local-content quotas increasing the demand for programming.

The National Film and Video Foundation develops and promotes the film and video industry in South Africa. It is also involved in the development of projects that appeal to targeted audiences and have greater commercial returns. The foundation disburses grants for developing and producing feature films,

In February 2008, the Soweto Gospel Choir won a Grammy award in the category Best Traditional World Music for their album *African Spirit*.

The Grammy awards ceremony took place at the Staples Centre in Los Angeles, United States of America (USA).

Since forming in 2002, the Soweto Gospel Choir has performed in Australia, New Zealand, the United Kingdom, the USA, Europe and Singapore, becoming an international, multi-award-winning sensation.

Drawing from the churches and communities of South Africa's most famous township, the 26-member group mixes earthy rhythms with rich harmonies to express the energy of South Africa.

Accompanied by a four-piece band and percussion section, the choir gives its own unique interpretation to both traditional and contemporary music, performing in six of South Africa's 11 official languages.

short films, television series, documentaries and animation projects, as well as for bursary students. This ensures a South African presence at major local and international film markets, festivals and exhibitions. By March 2007, grants awarded totalled R26 million.

In 2006/07, the Department of Arts and Culture hosted the African Film Summit, which brought film representatives together from all over the continent, as a contribution to the New Partnership for Africa's Development's Cultural Industries Programme.

In 2006/07, the Film and Publication Board classified 6 848 films and interactive games compared with 4 829 in the previous year.

Literature

South Africa has a vibrant and rich oral tradition. This form of expression goes back many centuries and has been passed down from generation to generation as an important way of sharing advice, remembering history, telling stories and reflecting on contemporary society.

Gross turnover in the publishing sector totals about R3 billion per year.

The department has launched an Indigenous Literature Publishing Project, aimed at producing a series of publications in

The annual Cape Town Book Fair (CTBF) is a huge cultural event for the general public, with more than 300 events taking place, including readings, book launches, panel discussions and seminars.

Attendance figures at the 2007 CTBF, held from 16 to 19 June 2007, were close to double those of the inaugural event the previous year. Over 49 000 visitors attended the four-day fair at the Cape Town International Convention Centre. This didn't include the many thousands of children who also attended the event.

Representatives from 25 countries were present at the fair, including trade delegations from Gemany, France, Russia, China, India, the United Kingdom, the Netherlands, Mauritius and Switzerland.

There were 354 exhibitors (Including collectives and exhibitors) on the convention floor, with a 74/16% split between South African and inernational exhibitors, and 4% from the rest of Africa. Pavilions at the 2007 event included a magical kids' zone and a comics section, aimed at comic lovers of all ages.

different languages, by writers from different backgrounds across South Africa. This is done to stimulate the growth and development of literature in indigenous languages and generate new readerships. The National Library of South Africa (NLSA) has been tasked with republishing out-of-print African-language classics by exploring the creation of partnerships with private companies.

Museums

More than 300 of the approximately 1 000 museums in Africa are in South Africa. The Department of Arts and Culture subsidises most museums, which are otherwise autonomous.

The department pays an annual subsidy to 13 national museums, ensuring the preservation of artefacts and collections that are important to all South Africans.

National Library of South Africa

The Pretoria campus of the new R374-million NLSA was expected to be completed in November 2007.

Some R1 billion will be made available over the next three years to fund public libraries.

In 2007, the Department of Arts and Culture made an additional R200 million available for the upgrading of libraries.

The three-month long *Africa Remix* exhibition started in Johannesburg in June 2007.

Featuring 137 artworks and more than 85 artists from 25 countries on the African continent and in the diaspora, the Johannesburg Art Gallery came alive with paintings, sculptures, installations, videos, drawings, photography and design, produced by the artists over the past 10 years.

Never before in the history of the continent had an exhibition of such magnitude, focusing exclusively on Africa, been shown to African audiences.

National anthem

The national anthem is a combined version of *Nkosi Sikelel' iAfrika (God bless Africa)* and *The Call of South Africa (Die Stem).*

The national anthem

Nkosi sikelel' i Afrika
Maluphakanyisw' uphondo lwayo,
Yizwa imithandazo yethu,
Nkosi sikelela, thina lusapho lwayo.

Morena boloka setjhaba sa heso,
O fedise dintwa le matshwenyeho,
O se boloke, O se boloke setjhaba
sa heso,
Setjhaba sa South Afrika –
South Afrika.

Uit die blou van onse hemel,
Uit die diepte van ons see,
Oor ons ewige gebergtes,
Waar die kranse antwoord gee.

Sounds the call to come together,
And united we shall stand,
Let us live and strive for freedom,
In South Africa our land.

National flag

The national flag of the Republic of South Africa was brought into use on Freedom Day, 27 April 1994. The design and colours are a synopsis of the principal elements of the country's flag history.

National symbols

South Africa's national symbols are:

National animal:
Springbok

National bird:
Blue Crane

National fish:
Galjoen

National flower:
King Protea

National tree:
Real Yellowwood

National orders

The Order of the Baobab

The Order of Mapungubwe

The Order of the Companions of OR Tambo

The Order of Luthuli

The Order of Mendi for Bravery

The Order of Ikhamanga

POCKET GUIDE TO SA 2007/08 | **TOURISM**

TOURISM

Often described as "a world in one country", South Africa offers the visitor a breathtaking variety of scenery, from desert and lush forest, to soaring mountains and vast empty plains. Culturally as diverse as the landscape, many visitors are drawn to experience for themselves the miracle of the peaceful overthrow of apartheid. Others are attracted by the endless golden beaches, big game, and activities such as diving and snorkelling, or birdwatching. Whatever their reasons, visitors will find South Africa positively inviting, with world-class infrastructure, transport and accommodation.

In 2006, South Africa received nearly 8,4 million tourists. Tourism's contribution to job creation in 2006 amounted to 947 530 jobs. This was an increase of 9,6% over 2005. Between January and May 2007, foreign arrivals grew by 10%. The positive trend in foreign arrivals was reflected in arrivals at airports, which increased by 4,4% during the first five months of 2007 compared with the same peroid in 2006 and across all the regions marketed by South African Tourism. According to statistics released by Statistics South Africa, 2007 saw the highest number of recorded arrivals for the first five months of a year since 1998.

Tourism has the potential to achieve Accelerated and Shared Growth Initiative for South Africa (AsgiSA) goals, which are to boost

Figures released by the International Congress and Convention Association (ICCA) in April 2007 showed that South Africa held 64 international congresses in 2006, with the country moving up to 31st spot on the international rankings.

According to the ICCA's *Meetings Market 2006 Statistics Report*, the leading destinations in the country were Cape Town, which hosted 42 congresses, Durban with seven and Pretoria with five congresses.

Vital to Cape Town's allure has been the Cape Town International Convention Centre (CTICC), which was constructed in 2003. According to the CTICC, bookings for congresses with more than 10 000 delegates have already been made for 2008, 2009, 2012 and 2014.

economic growth to 6% by 2010 and halve poverty and unemployment by 2014. The strategy has identified tourism as one of the key economic sectors, with excellent potential for growth. As part of the growth platform targeted by AsgiSA, tourism has been set some very steep goals for the next five years: 500 000 new jobs, 8,5 million international arrivals annually and a contribution to gross domestic product of at least R100 billion a year.

Travel formalities

- Foreign visitors should check before arriving whether a visa is required. Visas are free of charge.
- Visitors must have at least one blank page in their passports.
- Tourists must have return or onward tickets.
- Visitors from yellow-fever areas must have proof of inoculation.
- Foreign tourists may have their value-added tax refunded upon departure.
- For safety, emergency and other information, tourists can phone 083 123 2345 (24 hours a day) when they are in South Africa.

Tourism in the provinces

Western Cape

The Western Cape continues to be one of the destinations most favoured by foreigners. Everyone wants to see Cape Town, one of the world's most beautiful cities.

Some attractions in Cape Town are:

- the Victoria and Alfred Waterfront
- the Company's Gardens
- the District Six Museum
- the houses of Parliament and the South African National Gallery
- a boat trip to Robben Island, the place where former President Nelson Mandela spent most of his 27 years in jail.

Table Mountain is a popular site for visitors and provides a majestic backdrop to the vibrant and friendly "Mother City". The top of the mountain can be reached by an ultramodern cableway.

Newlands is home to the world-renowned Kirstenbosch National Botanical Garden, and a well-known rugby stadium.

Cape Point, part of the Table Mountain National Park, offers many drives, walks, picnic spots and a licensed restaurant. The park has a marine protected area encompassing almost 1 000 km^2.

Hout Bay is well known for its colourful working harbour, seafood outlets, round-the-bay trips to the nearby seal island, and a harbour-front emporium that attracts many visitors.

The wine routes outside Cape Town offer the chance to taste first-class wines in arguably the most beautiful winelands in the world. Superb accommodation is available in historic towns such as Paarl, Stellenbosch and Franschhoek, as well as on many estates and farms.

Garden Route

The Garden Route has well-developed tourist infrastructure, spectacular scenery and a temperate climate, making the region popular all year round.

Not to be missed

- The city of George is at the heart of the Garden Route and the mecca of golf in the southern Cape. It is home to the renowned Fancourt Country Club and Golf Estate.
- Knysna, nestling on an estuary, is one of South Africa's favourite destinations, famous for its indigenous forests, lakes and beaches.

A number of South Africa's top-end hotels feature regularly on some of the best-known "world's best" lists, such as the World Travel Awards, *Condé Nast Traveller's Readers' Choice Survey*, and *Travel & Leisure* magazine's World's Best Awards.

These include the Cape Grace, Arabella Sheraton Grand, Table Bay and Mount Nelson hotels in Cape Town; the Grande Roche in Paarl outside Cape Town; the Plettenberg on the Western Cape Garden Route; in Gauteng, the Grace in Rosebank; and Michelangelo, Saxon and Westcliff hotels in Johannesburg.

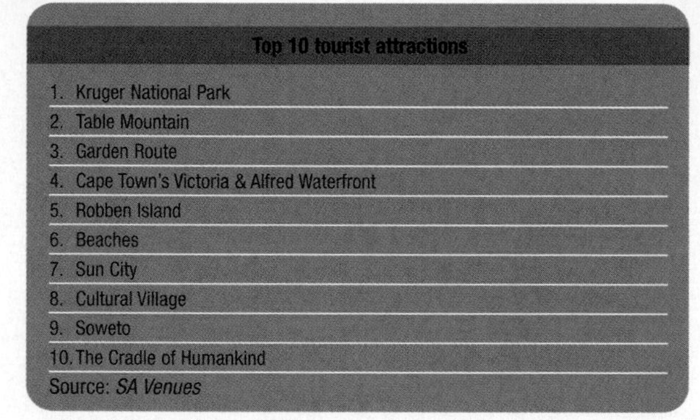

Top 10 tourist attractions

1. Kruger National Park
2. Table Mountain
3. Garden Route
4. Cape Town's Victoria & Alfred Waterfront
5. Robben Island
6. Beaches
7. Sun City
8. Cultural Village
9. Soweto
10. The Cradle of Humankind

Source: *SA Venues*

- Just 29 km from Oudtshoorn, the ostrich-feather capital of the world, at the start of the Cango Valley lie the Cango Caves, the only show caves in Africa that offer a choice of tours in various languages. The remarkable caves are a series of 30 spectacular subterranean limestone caverns. The cave system is 5,3 km long.

Central Karoo

The Central Karoo forms part of one of the world's most interesting and unique arid zones. This ancient, fossil-rich land, with the richest desert flora in the world, also has the world's largest variety of succulents.

Key attractions

- Matjiesfontein, a tiny railway village in the Karoo, offers tourists a peek into the splendour of colonial Victorian South Africa.
- Prince Albert is a well-preserved town, which nestles at the foot of the Swartberg mountains. The Fransie Pienaar Museum offers interesting cultural-history displays, a fossil room and an exhibit of gold-mining activities in the 19th century.
- The museum in Beaufort West, birthplace of heart surgeon Prof. Chris Barnard, depicts the story of the world's first heart

transplant. The Karoo National Park on the outskirts of the town is also worth a visit.

Northern Cape

The Augrabies Falls National Park, with its magnificent falls pressing through a narrow rock ravine, remains the main attraction of the Northern Cape. Game drives reveal a variety of birdlife and animals such as klipspringer, steenbok, wild cats and otters.

Key attractions

- The Big Hole in Kimberley is the largest man-made excavation in the world. The Kimberley Mine Museum is South Africa's largest full-scale open-air museum. Underground mine tours are a big attraction. The Freddy Tate Golf Museum at the Kimberley Golf Club was the first golfing museum in Africa. The Kimberley Ghost Trail has become a popular tourist attraction.
- The Robert Sobukwe House in Galeshewe was once the residence of Robert Sobukwe, an important figure in South African history and a major role-player in the rise of African political consciousness.
- The Orange River Wine Cellars Co-op in Upington offers wine-tastings and cellar tours. The South African Dried Fruit Co-operative is the second-largest in the world.
- Moffat's Mission in Kuruman is a tranquil place, featuring the house of missionary Robert Moffat, whose son-in-law was explorer David Livingstone.
- Namaqualand, the land of the Nama and San people, puts on a spectacular show in spring when its floral splendour covers vast tracts of desert in a riot of colour.
- A cultural centre at Wildebeestkuil outside Kimberley features !Xun and Khwe artwork for sale and a tour of rock engravings by these indigenous people.
- The 100-m high, 9-km long, and 2-km wide white sand dune at the Witsand Nature Reserve near Postmasburg should not be missed.

South Africa has eight world heritage sites, namely: Robben Island, iSimangaliso Wetland Park (formerly the Greater St Lucia Wetland Park), uKhahlamba-Drakensberg Park, Mapungubwe, Sterkfontein Cradle of Humankind, the Cape Floral Kingdom, the Vredefort Dome and the Richtersveld cultural and botanical landscape.

Free State

In the capital, Bloemfontein, the Eerste Raadsaal (First Parliament Building) was built in 1849 as a school and is the city's oldest surviving building that is still in its original condition. It is still used as the seat of the Provincial Legislature.

The National Women's Memorial is a sandstone obelisk, 36,5m high, which commemorates the women and children who died in concentration camps during the Anglo-Boer/South African War.

Not to be missed

- Clarens, the jewel of the Free State, is surrounded by spectacular scenery and boasts many art galleries.
- The Golden Gate Highlands National Park outside Clarens has beautiful sandstone rock formations.
- The King's Park Rose Garden in Bloemfontein boasts more than 4 000 rose bushes.
- The Vredefort Dome, a world heritage site, is the oldest and largest meteorite impact site in the world. It was formed about two billion years ago when a giant meteorite hit Earth.

Eastern Cape

The Eastern Cape is the only province in South Africa, and one of the few places on Earth, where all seven biomes (major vegetation types) converge.

What to see and do

- The rugged beauty of the Wild Coast, including Hole-in-the-Wall.
- Port Elizabeth, the sunshine capital of the Eastern Cape, with its friendly people and excellent beaches.
- The Red Location Museum of the People's Struggle in New Brighton, Port Elizabeth – winner of three international awards.
- The Tsitsikamma National Park, forests and rivers.
- East London, South Africa's only river port, originally established

as a supply port to serve the British military headquarters at King William's Town.
- The village of Qunu, former President Mandela's childhood home.
- The world's highest bungee jump (216 m) at the Bloukrans Bridge over the Storms River.
- Outstanding and varied game reserves, including the Addo Elephant, Mountain Zebra and Mkambati parks.

Limpopo

Limpopo is well endowed with cultural diversity, historical sites and tourist attractions, and an excellent destination for get-away-from-it-all luxury holidays in the bush.

Not to be missed

- The Mokopane vicinity has several nature reserves. The Arend Dieperink Museum offers a fine cultural-historical collection, while the Makapan caves are famous for their fossils. The Makapan Valley is the only cultural-heritage site of its kind. It reflects the history of the Ndebele people and resistance wars dating back 151 years. The fossil hominid sites of Sterkfontein include Makapan Valley.
- With its outstanding game reserves, the Thabazimbi district is one of the fastest-growing ecotourism areas in South Africa.
- Bela-Bela is well known among South Africans, and increasingly foreigners, for its hot-water springs, fun water slides and scenery.
- The Waterberg mountain range is rich in indigenous trees, streams, springs, wetlands, birdlife and dramatic vistas.
- The Modjadji Nature Reserve, north of Tzaneen, is named after the legendary Rain Queen, Modjadji, who inspired Rider Haggard's *She*.
- Phalaborwa has one of the country's top-rated golf courses – just watch out for animals on the fairways!
- The Schoemansdal Voortrekker Town and Museum, a short drive west of Makhado, is built on the site of an original

Voortrekker village and depicts their lifestyle in the mid-18th century.
- the Big Tree in the Mutale district is one of the largest known baobabs in southern Africa.

North West

The province abounds with attractions, including wild animals and fun nights at the famous Sun City and Lost City resorts.

Key attractions

- The Historic Route of Mafikeng includes the town of Mafikeng, which was besieged by the Boers during the Anglo-Boer/South African War.

In 2006, there was a 6,4% increase in occupancy rates at hotels and at other forms of accommodation, compared with 2005.

Figures in Statistics South Africa's (Stats SA) tourist accommodation survey, released in March 2007, showed that the number of stay unit nights sold during 2006 increased from 17 227 200 individual stays in 2005 to 18 330 900.

A stay unit is defined as a unit of accommodation available to be let out to guests, be it a hotel room or a powered site in a caravan park.

Furthermore, the number of stay unit nights sold during the fourth quarter of 2006 increased by 10,3%, from 4 544 300 to 5 014 500, compared with the fourth quarter of 2005.

The occupancy rate for 2006 compared with 2005 increased by 5,9%, Income from accommodation in the fourth quarter of 2006 increased by 25,3%, totalling R528,1 million, compared with the fourth quarter of 2005.

The major contributors to the increase of 25,3% were hotels (13,8%), other accommodation (6,6%) and guest houses and guest farms (4,9%).

The occupancy rate of 54,6% reported in November 2006 was the highest since the beginning of the survey in September 2004.

Stats SA's figures also indicated that income from accommodation in 2006 increased by 17,7%, totalling almost R1,3 billion, compared with 2005.The major contributors to the increase were hotels (10%), other accommodation (4,9%) and guest houses and guest farms (2,9%).

- The Groot Marico region, mampoer (moonshine) country, is associated with author Herman Charles Bosman.
- The Hartbeespoort Dam is popular for weekend outings, yachting and golf.
- The Pilanesberg National Park supports over 7 000 head of game, including the Big Five and 350 bird species.
- Sun City and the Palace of the Lost City are hugely popular tourist attractions offering gambling, golf, extravaganza shows, water sport and an artificial sea.
- The Taung skull fossil site is an extension of the Sterkfontein hominid sites. The site marks the place where the celebrated Taung skull – a specimen of the species *Australopithecus africanus* – was found in 1924.
- Madikwe Game Reserve, one of South Africa's largest game reserves, is home to 66 large mammal species, including the Big Five, and about 300 resident and migrant bird species.

Mpumalanga

Mpumalanga – the place where the sun rises – lies in the north-eastern part of South Africa, bordered by Mozambique to the east and the Kingdom of Swaziland to the south-east.

Scenic beauty and wildlife are abundant.

Tourist attractions

- Historical sites and villages, old wagon routes and monuments mark the lives of the characters who came to Mpumalanga seeking their fortune. The town of Pilgrim's Rest is a living monument reflecting the region's gold-fever period.
- The Blyde River Canyon Nature Reserve near Graskop has striking rock formations and a rich diversity of plants.
- Within the Blyde River Canyon Nature Reserve, the Bourke's Luck potholes were formed by river erosion and the action of flood water. The spectacular Blyde River Canyon is a 26-km long gorge carved out of the face of the escarpment. It is the world's third-largest canyon and the only green canyon.

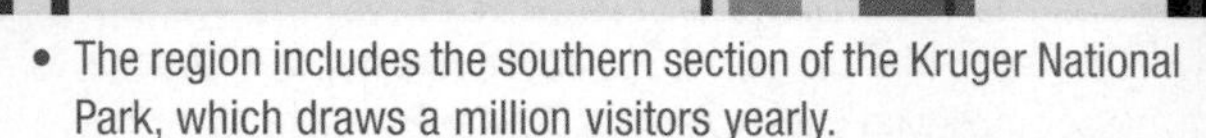

- The region includes the southern section of the Kruger National Park, which draws a million visitors yearly.
- An annual frog-watching festival is held at Chrissiesmeer, South Africa's largest freshwater lake.
- Dullstroom is popular with trout- and fly-fishing enthusiasts.

Gauteng

Gauteng, the economic heart of southern Africa, offers a vibrant business environment and many tourist attractions, including a rainbow of ecological and cultural diversity.

Key attractions

- The Vaal Dam covers some 300 km^2 and is a popular venue for water sport. Numerous resorts line the shore. The dam is also popular with birders and anglers.
- The Sterkfontein caves near Krugersdorp are the site of the discovery of the skull of the famous Mrs Ples, an estimated 2,5-million-year-old hominid fossil; and Little Foot, an almost complete hominid skeleton more than 3,3 million years old.
- The Walter Sisulu National Botanical Garden has a 70-m high waterfall, stunning indigenous plant displays and a breeding pair of black eagles.
- There is a ring of hills a kilometre in diameter and 100 m high just 40 km north of Pretoria. These hills are the walls of the Tswaing Meteorite Crater, left by an asteroid 200 000 years ago.
- The National Zoological Gardens in Pretoria is considered one of the 10 best in the world.
- The Constitution Hill Precinct is set to become one of South Africa's most popular landmarks.
- The old mining town of Cullinan is where the world's biggest diamond, the 3106-carat Cullinan diamond, was found.
- A guided tour of Soweto leaves a lasting impression of this vast community's life and struggle against apartheid.

- The Apartheid Museum in Johannesburg tells the story of the legacy of apartheid through photographs, film and artefacts.
- The Union Buildings in Pretoria was the venue for the inauguration of presidents Nelson Mandela and Thabo Mbeki.

KwaZulu-Natal

Also known as the Zulu Kingdom, KwaZulu-Natal is a combination of natural wonders, fascinating culture and ultra-modern facilities.

Durban's Golden Mile skirts the main beaches of the Indian Ocean. Drawcards include an amusement centre, paddling pools, paved walkways and fountains.

Enticing attractions

- The uShaka Marine World theme park comprises an oceanarium, dolphinarium and oceanographic research institute situated on Durban's Point.
- Spot dolphins or laze the days away on the coastline between the Umdloti and Tugela rivers – the Dolphin Coast.
- The Hluhluwe-Umfolozi Park, one of the largest game parks in South Africa is home to the Big Five, as well as cheetah and wild dogs.
- The eMakhosini Valley, birthplace of King Shaka, and the Valley of Zulu Kings give visitors insight into the Zulu nation's history and culture.
- The iSimangaliso Wetland Park (formerly the Greater St Lucia Wetland Park) is one of the highest forested dunes in the world, and has an abundance of fish and birds.
- The Banana Express runs between Umkomaas and the Wild Coast.
- The Royal Natal National Park offers many scenic highlights, including the Amphitheatre, Mont-aux-Sources and the Tugela falls.
- The Battlefields Route in northern KwaZulu-Natal has the

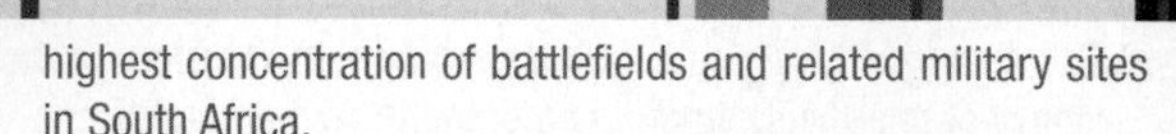

highest concentration of battlefields and related military sites in South Africa.

- Every year around June or July, millions of sardines leave their home on the Agulhas banks and move up to the coast of Mozambique. Thousands of dolphins, Cape gannets, sharks and game fish follow the "sardine run" northwards.

Things to see and do in South Africa

Just a few of the attractions that make South Africa an exceptional destination:

- breathtaking Cape Town with its laid-back, welcoming attitude and vibrant nightlife, nestling at the foot of Table Mountain
- Cape Point
- Robben Island in Cape Town's Table Bay where former President Mandela was incarcerated
- the delights of Sun City and the Lost City, and many other first-rate casino resorts
- walking in the spectacular Drakensberg mountains
- the chance to learn how to say "hello" in 11 official languages
- the country's Blue Flag beaches
- the variety of national parks and transfrontier conservation areas
- seven world heritage sites
- the lilac-breasted roller, the blue crane and the other 900 bird species to be spotted in southern Africa
- the Big Five and other wild animals found in the many parks and game reserves

The Tourism Enterprise Programme (TEP) is a public-private partnership between the Department of Environmental Affairs and Tourism and the Business Trust. TEP facilitates the growth of tourism small, medium and micro-enterprises (SMMEs) by establishing linkages between SMMEs and larger customers. For 2006/07, the department provided R42 million in funding to TEP. Some 1 683 SMMEs were trained, 6 525 jobs were created and 368 transactions were facilitated, of which 225 were Black Economic Empowerment transactions.

- the strange halfmens (half-human) and the exotic baobab, just some of South Africa's many amazing trees and plants
- battlefields on which imperial Britain fought Zulus, Xhosas and Boers
- the dazzling floral displays which carpet Namaqualand yearly
- the mountains, forests and beaches of the Garden Route
- the silence and solitude of the Karoo's wide-open spaces
- country hospitality (and home cooking) in hundreds of picturesque towns and villages across South Africa

- South Africa has the third-highest level of biodiversity in the world.
- The three-billion-year-old rocks around Barberton, Mpumalanga, are among the oldest in the world.
- The 850-m high Tugela Falls is the second-highest waterfall in the world.
- Most of the globe's proto-mammalian fossils are found In the Karoo, which has also yielded a 280-million-year-old fossilised shark.
- Known for its astronomy observatory, the Karoo town of Sutherland is one of the most geologically stable places on Earth, yet has a 66-million-year-old volcano that is not officially extinct.
- The Free State town of Jagersfontein has the deepest vertical man-made hole in the world.
- The world's smallest succulent plants (less than 10 mm) and the largest – the Baobab tree – are found in South Africa.
- Lake Funduzi in Venda might be te world's only inland freshwater lake formed by a landslide.
- Vilakazi Street in Soweto is the only street in the world where two Nobel Peace Prize winners, namely Mr Nelson Mandela and Archbishop Desmond Tutu, have houses.
- South Africa, Zimbabwe and Mozambique are removing fences between their countries' game parks to create a 35 000 km^2 game park that will become the world's largest conservation area.
- South Africa is ranked first in the world for its floral kingdom.

Source: South Africa The Good News

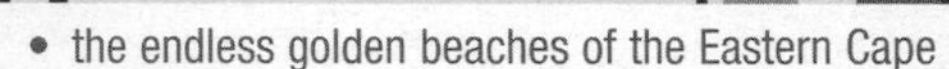

- the endless golden beaches of the Eastern Cape
- fly-fishing in stunning scenery with first-class accommodation
- fabulous golf courses that produced the likes of Gary Player, Ernie Els and Retief Goosen
- an array of cultural villages, arts festivals, rock paintings and museums
- the adrenaline rush of the many adventure-tourism opportunities available in the country.

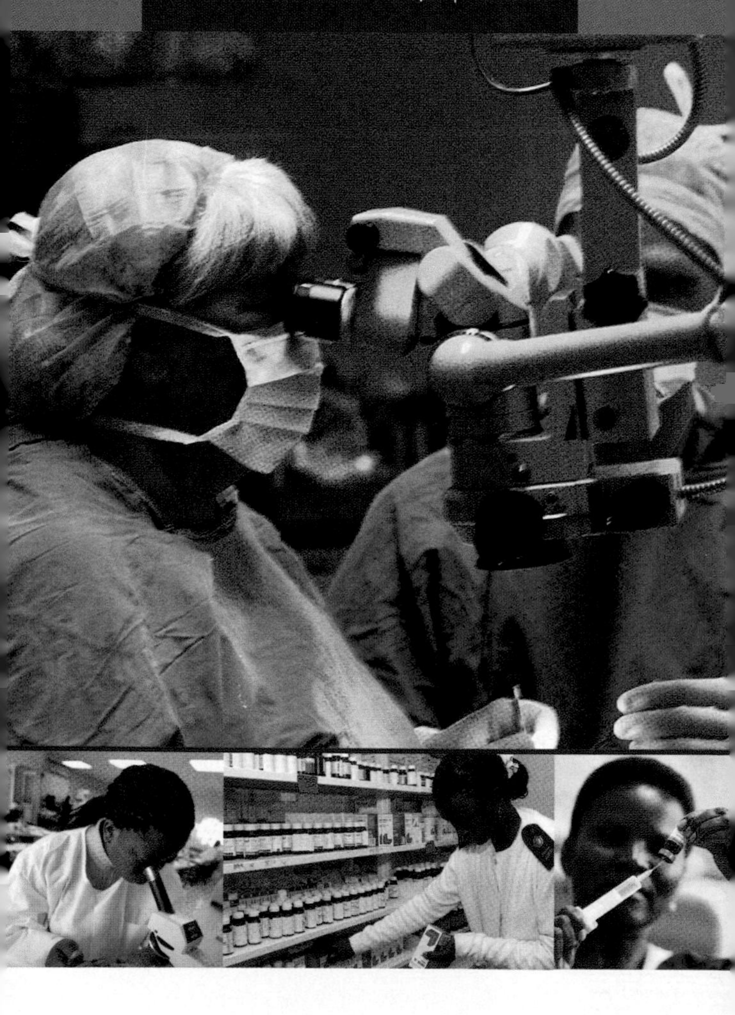

The Department of Health promotes the health of all South Africans through a caring and effective national health system (NHS) based on the primary healthcare (PHC) approach.

In 1994, government started providing free PHC services for children under six years, and pregnant and lactating women. During the same period, government initiated a programme that resulted in more than 1 500 clinics being built or upgraded between 1994 and July 2007.

Where necessary, patients with complications are referred to higher levels of care, such as hospitals.

PHC services include immunisation, communicable and endemic disease prevention, maternity care, screening of children, integrated management of childhood illnesses and child healthcare, health promotion, counselling, management of chronic diseases and diseases of older persons, rehabilitation, accident and emergency services, family planning, and oral health.

Districts countrywide are integrating mental health and substance abuse into their PHC services.

During 2006/07, the Healthy Lifestyles Campaign was expanded to districts and local municipalities, schools and places of work. Thousands of schools were assisted in establishing school-based food gardens, implementing tobacco-control programmes, and implementing a strategy on diet, physical activity and health. Health promoters in all provinces will be trained to implement this strategy.

Health-delivery system

The major emphasis in developing health services at provincial level has been the shift from curative hospital-based healthcare to heath services provided in an integrated, community-based manner. Patients in provincial hospitals pay for examinations and treatment in accordance with their income and number of dependants. A provincial government may partly or entirely finance patients' treatment.

Clinics
A network of mobile clinics run by government forms the backbone of primary and preventive healthcare.

Hospitals
In 2007, there were about 400 public hospitals in South Africa serving more than 47 million people, and 200 private hospitals with 26 00 beds.

Hospital management was strengthened in various ways in all nine provinces during 2006/07. In 2007/08, the Department of Health envisaged ensuring that at least 50% of hospital managers were enrolled in a formal hospital-management training programme.

The department also helped provinces implement cost centres in 27 hospitals during 2006/07, as part of the strategy to strengthen financial management and accountability. Four hospitals implemented electronic cost centres and 23 developed manual cost centres.

The Hospital Revitalisation Programme entered its fifth year in 2007, and continues to illustrate the importance of an integrated strategy for improving health-service delivery. The programme

As from January 2007, 4 565 professionals from 10 health professional groups commenced their internship and community service placements:
- dentists – 188
- pharmacists – 469
- clinical psychologists – 121
- dieticians – 140
- occupational therapists – 250
- physiotherapists – 340
- radiographers – 284
- speech, language and hearing therapists – 145
- doctors – 1 230
- medical interns – 1 398.

Nurses were expected to start their community service in January 2008.

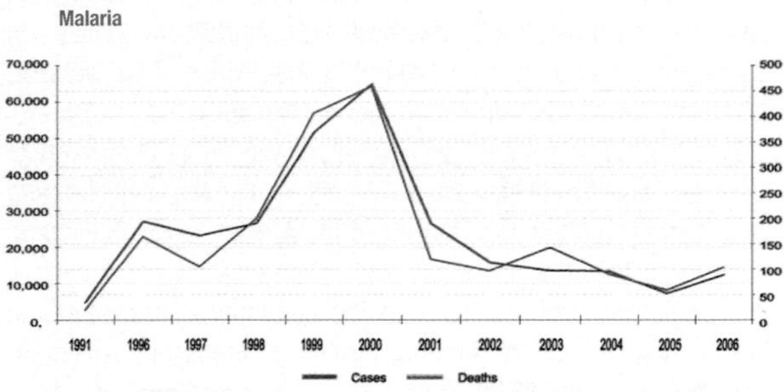

Source: *Development Indicators*

includes improving infrastructure, health technology (equipment), quality of care, and the management and organisational development within targeted hospitals in the programme. During 2006/07, four new hospitals were officially opened. A total of 43 hospital projects were active during 2006. In 2007/08, there were 39 active projects.

Emergency medical services (EMS)

Although provinces run their own EMS, including ambulance services, training is standardised nationally.

Private ambulance services also serve the community. Some of these also render aeromedical services.

By June 2007, the Department of Health had developed a national EMS plan for the 2010 FIFA World Cup™.

Legislation

The National Health Act, 2003 provides a framework for a single health system for South Africa. It highlights the rights and responsibilities of health-providers and users, and ensures broader community participation in healthcare delivery from the level of health facility up to national level.

The Department of Health has established a traditional medicine directorate to develop and implement policy on traditional medicine and co-ordinate the activities of the National Reference Centre for African Traditional Medicine.

President Thabo Mbeki appointed a presidential task team to institutionalise African traditional medicine. The Minister of Health was elected to chair the Bureau of the African Health Ministers' meeting of the African Union (AU), charged with conducting a mid-term review of progress on the continent in implementing the African Decade of African Traditional Medicine, which AU heads of state adopted.

The Nursing Act, 2005 addresses developments in nursing education and the classification of nurses into categories. This Act also assists in introducing the nursing profession to the

Registered medical interns, practitioners and dentists, 2002 – 2007

	2002	April 2007
Dentists	4 560	4 799
Medical interns	2 306	2 864
Medical practitioners	30 271	33 220

Source: Health Professions Council of South Africa

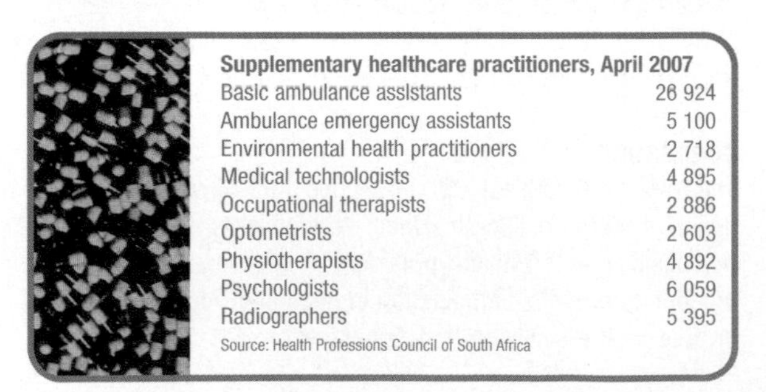

Supplementary healthcare practitioners, April 2007

Basic ambulance assistants	26 924
Ambulance emergency assistants	5 100
Environmental health practitioners	2 718
Medical technologists	4 895
Occupational therapists	2 886
Optometrists	2 603
Physiotherapists	4 892
Psychologists	6 059
Radiographers	5 395

Source: Health Professions Council of South Africa

Registered and enrolled nurses, 2007	
	2007
Registered nurses and midwives	101 295
Enrolled nurses and midwives	39 305
Nursing auxiliaries	56 314
Students in training	27 924

Source: South African Nursing Council

community-service programme, which already covers all other categories of health professionals.

The Mental Healthcare Act, 2002 enforces the culture of human rights within the mental-health service and ensures that mental-health patients are treated with respect and dignity.

Health team

The core team of practising medical practioners in South Africa consists of:

- 33 220 registered doctors (April 2006)
- 4 799 dentists (April 2006)
- 10 948 pharmacists (2007)
- 101 295 registered nurses and midwives (2006).

South Africa has a shortage of certain health professionals such as physiotherapists, dieticians and radiographers.

National Health Laboratory Service (NHLS)

The NHLS is the largest diagnostic pathology service in South Africa with over 250 laboratories serving 80% of the country's population. All laboratories provide laboratory diagnostic services to the national and provincial departments of health, provincial hospitals, local governments and medical practitioners.

The NHLS conducts health-related research appropriate to the needs of the broader population, including research into HIV and AIDS, tuberculosis (TB), malaria, pneumococcal infections,

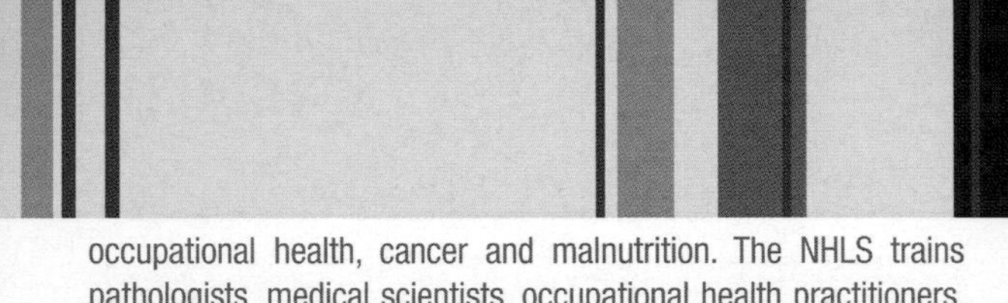

occupational health, cancer and malnutrition. The NHLS trains pathologists, medical scientists, occupational health practitioners, technologists and technicians in pathology disciplines.

Medical schemes

The Council of Medical Schemes regulates more than 160 registered private medical schemes, with a total annual contribution of about R35 billion.

Community health

The most common communicable diseases in South Africa are TB, malaria, measles and sexually transmitted infections (STIs).

In South Africa, it is recommended that children under the age of five be immunised against the most common childhood diseases. Immunisation should be administered at birth, six, 10 and 14 weeks, nine months, 18 months and five years of age. Children are inoculated against polio, TB, diphtheria, pertussis, tetanus, *haemophilus influenzae* type B, hepatitis B and measles.

The set routine immunisation coverage target for fully immunised children under one year is 90%. In 2007, the overall routine immunisation coverage for South Africa was 83%. The last confirmed case of polio was reported in 1989.

Malaria is endemic to the low-altitude areas of Limpopo, Mpumalanga and north-eastern KwaZulu-Natal. About 10% of the population lives in malaria-risk areas. The highest-risk area

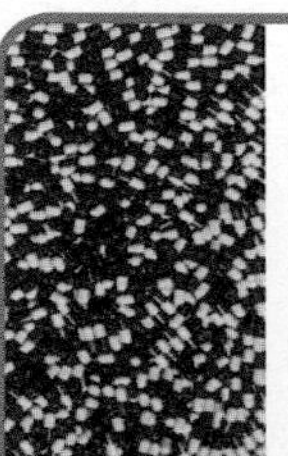

During 2006/07, the Department of Health undertook various activities to reduce the burden of disease from non-communicable diseases, including:
- a number of health-screening activities
- the "Move for Health" Programme to encourage physical activities
- nutrition programmes, including the provision of vitamins and the establishment of food gardens
- programmes to reduce risky behaviour such as smoking, and alcohol and drug abuse.

is a strip of about 100 km along the Zimbabwe, Mozambique and Swaziland borders.

The success of the country's malaria-control programme has not been limited to affected areas in South Africa, but extended to other countries in the Southern African Development Community (SADC) region, where South Africa has initiated joint efforts with its neighbours to control malaria.

The department has strengthened the roll-back malaria strategy in KwaZulu-Natal, Limpopo and Mpumalanga, where malaria is endemic.

Integrated Management of Childhood Illnesses (IMCI)

IMCI promotes child health and improves child survival as part of the National Plan of Action for Children. It is being instituted as part of the Department of Health's policy on the NHS for Universal Primary Care.

South Africa's nurses and doctors are well trained to treat all diseases by using the IMCI Strategy. Diseases such as pneumonia, malaria, meningitis, diarrhoea and malnutrition are easily managed. In South Africa, the IMCI Strategy has been adapted to include HIV assessment and classification.

The strategy tries to integrate all interventions relating to children to ensure that a package of care is offered to each child.

During 2006, the department expanded the IMCI Strategy to health subdistricts, having attained 100% saturation at health-district level in 2005. More than 60% of healthcare-providers managing children in 48% of the subdistricts were IMCI-trained. By June 2007, 60% of healthcare facilities had at least one IMCI-trained healthcare-provider. Another strategy to improve child health is to provide vitamin A supplementation to all infants between six and 11 months of age.

Tuberculosis

In 2006, there were more than 300 000 TB cases. Free testing is available at public clinics countrywide.

Efforts have now been brought to bear on this disease. These include:

- implementing the Directly Observed Treatment Strategy
- establishing a national TB team
- establishing a countrywide reporting system
- creating a TB crisis-management plan
- providing free testing at public clinics.

HIV and AIDS

The Department of Health has developed the National Strategic Plan (NSP) for HIV and AIDS and STIs for 2007 to 2011, which builds on the gains of the Strategic Plan for 2000 to 2005.

The plan places a new emphasis on treatment and prevention. It also spells out clear, quantified targets, and places a high priority on monitoring and evaluation.

The newly restructured South African National AIDS Council (SANAC), headed by Deputy President Phumzile Mlambo-Ngcuka, endorsed the plan.

The primary goal of the NSP is to reduce the rate of new HIV infections and to mitigate the impact of AIDS on individuals, families and communities.

The new plan aims to reduce new infections by 2011 and provides an appropriate package of treatment, care and support services.

The package provided by the plan includes counselling and testing services as an entry point, healthy lifestyle interventions,

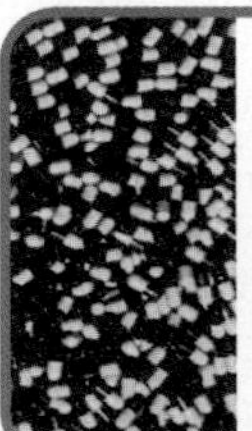

In 2006, South Africa was declared free of the wild polio virus by the Africa Regional Certification Commission, a subcommittee of the Global Certification Commission.

This is an independent commission that works closely with the World Health Organisation. During 2007/08, the department continued its surveillance of polio-free certification indicators, which will be sustained until the Global Certification Commission declares global eradication of polio.

including nutritional support, treatment of opportunistic infections, antiretroviral (ARV) therapy and monitoring, and evaluation to assess progress and share research.

The Government first announced South Africa's ARV treatment programme in 2006. At that time, over 130 000 people were receiving ARV treatment through government programmes, on top of the more than 80 000 people receiving ARV treatment from the private healthcare sector. By the end of April 2007, 282 200 patients were receiving ARVs. At least 335 public health facilities had been accredited to provide this service, including nine correctional service centres.

In the 2007/08 Budget presented In February 2007, the Minister of Finance, Mr Trevor Manuel, announced an additional R1,65 billion for comprehensive treatment. With this additional funding over a three-year period, the number of people receiving comprehensive treatment against HIV and AIDS is expected to double, according to the *2007 Budget Review*.

Government departments are expected to spend in excess of R5 billion on dedicated HIV and AIDS programmes yearly by 2009/10.

During 2006/07, the department published the *2005 National HIV and Syphilis Antenatal Sero-Prevalence Survey*, which revealed that HIV prevalence in South Africa was stabilising. Furthermore, HIV prevalence among women younger than 20 years continued to decline, which suggested a decline in new cases.

SANAC has served as an important platform for partnerships

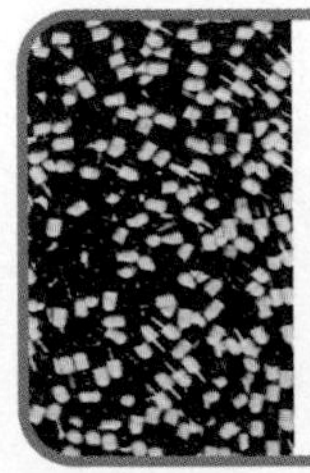

Efforts to control malaria continue to pay dividends. Between June 2006 and April 2007, 4 404 malaria cases were reported, compared with 11 246 cases reported for June 2005 to April 2006. During the same time, the number of deaths decreased from 88 to 31. The main reasons for this decline include indoor residual spraying using DDT, which has now been accepted by the World Health Organisation as the significant tool in malaria control after many years of South Africa's engagement on this issue.

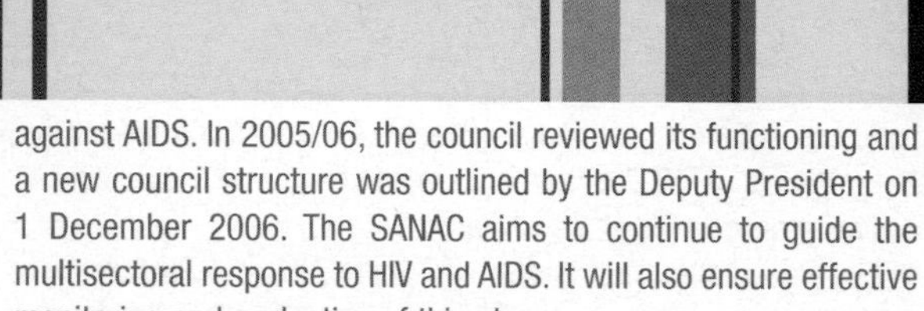

against AIDS. In 2005/06, the council reviewed its functioning and a new council structure was outlined by the Deputy President on 1 December 2006. The SANAC aims to continue to guide the multisectoral response to HIV and AIDS. It will also ensure effective monitoring and evaluation of this plan.

In its capacity as the country's co-ordinating mechanism for the Global Fund to Fight AIDS, TB and malaria, the SANAC supported a successful application for approximately R200 million towards the fight against HIV and AIDS in KwaZulu-Natal, where government, non-governmental organisations (NGOs), academia and the private sector will collaborate to implement programmes aimed at capacity-building, and preventing and treating HIV and AIDS.

In 2006/07, 439 million male condoms and three million female condoms were distributed.

HIV and AIDS vaccine research and development

The South African AIDS Vaccine Initiative was established in 1999 to develop and test an affordable, effective, and locally relevant HIV and AIDS vaccine for southern Africa.

Home- and community-based care (HCBC)

HCBC is a central tenet of the care component of the comprehensive response to HIV and AIDS. This service is provided mainly through NGOs and community-based organisations.

The objective of the HCBC Programme is to ensure:

- access to care, and follow-up through a functional referral system
- that children and families who are affected and infected by HIV and AIDS access social-welfare services within their communities.

In 2006/07, the Department of Health supported HCBC programmes in 60% of subdistricts and more than 493 000 patients with debilitating conditions received nutritional support.

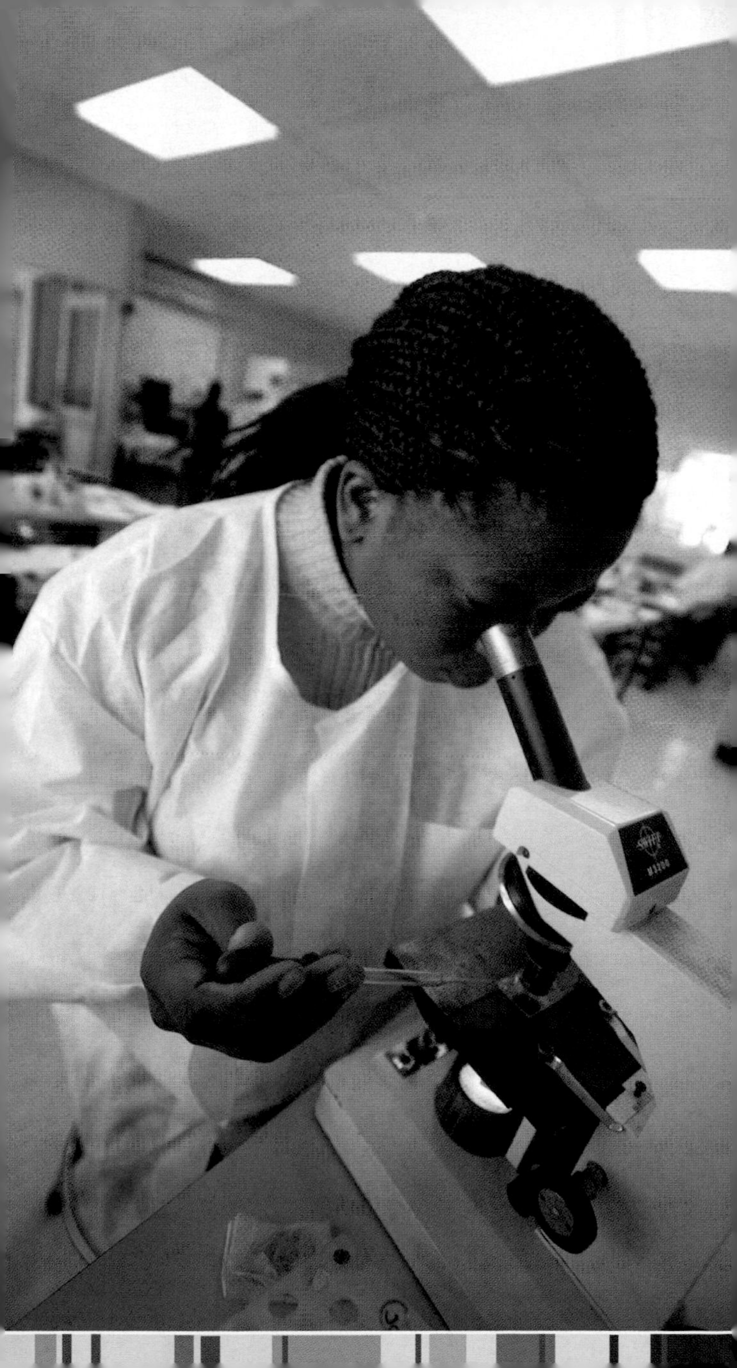

GM
NOKIA
PEPSI
NOKIA
PEPSI
NOKIA
PEPSI
NOKIA
PEPSI

2010 FIFA WOR
ZUR
SOUTH AFRICA

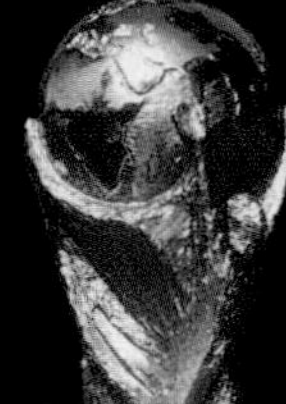

SPORT AND RECREATION

South Africans have more than made their mark in international sport. The country has successfully hosted major international events, including the rugby, cricket and women's golf world cups and will be sure to impress when it hosts the FIFA World Cup in 2010™.

Sport is a unifying factor as was proven again in 2007, when South Africa won the Rugby World Cup for the second time.

Sport in South Africa is a multibillion-rand industry and contributes more than 2% to the country's gross domestic product.

Sport and Recreation South Africa (SRSA) aims to improve the quality of life of all South Africans by promoting participation in sport and recreation in the country, and through the participation of sportspeople and teams in international sporting events.

Mass participation

The Siyadlala Mass Participation Programme (SMPP) is the cradle of community sports in South Africa. The programme was launched in 2005 to facilitate access to sport and recreation to as many South Africans as possible, especially those from historically disadvantaged communities.

SRSA launched the programme with a budget of R20 million. The budget has since increased to R194 million with the inclusion of school sport and club development. Hubs (centres of activity) increased from 36 to 289 with over two million participations in various activities, ranging from indigenous games, rugby, soccer, netball, baseball, general gymnastics, hockey, aerobics, handball, boxing, cricket, swimming, dance sport, volleyball, and basketball. The eventual aim is to ensure that no child has to walk more than five kilometres to access an activity hub anywhere in the country. The ideal is to establish at least one hub in every ward in every municipality across South Africa.

The SMPP is expected to enable the sport sector to contribute to the Accelerated and Shared Growth Initiative for South Africa. Some 8 000 unemployed young people were expected to be recruited and trained by mid-2007. The trained youth will then be employed as activity co-ordinators. Research done in the hubs indicates that small stipends given to these co-ordinators contribute to feeding up to eight families in some instances. The SMPP has also trained over 2 000 young volunteers in sport and recreation administration, over 1 500 entry-level coaches, over 1 200 referees, and over 2 000 people in event management and first aid.

Indigenous games

The forth annual National Indigenous Games Festival took place in Mdantsane, East London, in August 2007. The festival was titled *Celebrating South African Poetry, Demonstrating Our Heritage Through Indigenous Games.* The festival started on 31 August and ended on 2 September 2007. It was won by North West.

The indigenous games are ugqaphu/kgati/ntimo, diketo/upuca/magave, morabaraba/mlabalaba, ncuva/ntijwa/tsoro/tshimaya/moruba, dibeke/diwiki/snuka/skununu/umabhorisha, Jukskei, and kho-kho. The eighth game, lintonga/melamu/Izinduku, was introduced at a later stage.

School sport

In 2005, the ministries of education and of sport and recreation signed a partnership agreement to resuscitate and revitalise school sports and physical education programmes. The SRSA has established the DIrectorate of School Sport within the Chief Directorate: Mass Participation. It consists of two sections: Competitive School Sport and Mass Participation in Schools Sport. This programme reaches about 1 600 schools nationally and focuses on capacity-building, providing sports equipment for use at events, sustaining the programme by suppporting local sports assistants and local leagues, and providing logistical support.

International achievements in 2007

All Africa Games

The All Africa Games were held in July 2007 in Algiers, Algeria. Egypt beat Algeria on the medals table, with South Africa securing third spot behind the two North African nations.

In total, 27 sporting disciplines were contested, with about 8 000 athletes from 52 countries participating.

South Africa dominated in the swimming pool, winning 53 medals, with the next best being Algeria's 16 and Zimbabwe's 15. South Africa's men won 12 golds, seven silvers and seven bronzes, while the women claimed 13 gold medals, nine silvers, and five bronzes.

Paraplegic superstar Natalie du Toit excelled in the relays and won individual gold in the 1 500-metres (m) freestyle.

South Africa also performed well in athletics, winning the most medals with 24, although Algeria won the most golds – nine to South Africa's seven.South Africa's men achieved the best results of any country, with the highlight provided by the 400-m hurdlers.

They finished 1-2-3, with LJ van Zyl taking gold in 48,74 seconds (sec), while Pieter de Villiers was awarded silver ahead of Alwyn Myburgh, even though both athletes were timed at 48,91 sec.

In wheelchair athletics, South Africa finished second on the table, picking up 14 medals, of which eight were for wins. There was also a gold medal for the wheelchair basketball team.

South African sailors led the way in a competition that featured women's and mixed racing. Of the nine golds on offer, South Africa picked up six. In another water-based sport, rowing, South Africa finished just one gold behind Algeria, although the team's seven-medal achievement was one better than the hosts.

After a tight fight against Nigeria, South Africa's badminton team finished top of the table, winning two golds, three silvers, and three bronzes.

South Africa was also number one in cycling, with three gold medals out of the six on offer, and six medals in all.

The wrestling team secured three gold medals and five bronzes to total eight medals.

South Africa's gymnasts claimed 12 medals, with two golds amongthem.

In chess, South Africa picked up 10 medals, but only one of them was gold.

Due to a lack of hockey facilities in Algeria, an Olympic qualifying tournament was held in Nairobi at the same time as the All Africa Games. Only the winners would qualify for Beijing 2008.

South Africa's women had no problems whatsoever in securing their spot, beating Kenya 5-0 in the final.

Matters were tougher for the men who faced their traditional rivals Egypt for the prized Olympic place as African champions.

The Egyptians took the lead in the 34th minute through Sameh Metwaly, but just five minutes later Emile Smith levelled for South Africa. With only six minutes remaining, Geoff Abbot scored the winner for South Africa.

Taking place every four years, in the year before the Olympic Games, the next All Africa Games, the 10th edition, will be hosted by Lusaka, Zambia, in 2011.

Rugby World Cup

In September 2007, in its first match of the 2007 Rugby World Cup, South Africa beat Samoa 59-7. Wing Bryan Habana scored four tries.

Any lingering doubts as to South Africa's ability to reach the World Cup final were swept away in a 36-0 thrashing of title holders England.

In their third game, South Africa beat Tonga 30-25.

South Africa went through to the quarter final by beating the United States of America (USA) 64-15 in the Pool A game at *Stade de la Mosson*. The Springboks then beat Fiji 37-20 at the *Stade Vèlodrome* in Marseille to advance to the semi-finals.

National orders are the highest awards that the country can bestow on individual South Africans.

In September 2007, four South Africans were honoured for their contributions to sport in the country at a national orders ceremony held in Pretoria. President Thabo Mbeki presented the Order of Ikhamanga in Silver to Kitch Christie (posthumously), Morné du Plessis, Sam Ramsamy and Roland Schoeman.

South Africa and Argentina, the last unbeaten southern hemisphere teams at the Rugby World Cup, met in the semi-finals. The Springboks took advantage of the Pumas' errors to cruise to a 37-13 victory, and book a place in the final against England, who defeated France in the other semi-final.

On 20 October 2007, in the final, the Springboks defeated England 15-6 at the *Stade de France* in Paris to clinch the William Webb Ellis trophy.The Springboks' return was held back by a day as the team remained in Paris for the annual International Rugby Board (IRB) Awards Gala, where the team picked up three major awards.

Bryan Habana was named IRB Player of the Year, following in the footsteps of his teammate Schalk Burger, who won the award in 2004. Jake White was named Coach of the Year, and the Springboks were named Team of the Year.

After their World Cup final victory, they also surpassed the All Blacks to number one in the world rankings.

Other achievements in 2007

- In January 2007, Jordy Smith, a Durban surfer, claimed the Billabong Association of Surfing Professionals (ASP) World Junior Championship title after a hard-fought victory over Brazil's Adriano de Souza, ranked 20th in the world.
- In January 2007, Retief Goosen claimed the Qatar Masters golf tournament by sinking a 15-m putt to steal a spectacular victory with a three-under-par 69. The win was worth over R2,4 million.

- In January 2007, at the Australian Tennis Open, Liezel Huber teamed up with Zimbabwe's Cara Black to win the women's doubles title.
- In March, up-and-coming golfer, Anton Haig, won the Johnnie Walker Classic in Phuket.
- In March, Roland Schoeman won gold in the 50-m butterfly at the Fina World Championships in Melbourne, Australia, in a time of 23,18 sec.
- Also in March, Bafana Bafana recorded a convincing 3-0 win over Chad in an African Nations Cup qualifier in N'Djamena.
- In March, Jordy Smith claimed his maiden win in the ASP World Qualifying Series (WQS) by defeating a top-class international field in the four-star, R550 000 – Hot Tuna Central Coast Pro in Australia.
- In April, Gerhard Zandberg won the men's 50-m backstroke gold medal at the world swimming championships in Melbourne, touching in 24,98 sec.
- In April, Oscar Pistorius broke three world records at the Nedbank Championships for the Physically Disabled held in Johannesburg.
- The South African cricket team, the Proteas, advanced to the semi-finals of the International Cricket Council (ICC) Cricket World Cup hosted in the West Indies. However, they lost to Australia in the final.

South Africa has hosted a number of international sporting events since 1994:

- Rugby World Cup 1995
- African Cup of Nations 1996
- IAAF World Cup in Athletics 1998
- All Africa Games 1999
- Cricket World Cup 2003
- President's Cup 2003
- Women's World Cup of Golf 2005, 2006, 2007 and 2008
- Women's World Cup of Cricket 2005
- World Amateur Golf Championships 2006
- Twenty20 Cricket World Cup 2007.

- Charl Schwartzel captured his second European Tour golf title, and his first in mainland Europe, when he won the 2007 Spanish Open in April.
- In May 2007, the Sharks and the Bulls rugby teams played in the final of the Super 14. It was the first time that two South African sides contested the final, the first final held on South African soil and the first final won by a South African team. The Bulls won 20-19 during the last minutes of the match.
- In May, the South African rugby team beat England 53-3 in a test in Bloemfontein.
- South African Rory Sabbatini sank a 15-foot birdie putt on the first play-off hole to win the USA PGA Crowne Plaza Invitational in May, beating veterans Bernhard Langer and Jim Furyk.
- The South African Sibusiso Vilane became the first black man to climb the seven highest peaks on seven continents. He reached the peak of Denali in Alaska in May 2007. The seven mountains are Denali, Kilimandjaro in Africa, Aconcagua in South America, Elbroes in Europe, Kosciuszko in Australia, Everest in Asia and Vinson Masif in Antarctica.

The South African Government launched a website (*www.sa2010.gov.za*) to provide information on government preparations for the 2010 World Cup. The site is complementary to the website of FIFA and the Organising Committee, and was conceived in consultation with FIFA.

It also provides information about the country and the continent in the context of the first African World Cup.

This is a government initiative to take advantage of the World Cup communication opportunity for the benefit of the country and continent. South Africa has committed to being Africa's stage, and to making the World Cup part of a 21st century of African growth and development.

The site provides an entry point to other sources of information about the country – such as the South African Tourism and International Marketing Council gateway, and provincial and host-city websites.

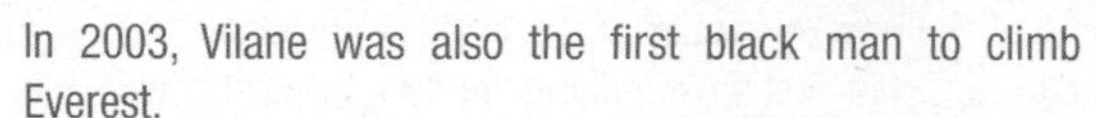

In 2003, Vilane was also the first black man to climb Everest.

- A birdie on the final hole at Celtic Manor earned South African Richard Sterne a one-stroke Wales Open victory in June 2007.
- In June, the South African rugby team beat England 55-22 in a test in Pretoria, and Samoa in a test in Johannesburg. The final score was 35-8.
- Bafana Bafana consolidated their position at the top of Group 11 standings when they beat Chad 4-0 in the African Cup of Nations qualifier at Durban's Absa Stadium in June.
- Ashleigh Simon (18) won the Catalonia Masters in June 2007. It was her first golfing title and came only a month after she turned professional.
- Bafana Bafana drew one all with the Congo in June 2007.
- Robert Hunter became the first South African to win a stage of the Tour de France. He won the 11th stage ahead of Swiss time trial world champion Fabian Cancellara and Brazil's Murilo Fischer.
- The Springboks beat Namibia 105-13 in a World Cup warm-up match at Newlands in August.
- Jordy Smith captured the first six-star-rated surfing event of his career in France to rocket back into the lead on the ASP WQS ratings.
- South Africa beat Irish provincial side Connacht 18-3 in a World Cup warm-up match in August. They also beat Scotland 27-3 in their warm-up international played at Murrayfield in Edinburgh.
- Swimmer Riaan Schoeman won the 400-m individual medley final in a new South African record time, on the second day of an international swimming meeting in Tokyo, Japan.
- In September 2007, South Africa hosted the inaugural ICC

Twenty20 World Cup. The opening match, between South Africa and the West Indies, was won by eight wickets by the home side.
South Africa cruised to a seven-wicket win over Bangladesh in their Twenty20 match in Cape Town.
Albie Morkel was the star of South Africa's 19-run win over England in the Super Eights match in Cape Town.
A few days later, Justin Kemp hit six sixes in an astonishing 89 not-out that set up a six-wicket victory over New Zealand in the Super Eights match at Kingsmead in Durban.
However, a few days later South Africa crashed to a 37-run defeat at India's hands, which knocked them out of the semi-final race on net run-rates. India went on to win the tournament.

- Also in September, Bafana Bafana beat Botswana 1-0 in a Cosafa Castle Cup semi-final game at the Super Stadium in Atteridgeville, west of Pretoria, and went through to the final against Zambia.
- In October 2007, paddler Barry Lewin won the USA national double-ski title with Tahitian star Lewis Laughlan to end his month-long international tour on a high note – which also included a win in the Souliga Challenge in the Caribbean Netherlands Antilles and victory in the Liffey Descent in Ireland.

The Garden Route plans on using its identity as a prime golf-tourism draw-card to assist the Western Cape to position itself as the leading tourism destination in the two years leading to the FIFA World Cup in 2010. The Garden Route was named the 2006 Golf Destination of the Year for Africa and the Middle East at the International Golf Travel Market in Spain, beating top destinations such as Dubai and Mauritius. It also has international standard golf courses designed by some of the world's best players, including Ernie Els, Gary Player and Jack Nicklaus.

- In October 2007, Dale Steyn took five wickets to dismiss Pakistan for 263 as South Africa won the first test in Karachi by 160 runs. South African cricketer Mark Boucher set a new world record for the most test dismissals by a wicketkeeper. Boucher's record of 396 dismissals (378 catches and 18 stumpings) in 103 tests surpassed the record previously held by Ian Healy of Australia, who made 395 dismissals in 119 tests. Jaques Callis scored two test centuries. South Africa went on to win the test series and one-day international series.
- In October, Ernie Els won his seventh World Match Play Championship title by beating Angel Cabrera 6 and 4. The win earned Els one million pounds.

South African sports awards

The South African Sports Awards recognise and honour individuals and teams who have excelled both on and off the field each year. They are presented by the SRSA, the South African Sports Federation and Olympic Committee (Sascoc) and the SABC.

South African Sports Confederation and Olympic Committee

Sascoc is responsible for:

- affiliating to and/or being recognised by the appropriate international, continental and regional sport organisations for high-performance sport
- initiating, negotiating, arranging, financing and controlling multisport tours to and from South Africa
- ensuring and, if necessary, approving that the bidding process relating to the hosting of international or any other sporting events in South Africa complies with the necessary rules and regulations
- facilitating the acquisition and development of playing facilities, including the construction of stadiums and other sports facilities

- ensuring close co-operation between government and the private sector relating to all aspects of Team South Africa
- ensuring the overall protection of symbols, trademarks, emblems or insignia of the bodies under its jurisdiction.

South African Institute for Drug-Free Sport (Saids)

Saids is the South African national anti-doping organisation. It is a public entity established by the Saids Act, 1997 and funded by the SRSA, with a mandate to promote participation in sport free from the use of prohibited substances or methods intended to artificially enhance performance, in the interest of the health and well-being of sportspeople.

Saids is responsible for developing an anti-doping policy and implementing a national anti-doping programme across all South Africa's sports codes. It has 54 part-time, accredited doping-control officers based throughout South Africa, who are trained to international standards and who conduct in- and out-of-competition testing on athletes from 57 sporting disciplines. A total of 76 trained and accredited chaperones assist the doping-control officers.

In 2010, South Africa will host the world's biggest sporting event. The 2010 FIFA World Cup™ is an opportunity for South Africa to showcase its people, talent, natural beauty, culture and organisational abilities.

The World Cup also provides an opportunity to improve the public-transport infrastructure, road networks, policing capacity and communications facilities. Many of these projects will leave a lasting impact on communities and on the quality of life for many.

The national budget makes available R17,4 billion for infrastructure related to the tournament. Of this amount, R8,4 billion is for stadiums and R9 billion is for transport infrastructure and to upgrade areas around the stadiums.

The money allows for new stadiums to be built in Cape Town; Durban; Nelson Mandela Bay; Mbombela, Nelspruit; and Polokwane. Stadiums in Johannesburg (Soccer City and Ellis Park), Mangaung, Rustenburg and Tshwane will be upgraded to meet World Cup standards.

Saids is one of the few national anti-doping agencies worldwide with ISO 9001:2000 certification in compliance with the International Testing Standards. This is the internationally recognised benchmark for quality assurance and excellence, and represents world best practice in doping control in sport.

Sport Tourism Project

The SRSA launched the Sport Tourism Project at the Durban Tourism Indaba in May 2006. The primary motivation of the project is to exploit the substantial benefits that the tourism industry presents for job creation in South Africa.

It combines the Veza route-finder tool, developed by the Council for Scientific and Industrial Research, with sports information, enabling users to plan attendance of sports events, including mapping the route to the venue, booking accommodation and selecting restaurants and other tourist attractions in the vicinity of the venue or elsewhere in South Africa.

Tourism is widely recognised as a major growth sector internationally, and it is estimated that 30% of all tourism comprises sports tourism.

The SRSA aims to enhance the sustainability of the project by:

- promoting "home-grown" events such as the Dusi Canoe Marathon and Argus Cycle Tour, which attract large numbers of international participants and spectators
- working closely with South African Tourism and the Department of Environmental Affairs and Tourism to promote more attractive tourist packages for spectators who want to accompany touring sports teams to South Africa
- assisting agencies, in line with a major events strategy and the hosting and bidding regulations, to attract major international sports events to South Africa
- marketing South Africa's sport and recreation facilities abroad
- producing an interactive CD-ROM to provide information on sport and recreation events and associated information on South Africa.

SINGER

READING LISTS

South Africa today

Buhlungu, S *et al.* eds. *State of the Nation: South Africa 2007.* Cape Town: Human Sciences Research Council (HSRC) Press, 2007.

Burger, D. ed. *South Africa Yearbook 2006/07.* Pretoria: Government Communication and Information System, 2005. Issued annually.

South African Survey 2003-2004.

Johannesburg: South African Institute of Race Relations, 2004. Issued annually.

World Economic Forum. South African at 10: Perspectives by Political, Business and Civil Leaders. Cape Town: Human and Rousseau, 2004.

Land and its people

Afolayan, F. *Culture and Customs of South Africa.* Westport, Connectlcut: Greenwood, 2004.

Bowes, B and Pennington, S. *The Good News.* Johannesburg: Good News, 2002.

Bowes, B and Pennington, S. *South Africa: More Good News.* Johannesburg: Good News, 2003.

Distiller, N and Steyn, M. *Under Construction: Race and Identity in South Africa Today.* Sandton, Heinemann, 2004.

Magubane, P. *Vanishing Cultures of South Africa: Changing Customs in a Changing World.* Cape Town: Struik, 1998.

Mitchley, C. ed. *South African Heritage: A Guide to Our Land, Our People, History and Culture* Caledon: Mill Street Publications, 2005.

Oduyoye, M and Kanyoro, M. *The Will to Arise: Women, Tradition and the Church in Africa.* Pietermaritzburg: Cluster Publications, 2006.

Raper, P. *New Dictionary of South African Place Names.* 3rd rev ed. Johannesburg: Jonathan Ball, n.d.

Tyson, PD and Preston-Whyte, RA. *Weather and Climate of Southern Africa.* 2nd ed. Cape Town: Oxford University Press of Southern Africa, 2004.

Webb, V and du Plessis, T. eds. *The Politics of Language in South Africa.* Pretoria: Van Schaik, 2006.

Arts and culture

Ansell, G. *Soweto Blues: Jazz, Popular Music and Culture in South Africa.* London: Continuum, 2005.

Gaylard, G. *After Colonialism: African Post-modernism and Magical Realism.* Johannesburg: Wits University Press, 2006.

Gray, S. *Indaba: Interviews with African Writers.* Pretoria: Protea Book House, 2005.

Levine, L. *Traditional Music of South Africa.* Johannesburg: Jacana, 2005.

Mangcu, X. ed. *The Meaning of Mandela: A Literary and Intellectual Celebration.* Cape Town: HSRC Press, 2006.

Meiring, H. *My Country in Line and Colour.* Cape Town: Fernwood Press, 2004.

Nuttall, S. *Beautiful Ugly: African Diaspora Aesthetics.* Cape Town: Kwela, 2006.

Perryer, S. ed. *10 Years 100 Artists: Art in a Democratic South Africa.* Cape Town: Bell Roberts, 2004.

Van Eeden, J and du Preez, A. eds. *South Africa's Visual Culture.* Pretoria: Van Schaik, 2005.

Van Graan, M and Ballantyne, T. *The South African Handbook on Arts and Culture 2002-2003.* Cape Town: David Philip, 2002.

History

Beinart, W. *Twentieth Century South Africa.* 2nd ed. Cape Town: Oxford University Press, 2001.

Bozzoli, B. *Theatre of Struggle and the End of Apartheid.* Johannesburg: Witwatersrand University Press, 2004.

Davenport, TRH and Saunders, C. *South Africa: A Modern History.* 5th ed. London: Macmillan, 2000.

Gumede, W. *Thabo Mbeki and the Battle for the Soul of the ANC.* Cape Town: Zebra Press, 2005.

Harvey, R. *The Fall of Apartheid: The Inside Story from Smuts to Mbeki.* Basingstoke: Palgrave Macmillan, 2005.

Heunis, J. *The Inner Circle: Reflections on the Last Days of White Rule.* Cape Town: Jonathan Ball, 2007.

Johnson, RW. *The First Man, The Last Nation.* Johannesburg: Jonathan Ball, 2005.

Khangela, A. *et al.* eds. *Soweto '76: Reflections on the Liberation Struggles.* Johannesburg: Pan Macmillan, 2006.

Maylam, P. *A History of the African People of South Africa: A Short History.* Cape Town: David Philip, 1995.

Meredith, M. *Diamonds, Gold and War: The Making of South Africa.* New York: Simon & Shuster, 2007.

Meredith, M. *The State of Africa: A History of Fifty Years of Independence.* Johannesburg: Jonathan Ball, 2005.

Saadi, S and McInerne, C, eds. *Freedom Spring Ten Years On: Celebration and Commemoration of Ten Years of Freedom in South Africa.* Glasgow: Waverley Books, 2005.

Saunders, C and Southey, N. *A Dictionary of South African History.* 2nd ed. Cape Town: David Philip, 2001.

Segal, L. ed. *Number Four: The Making of Constitution Hill.* Johannesburg: Penguin, 2006.

Stolten, HE. *History Making and Present Day Politics: The Meaning of Collective Memory in South Africa.* Uppsala: Nordiske Afrikainstituut, 2007.

Terreblanche, S. *History of Inequality in South Africa, 1652 - 2002.* Pietermaritzburg: University of Natal Press, 2002.

Thompson, L. *History of South Africa.* Johannesburg: Jonathan Ball, 2006. Reprint of 2001 edition.

Turok, K. *Life and Soul: Portraits of Women Who Move South Africa.* Cape Town: Double Storey, 2006.

Government

Bond, P. *Elite Transition: From Apartheid to Neoliberalism in South Africa.* 2nd ed. Scottsville: University of KwaZulu-Natal Press, 2005.

Calland, R. *Anatomy of South Africa. Who Holds the Power?* Cape Town: Zebra Press, 2006.

Calland, R and Graham, P. eds. *Democracy in the Time of Mbeki;* . Cape Town: Institute for Democracy in South Africa, 2005.

Chipkin, I. *Do South Africans Exist? Nationalism, Democracy and the Identity of "The 'People".* Johannesburg: Wits University Press, 2007.

Constitution of the Republic of South Africa; edited by Juta's Statutes Editors: Reflecting the Law as at October 2004. Lansdowne: Juta, 2004.

Daniel, J. *et al.* eds. *State of the Nation: South Africa;* Pretoria: HSRC 2004.

Lodge, T. *Politics in South Africa: From Mandela to Mbeki.* Cape Town: David Philip, 2002.

Marganui, C. ed. *On Becoming a Democracy: Transition and Transformation in South African Society.* Pretoria: Unisa Press, 2004.

Saul, JS. *Development After Globalisation: Theory and Practice for the Embattled South in a New Imperial Age.* Scottsville: University of KwaZulu-Natal Press, 2006.

Seepe, S. *Speaking Truth to Power: Reflections on Post-1994 South Africa.* Pretoria: Vista University and Skotaville Publishers, 2004.

Shain, M. ed. *Opposing Voices: Liberalism and Opposition in South Africa Today.* Cape Town: Jonathan Ball, 2006.

Slober, P and Ludman, B. eds. *Mail and Guardian A-Z of South African Politics* Johannesburg: Jacana, 2004.

Sparks, A. *Beyond the Miracle: Inside the New South Africa.* Johannesburg: Jonathan Ball, 2003.

Sparks, A. *Tomorrow is Another Country: The Inside Story of South Africa's Negotiated Revolution.* Cape Town: Struik, 1995.

READING LISTS

Tourism

Erasmus, BJP. *En Route in South Africa: A Region By Region Guide.* Cape Town: Sunbird (Jonathan Ball), c. 2007.

Greenwood Guide to South Africa: Hand-Picked Accommodation. London: Greenwood Guides, 2005.

Kellett, F and Williams, L. eds. *Footprint South Africa* 7th ed. Bath, England: Footprint Books, 2004.

Kramer, P. ed. *Illustrated Guide to Places to Visit in Southern Africa.* Cape Town: Readers' Digest, 2001.

Road Atlas of South Africa. Johannesburg: Automobile Association, 2004.

Travel Guide to South African Craft Sites. Erasmuskloof: Eskom Due-South Craft Route Project, 2004.

Viljoen, J and Tlabela, K. *Rural Tourism Development in South Africa: Trends and Challenges.* Cape Town: HSRC Press, 2006.

Economy

Bertelsmann-Scott, T and Draper, P. *Regional Integration and Economic Partnership Agreements: Southern Africa at the Crossroads.* Johannesburg: South African Institute of International Affairs, 2006.

Chipp, K and Ismail, Z. *E-Commerce: A Southern African Perspective.* Cape Town: New Africa Books, 2004.

Levin, A. *The Art of African Shopping.* Cape Town: Struik, 2005.

Marais, H. *South Africa: Limits to Change: The Political Economy of Transition.* 2nd ed. Cape Town: University of Cape Town, 2001.

Opperman, I. ed. *Buy Right: Consumer Guide for South Africa.* Pretoria: Protea Book House, 2006.

Padayachee, V. ed. *The Development Decade: Economic and Social Change in South Africa, 1994 - 2004.* Cape Town: HSRC Press, 2006.

Zegeye, A and Maxted, J. *Our Dream Deferred: The Poor in South Africa.* Pretoria: SAHO and Unisa. 2003.

Finance

Collins, G. *Managing Your Money: Starting on the Right Track.* Durban: Butterworths, 2002.

Fourie, IJ *et al.* eds. *Student Guide to the South African Financial System;* 2nd ed. Cape Town: Oxford University Press Southern Africa, 2004.

Kohn, M. *Financial Institutions and Markets.* 2nd ed. Cape Town: Oxford University Press Southern Africa, 2004.

Musava, C. ed. *Behind Closed Doors: Secrecy in International Financial Institutions.* Cape Town: Institute for Democracy in South Africa 2006.

Parsons, R. ed. *Manuel, Markets and Money: Essays in Appraisal.* Cape Town: Double Storey, 2004.

Porteous, D and Hazelhurst, E. *Banking on Change: Democratizing Finance in South Africa 1994 - 2004.* Cape Town: Double Storey, 2004.

Van Zyl, C. ed. *Understanding South African Financial Markets,* Pretoria: Van Schaik, 2006.

Foreign affairs

Adebajo, A, Adedeji, A and Landsberg, C. eds. *South Africa in Africa: The Post-Apartheid Era. Scottsville*: University of KwaZulu-Natal Press, 2007.

Adebajo, A and Scanlon, H. eds. *A Dialogue of the Deaf: Essays on Africa and the United Nations.* Johannesburg: Fanele (Jacana Media) 2006.

Bond, P. *Talk Left, Walk Right: South Africa's Frustrated Global Reforms.* Scottsville: University of KwaZulu-Natal Press, 2004.

Landsberg, C. *The Quiet Diplomacy of Liberation: International Politics and South Africa's Transition.* Johannesburg: Jacana, 2004.

Murray, R. *Human Rights in Africa: From the OAU to the African Union.* Cambridge: University of Cambridge Press, 2004.

READING LISTS

Transport

Harris, CJ and Ingpen, BD. *Mailships of the Union-Castle Line*. Cape Town: Fernwood, 1994.

Illsley, J. *In Southern Skies: A Pictorial History of Early Aviation in Southern Africa.* Cape Town: Jonathan Ball, 2003.

Moore, D. *Sunset of Steam: A Tribute in Colour to the Golden Years of Steam Locomotives in South Africa.* Johannesburg: Chris van Rensburg, 1990.

Potgieter, C, Pillay, R and Rama, S. *Women, Development and Transport in Rural Eastern Cape, South Africa.* Cape Town: HSRC Press, 2006.

Schnettler, FA. *Century of Cars.* Cape Town: Tafelberg, 1997.

Stirling, WGM and House, JA. *They Served Africa with Wings: 60 Years of Aviation in Central Africa.* Saanichton BC Canada: Bookmark Publishing, 2004.

Agriculture, forestry and land

Devereux, S and Maxwell, S. eds. *Food Security in Sub-Saharan Africa.* Pietermaritzburg: University of Natal Press, 2003.

Du Toit, P. *The Great South African Land Scandal.* Centurion: Legacy Publications, 2004.

Lawes, MJ *et al.* eds. *Indigenous Forests and Woodlands in South Africa.* University of KwaZulu-Natal Press, 2004.

Lee, M and Colvard, K. eds. *Unfinished Business: The Land Crisis in Southern Africa.* Pretoria: Aisa, 2004.

Moyo, S and Yeros, P. eds. *Reclaiming the Land: The Resurgence of Rural Movements in Africa, Asia and Latin America.* London: Zed Books; Cape Town: David Philip, 2005.

Nieuwoudt, L and Groenewald, J. *The Challenge of Change: Agriculture, Land and the South African Economy.* Pietermaritzburg: University of Natal Press, 2003.

Ntsebeza, L and Hall, R. eds. *The Land Question in South Africa: The Challenge of Transformation and Redistribution.* Cape Town: HSRC Press, 2007.

Pakenham, T. *Meetings with Remarkable Trees.* Cape Town: Sunbird (Jonathan Ball) 1998.

Smith, B. *The Farming Handbook.* Scottsville: University of KwaZulu-Natal Press, c.2006.

Van Onselen, C. *The Seed is Mine: The Life of Kas Maine: A South African Sharecropper 1894 - 1985.* Cape Town: David Philip, 1996.

Environment

Bond, P. *Unsustainable South Africa: Environment, Development and Social Protest.* Pietermaritzburg: University of Natal Press, 2002.

Dovers, S. ed. *South Africa's Environmental History: Cases and Comparisons.* Cape Town: David Philip, 2002.

Joubert, L. Scorched: *South Africa's Changing Climate.* Johannesburg: Wits University Press, 2006.

Kok, P and Pietersen, J. *Environmental Management.* Pretoria: HSRC, 2000.

McDonald, D. ed. *Environmental Justice in South Africa.* Cape Town: University of Cape Town Press, 2002.

Science and technology

Bonner, P *et al.* eds. *The Search for Origins: Science, History and South Africa's "Cradle of Humankind".* Johannesburg: Wits University Press, 2006.

Harrison, P. *South Africa's Top Sites: Science.* Cape Town: Spearhead, 2004.

Harrison, I and Joyce, P. eds. *The Book of Firsts: South African Edition.* Cape Town: Jonathan Ball, 2005.

Macrae, C. *Life Etched in Stone: Fossils of Southern Africa.* Johannesburg: Geological Society of South Africa, 1999.

McCarthy, T and Rubidge, B. *The Story of Earth and Life: A Southern African Perspective on a 4,6-Billion-Year Journey.* Cape Town: Struik, 2005.

Pillay, U, Roberts, B and Rule, S. eds. *South African Social Attitudes.* Cape Town: HSRC Press, 2006.

Communications

Evans, N and Seeber, M. eds. *The Politics of Publishing in South Africa;* Scottsville: University of KwaZulu-Natal Press, 2000. Goldstuck, A. *Hitchhiker's Guide to the Internet: A South African Handbook.* Wynberg: Sandton: Zebra Books, 1995.

Hadland, A, Aldridge, M and Ogada, J. *Re-visioning Television: Policy, Strategy and Models for the Sustainable Development of Community Television in South Africa.* Cape Town: HSRC Press, 2007.

Merrett, C. *A Culture of Censorship: Secrecy and Intellectual Repression in South Africa.* Cape Town: David Philip and University of Natal Press, 1994.

Nel, F. *Writing for the Media in South Africa.* 2nd ed. Oxford: Oxford University Press, 2003.

Oosthuizen, L. *Media Ethics in the South African Context.* Cape Town: Juta, 2002.

Steyn-Barlow, C. *Publish and Be Damned: Two Decades of Scandals.* Alberton: Galago, 2006.

Switzer, L and Adhikari, M. eds. *South Africa's Resistance: Press: Alternative Voices in the Last Generation Under Apartheid.* Ohio: Ohio University Centre for International Studies, 2000.

Thlabela, K *et al.* eds. *Mapping ICT Access in South Africa.* Cape Town: HSRC Press, 2006.

Young, L. *The All Africa Internet Guide.* Johannesburg: M & G Books, 2002.

Housing

Bond, P. *Cities of Gold: Townships of Coal: Essays on South Africa's New Urban Crisis.* Trematon, NJ: African World Press, 2000.

Boraine, A. ed. *State of the Cities Report 2004,* Johannesburg: South African Cities Network, 2004.

Harrison, P *et al.* eds. *Confronting Management: Housing and Urban Development in a Democratising Society.* Cape Town: University of Cape Town Press, 2003.

Safety, security and defence

Altbeker, A. *The Dirty Work of Democracy.* Cape Town: Jonathan Ball, 2006.

Bezuidenhout, C and Joubert, S. eds. *Child and Youth Misbehaviour in South Africa: A Holistic View.* Pretoria: Van Schaik, 2003.

Dixon, B and van der Spuy E. *Justice Gained? Crime and Crime Control in South Africa's Transition.* Cape Town: University of Cape Town Press, 2004.

Gamba, V. ed. *Governing Arms: The Southern African Experience* Pretoria: Institute for Security Studies, 2000.

Marks, M. *Transforming the Robocops: Changing Policy in South Africa.* Scottsville: University of KwaZulu-Natal Press, 2005.

Marks, M. *Young Warriors: Youth Politics, Identity and Violence in South Africa.* Johannesburg: Wits University Press, 2004.

Pelser, E. ed. *Crime Prevention Partnerships: Lessons from Practice.* Pretoria: Institute of Strategic Studies, 2003.

Solomon, H. ed. *Towards a Common Defence and Security Policy in the Southern African Development Community.* Pretoria: Africa Institute of South Africa 2004.

Steinberg, J. *The Number: One Man's Search for Identity in the Cape Underworld and Prison Gangs.* Johannesburg: Jonathan Ball, 2004.

Straw, M. *Crime and Policing in Post-Apartheid South Africa.* Cape Town: David Philip, 2002.

Justice and correctional services

Asmal, K *et al. Legacy of Freedom: The ANC's Human Rights Tradition: Africans' Claim in South Africa, the Freedom Charter, the Women's Charter and the Human Rights Landmarks of the African National Congress.* Johannesburg: Jonathan Ball, 2005.

Bennett, TW. *Customary Law in South Africa.* Cape Town: Juta, 2004.

Bizos, G. *Odyssey to Freedom.* Johannesburg: Random House, 2007.

Burger, J. *Strategic Perspectives on Crime and Policing in South Africa.* Pretoria: Van Schaik, 2006.

Doxator, E and Villa-Vicence, C. eds. *Repairing the Unforgivable: Reparations, Restoration and Renewal,* C. Cape Town: David Philip, 2003.

Edelstein, J. *Truth and Lies: Stories from the Truth and Reconciliation Commission in South Africa.* Johannesburg: M & G Books, 2001.

Glauber, I. *The Death Penalty as a Deterrent.* Johannesburg: The Author, 2004.

Krog, A. *Country of My Skull.* Johannesburg: Random House, 1998.

McQuoid-Mason, D. ed. *Street Law South Africa: Practical Law for South Africans.* Cape Town: Juta, 2004.

Turrell, R. *White Mercy: A Study of the Death Penalty in South Africa.* Westport, Cape Town: Praeger, 2004.

Vale, P. *Security and Politics in South Africa: The Regional Dimension,* Cape Town: University of Cape Town Press, 2003.

Van der Walt, J. *Law and Sacrifice: Towards a Post-Apartheid Theory of Law.* Johannesburg: Wits University Press, 2006.

Minerals and mining

Fig, D. *Uranium Record: Questioning South Africa's Nuclear Direction.* Johannesburg: Jacana, 2005.

Fig, D. *Uranium Road: Questioning South Africa's Nuclear Direction.* Johannesburg: Jacana, 2005.

Simons, PB. *Cullinan Diamonds: Dreams and Discoveries.* Vlaeberg, Cape: Fernwood Press, 2004.

Strategic Overview of the South African Mining Industry: Gold, Coal, Platinum-Group Metals, Diamonds, Vanadium. Johannesburg: Industrial Development Corporation, 2000.

Education

Every Step of the Way: The Journey to Freedom in South Africa. Cape Town: HSRC Press, 2004. Commissioned by the Ministry of Education to commemorate 10 years of freedom in education.

Fleisch, B. *Managing Educational Change: The State and School Reform in South Africa.* Sandown: Heinemann, 2005.

Morrow, W. *Learning to Teach in South Africa.* Cape Town: HSRC Press, 2007.

Wolhuter, CC *et al.* eds. *Comparative Education: Education Systems and Contemporary Issues.* Pretoria: Van Schaik, 2007.

Health

Abdool Karim, SS and Abdool Karim, Q. eds. *HIV/AIDS in South Africa.* New York: Cambridge University Press, 2005.

Barnett, T and Whiteside, A. *AIDS in the 21st Century: Disease and Globalisation.* 2nd ed. Basingstroke: Palgrave Macmillan, 2006.

De Haan, M *et al. The Health of Southern Africa.* 9th ed. Cape Town: Juta, 2005.

Dennil, K, King, L and Swanepoel, T. *Aspects of Primary Healthcare.* 2nd ed. Cape Town: Oxford University Press of Southern Africa, 2004.

Evian, C. *Primary Health Care.* 4th rev. ed. Johannesburg: Jacana, 2006.

Evian, C. *Primary HIV/AIDS Care.* 4th rev. ed. Johannesburg: Jacana, 2006.

Kauffman, KD and Lindauer, DL. eds. *AIDS and South Africa: The Social Expression of a Pandemic;* Basingstoke, Hampshire: Palgrave Macmillan, 2004.

Hassim, A, Heywood, M and Bergen, J. *Health and Democracy: A Guide to Human Rights, Health Law and Policy in Post-Apartheid South Africa.* Tokai, Cape: Siberlink , 2007.

Van Rensburg, HCJ. *Health and Health Care in South Africa.* Pretoria: Van Schaik, 2004.

Social development

Amoateng, AY and Heaton, TB. eds. *Families and Households in Post-Apartheid South Africa.* Cape Town: HSRC Press, 2007.

Brown, D. *To Speak of This Land: Identity and Belonging in South Africa and Beyond.* Scottsville: University of KwaZulu-NatalPress, 2006.

Chidester, D, Dexter, P and Wilmot, J. *What Holds Us Together: Social Cohesion in South Africa.* Pretoria: HSRC, 2003.

Geisler, G. *Women and the Remaking of Politics in Southern Africa: Negotiating Autonomy, Incorporation and Representation.* Uppsala: Nordiska Afrikainstituut, 2004.

Sewpaul, V and Hischer, D. *Social Work in Times of Neotribalism: A Postmodern Discourse.* Pretoria: Van Schaik, 2004.

Patel, L. *Social Welfare and Social Development in South Africa.* Cape Town: Oxford University Press, 2005.

Zegeye, A and Kriger, R. eds. *Culture in the New South Africa: After Apartheid: Volume 2;* Cape Town: Kwela Books and South African History Online, 2001.

Zegeye, A. ed. *Social Identities in the New South Africa: After Apartheid: Volume 1.* Cape Town: Kwela Books and South African History Online, 2001.

Sport

Alegi, P. *Laduma! Soccer, Politics and Society in South Africa.* Scottsville: University of KwaZulu-Natal Press, 2004.

Black, B. *Fly-Fishing South Africa's Rivers, Lakes and Surf.* Cape Town: Struik, 2007.

Colquhoun, A. ed *Sasol South African Rugby Annual 2006.* Cape Town: SA Rugby and MWP Media, 2005.

Jaffee, J and Wolfaardt, F. *And Away They Go.* Johannesburg: Sharp Sharp Media, 2004.

Mazwai, T. ed. *Thirty Years of South African Soccer;* Cape Town and Randburg: Sunbird Publishing and Mafube Publishing, 2003.

Meintjies, M. *Remarkable Flyfishing Destinations of Southern Africa.* Cape Town: Struik, 2005.

Murray, B and Christopher M. *Caught Behind: Race and Politics in Springbok Cricket.* Johannesburg: Wits University Press and Scottsville: University of KwaZulu-Natal Press, 2004.

Wolhunter, L. ed. *Nedbank Guide to Flyfishing in Southern Africa.* 5th ed. Np: Federation of Southern African Flyfishers, 2004.

Cottrell, T. ed. *Nedbank Runners' Guide to Road Races in South Africa;* Parklands: Guide Book Publications, 2005.

Osborne, P. *Basil d'Oliviera: Cricket and Conspiracy: The Untold Story.* London: Little Brown, 2004.

Raath, P. *Soccer Through the Years 1862 - 2002: The First Official History of South African Soccer.* Cape Town: The Author, 2002.

Ramsamy, S. *Reflections on a Life in Sport.* Cape Town: Publishing Partnership for Greenhouse, 2004.

Important telephone numbers and notes

Important telephone numbers and notes